MW01235376

WISDOM
AND DOMINION

WISDOM
AND DOMINION

AN ECONOMIC COMMENTARY ON PROVERBS

GARY NORTH

POINT FIVE PRESS
Dallas, Georgia

Wisdom and Dominion: An Economic Commentary on Proverbs

Copyright © 2012, 2021 by Gary North

This work is licensed under the Creative Commons Attribution 4.0 International License. To view a copy of this license, visit creativecommons.org/licenses/by/4.0/.

Published by
Point Five Press
P.O. Box 2778
Dallas, Georgia 30132

Typesetting by Kyle Shepherd

This book is dedicated to

Dennis Peacocke

A revolutionary who switched sides

TABLE OF CONTENTS

PREFACE

This book is part of a series, *An Economic Commentary on the Bible*. There has never before been an economic commentary on the Bible. This series is preliminary to what I hope will be a comprehensive volume on Christian economics. I decided in 1973 that I should not write such a book until I had completed the exegetical work. I wrote monographs on Christian economics, most notably *An Introduction to Christian Economics* (1973), *Honest Money* (1986), *Inherit the Earth* (1987), and *The Coase Theorem* (1991) before I completed my exegetical work in 2010.

In working with the texts of the Pentateuch, I discovered a hermeneutic[1] for assessing which Mosaic economic laws apply in the New Covenant and which do not. I summarized these in the Conclusion of my 1994 commentaries on Leviticus: the shorter *Leviticus: An Economic Commentary* and *Boundaries and Dominion*. These are:

1. Seed laws (annulled)
2. Land laws (annulled)
3. Priestly/holiness laws (annulled)
4. Cross-boundary laws (permanent)

The rules in the Book of Proverbs rest on cross-boundary laws. They are still in force.

As you will see when you read this book, I refer back to the Mosaic law when I discuss many of the economic proverbs. I sometimes also refer forward to the teachings of Jesus and Paul. I do this in order to establish my general point, namely, that these are permanent rules of action that rest on cross-boundary laws.

The proverbs are brief aphorisms that summarize or apply either a specific Mosaic law or else a principle undergirding the Mosaic law

---

1. Principle of interpretation.

as a whole. They repeatedly call people to exercise wisdom, but a specific kind of wisdom: prudence.

This commentary can be read from start to finish as a unit. It can also be read one proverb at a time. Most commentaries survive because they are read one verse at a time. Pastors read commentaries because they want help writing a sermon, and a sermon can cover only a few verses in detail. But a commentary that focuses on a particular academic discipline is more likely than most commentaries to be read from start to finish, because readers other than pastors are likely to attempt this. The readers want insight into a particular field, not just insight into the meaning of a few verses. This series is the first such commentary in 1900 years on a specific academic discipline.

Each chapter in this commentary can stand alone. Someone who seeks information about a single proverb or a related group of proverbs will find an exposition that deals with the passage. There is repetition in the book as a whole, because each chapter was written to stand alone. I will post each chapter separately on the Web: at GaryNorth.com and at biblicaleconomics.wordpress.com. As I have said, I do not expect everyone to read this commentary from start to finish. I expect a few people to do this—those who are ready to learn the Bible's comprehensive plan for personal success. This, we find in Proverbs.

Handbook for personal success

INTRODUCTION

The Book of Proverbs can legitimately be regarded as the original self-help manual. It is a handbook for personal success. No comparable handbook has come down to us from the ancient world.

The section from chapter 10 through chapter 30 offers aphorisms. An aphorism can encapsulate great wisdom in a short, memorable, and memorizable phrase. The Book of Proverbs has lots of them.

There are three major problems with any compilation of aphorisms. *First*, it is not easy to keep them all in the back of your mind, ready to apply in a specific situation. The decision-maker must select the applicable aphorism and then apply it to a specific set of circumstances. This is not easy. This is why a young man who memorizes Sun Tzu's *Art of War* probably will not wind up as a successful general. A few may; most will not. *Second*, the collected aphorisms may not be consistent with each other. This will lead to inconsistencies in any comprehensive program of applied wisdom. *Third*, it is not always clear what the overall collection's integrating conceptual framework is, if there is one.

A. The Integrating Framework

There is an integrating conceptual framework for the Book of Proverbs: the contrast between the righteous man and the unrighteous man, meaning between the wise man and the fool, between the covenant-keeper and covenant-breaker. This theme is applied to economic issues in well over a hundred proverbs. Some of these proverbs are repeated. In this book, I discuss how the basic theme applies to more than 80 separate proverbs.

There are numerous sub-themes in those proverbs that are devoted to economics. Among these are:

1. The steps to personal success
2. The standards of personal success
3. Success indicators
4. Failure indicators
5. The function of riches
6. The basis of riches
7. The concept of ownership
8. The nature of economic causation
9. The marks of a biblical economy
10. The purposes of inheritance

Each of these themes has several proverbs associated with it. All of these themes are important for devising and implementing a lifelong plan of personal success.

As with all of the books of the Bible, the Book of Proverbs is theo-centric. God is central; man is not. "The king's heart is in the hand of the LORD, as the rivers of water: he turneth it whithersoever he will" (Prov. 21:1) The proverbs focus on what God demands from men—*holiness*—not what men want from God. Yet numerous proverbs appeal openly to personal self-interest. So, the book reflects a fundamental theme in the entire Bible: *the consistency between what God wants from men and what men want in this life.* "But seek ye first the kingdom of God, and his righteousness; and all these things shall be added unto you" (Matt. 6:33).[1]

B. Economic Theory

The covenantal laws of society are found in the Mosaic covenant. These are the basis of the Proverbs. The Book of Proverbs encapsulates these laws in a way that we can more easily recall them.

This book makes clear that the society we live in is governed by ethical cause and effect. It is not governed by impersonal natural law. It is not governed by an evolving system of impersonal social laws. It is not governed by impersonal fate or impersonal chance. It is not governed by luck, either personal or impersonal. It is governed by God's covenants. It is therefore governed by a comprehensive system of biblical law and the sanctions associated with this law.

This leads to a conclusion: *there is no value-free economic theory*. God is not neutral. His universe is not neutral. Any attempt to interpret the universe, including economic theory, in terms of the doc-

---

1. Gary North, *Priorities and Dominion: An Economic commentary on Matthew*, 2nd ed. (Dallas, Georgia: Point Five Press, [2000] 2102), ch. 15.

trine of value-neutrality is an assertion of man's autonomy—collective mankind as well as the individual. Such an assertion is an act of covenant-breaking.

God, not man, imputes final economic value to everything.

Conclusion

The Book of Proverbs presents a view of economic causation that is in opposition to all modern academic economic theory, which was a self-conscious attempt to strip God and morality out of economic science.[2] This view insists that God, not man, imputes final economic value to everything. Men impute economic value as image-bearers of God. They do not do this autonomously.

The free market social order first appeared in Western Europe because Western Europe and colonial America were more consistently biblical in their related concepts of law and causation than other societies were in the eighteenth century. Their legal order reflected biblical law's dual affirmation of private property and personal responsibility.

The Bible is hostile to all forms of socialism and the welfare state. I have spent over three decades proving this, verse by verse. So far, Christian socialists refuse to present detailed exegetical support for their case. They do not respond to me. Meanwhile, socialism has visibly died. Communism is defunct. There was never an intellectually coherent theoretical defense of socialism, and now it has failed visibly. It impoverished those nations that adopted it. Socialism is a dead mule. It was always sterile. It is time to bury the carcass.

Men impute economic value as image-bearers of God. They do not do this autonomously

The Bible is hostile to all forms of socialism and the welfare state.

---

2. William Letwin, *The Origins of Scientific Economics* (Cambridge, Massachusetts: MIT Press, 1963).

1

PERSONAL MOTIVATION FOR HOLINESS

The proverbs of Solomon the son of David, king of Israel; To know wisdom and instruction; to perceive the words of understanding; To receive the instruction of wisdom, justice, and judgment, and equity; To give subtilty to the simple, to the young man knowledge and discretion.

PROVERBS 1:1–4

A. A Holy Kingdom

God wants His covenant people to be holy, for He is holy. "Speak unto all the congregation of the children of Israel, and say unto them, Ye shall be holy: for I the LORD your God am holy" (Lev. 19:2). This requirement extends into the New Covenant era. Peter affirmed this principle. "Because it is written, Be ye holy; for I am holy" (I Pet. 1:16).

Holiness is made visible by obeying God's Bible-revealed laws.

> This day the LORD thy God hath commanded thee to do these statutes and judgments: thou shalt therefore keep and do them with all thine heart, and with all thy soul. Thou hast avouched the LORD this day to be thy God, and to walk in his ways, and to keep his statutes, and his commandments, and his judgments, and to hearken unto his voice: And the LORD hath avouched thee this day to be his peculiar people, as he hath promised thee, and that thou shouldest keep all his commandments; And to make thee high above all nations which he hath made, in praise, and in name, and in honour; and that thou mayest be an holy people unto the LORD thy God, as he hath spoken (Deut. 26:16–19).

God wants all those who do obey His laws to become visibly successful as members of a uniquely holy people in a social order that has been established by means of *a public, corporate, oath-bound cove-*

nant. Visible blessings are basic (Deut. 28:1–14).[1] He wants people to use their success in this life to extend His kingdom in history. "But seek ye first the kingdom of God, and his righteousness; and all these things shall be added unto you" (Matt. 6:33).[2]

God has gone to extreme lengths to enable people to do this, even to the extent of sending His Son into this world to live the life required of all people, then to die on behalf of mankind in general (common grace)[3] and for His covenant people in particular (special grace). God is highly motivated. "For God so loved the world, that he gave his only begotten Son, that whosoever believeth in him should not perish, but have everlasting life" (John 3:16).

B. Personal Motivation

In order to persuade His covenant people to become highly motivated to discover, develop, and implement their individual talents in a program of kingdom extension, God offers a comprehensive program of personal self-improvement. This program is presented in the Book of Proverbs. This book is God's handbook for self-improvement. There is none like it in the literature of the ancient world.

Because the Book of Proverbs is deliberately motivational, we should expect to find in the book examples of highly motivational communications. Perhaps the book could even become a model for motivational communications, yet suitable for kingdom use. This is exactly what we find.

There is a rule governing direct-response advertising, which is a highly specific form of motivational literature: "Lead with the benefits. Follow with the proof." Benefits motivate people to read your advertisement. If they are not motivated early, they will not read it. There is second rule: "Be explicit regarding the benefits unless the benefits are obvious to virtually everyone in your targeted audience." The more obvious the benefits, the better. You then do not have to devote space to persuade people to read your advertisement. People are already highly motivated with respect to these benefits. There is a third rule: "Offer people hope." If they have no hope, they will not act. If they will not act, they will not change.

---

1. Gary North, *Inheritance and Dominion: An Economic Commentary on Deuteronomy*, 2nd ed. (Dallas, Georgia: Point Five Press, [1999] 2012), ch. 69.

2. Gary North, *Priorities and Dominion: An Economic Commentary on Matthew*, 2nd ed. (Dallas, Georgia: Point Five Press, [2000] 2012), ch. 15

3. Gary North, *Dominion and Common Grace: The Biblical Basis of Progress* (Tyler, Texas: Institute for Christian Economics, 1987).

The introductory words of the Book of Proverbs adhere to all three rules. This passage identifies the author, who has a reputation for possessing two major benefits that are widely desired: wisdom and wealth. These benefits need no explanation. Because the reader knows who Solomon was, these two benefits are implicit rather than explicit. This also saves space. Finally, the passage motivates the reader by appealing to his hope that he, too, can become successful.

Only after doing this does the book present a long list of specific motivations: gaining specific benefits and avoiding specific liabilities. This motivational strategy conforms to direct-response advertising's fourth rule: "People respond to their immediate concerns. The more specific these concerns are addressed in the ad, the more likely people will take action." This is sometimes referred to as *the hot-button rule.*

So, there must be a combination of universally recognized benefits and highly specific benefits. The Book of Proverbs offers this combination as no other surviving document from the ancient world does.

C. Implied Benefits

The opening words of the book list the benefits.

> The proverbs of Solomon the son of David, king of Israel; To know wisdom and instruction; to perceive the words of understanding; To receive the instruction of wisdom, justice, and judgment, and equity; To give subtilty to the simple, to the young man knowledge and discretion.

Solomon does not spell out these benefits. He merely lists them. He assumes that they are well known by his targeted audience. This saves space.

1. Wisdom   How to make decisions

The first benefit for reading this book is implied: to discover how Solomon, the son of David and the king of Israel, made his decisions. This is why the book begins with the identification of its source: Solomon. The text does not say that Solomon wrote the book, only that these are his proverbs. Beginning with chapter 25 and continuing through chapter 30, the proverbs are said to be Solomon's, but they were copied by scribes in King Hezekiah's reign. "These are also proverbs of Solomon, which the men of Hezekiah king of Judah copied out" (Prov. 25:1). Hezekiah's reign lasted from about 716 B.C. to 687.[4] This was over two centuries after Solomon's reign. Either the

---

4. This is the estimate of E. R. Thiele. W. F. Albright dated this from 715 to 686.

proverbs had been memorized and passed down orally, or else they had been written down, passed down, and compiled at the later date. The author of the book's opening words was intimately familiar with these proverbs—so intimate that he risked attributing them to the king. The presumption is that the compiler was Solomon or someone very close to him.

This identification of the source of the proverbs brings great authority to this collection within a targeted audience: *covenant-keepers*. They know who Solomon is. Not everyone does. Those who have read the Bible know. In his day, his reputation extended beyond the borders of Israel. He was internationally known for his wisdom, especially his good judgment as a ruler. Other rulers from the region came to see him execute judgment, and they marveled. The queen of Sheba came and witnessed his abilities as a judge. "And she said to the king, It was a true report that I heard in mine own land of thy acts and of thy wisdom. Howbeit I believed not the words, until I came, and mine eyes had seen it: and, behold, the half was not told me: thy wisdom and prosperity exceedeth the fame which I heard" (I Kings 10:6–7).

2. Wealth

The queen of Sheba was so impressed that she gave a large gift to him, "an hundred and twenty talents of gold, and of spices great abundance, and precious stones: neither was there any such spice as the queen of Sheba gave king Solomon" (II Chron. 9:9).

His career testified visibly to a close relationship between judgment and wealth. Great wealth came to him because of his wisdom, as the queen's visit exemplifies. His life was a living testimony to the entire region that wisdom in judgment produces benefits for all, including the ruler who possesses such wisdom.

So, the second benefit is also implied: how to attain great wealth, just as Solomon did. This is a universally recognized benefit. These proverbs were compiled by a very rich man. *No book in the Bible provides more information regarding the way to wealth*. Yet what is striking about the Book of Proverbs is the centrality of its ethical framework. It initially focuses on ethics. Only when this issue is settled early in the book does Solomon move on to the practical implementation of his strategy of success, which is at bottom ethical.

"Hezekiah." *Wikipedia*, Wikimedia Foundation, January 16, 2021; en.wikipedia.org/wiki/hezekiah.

So, the introduction is both universal and specific. It offers wisdom and wealth on the authority of a man renowned as possessing both, a man whose name is recognized by members of a targeted audience. This combination of universal and specific is essential for a direct-response motivational communication.

3. Hope

Simple people recognize that they are simple. From long experience, they have learned that others are quicker to perceive the decisive conditions of social relationships. Others can make self-seeking decisions through this perception and their wits. How can a simple person compete in such a competitive world? This proverb says that the solution is instruction in wisdom, justice, judgment, and equity. These topics seem to be aspects of a realm of high-level decision-making. But this proverb says that simple people can be elevated into this realm as successful practitioners.

Jesus recognized this aspect of success in God's kingdom.

> And Jesus called a little child unto him, and set him in the midst of them, And said, Verily I say unto you, Except ye be converted, and become as little children, ye shall not enter into the kingdom of heaven. Whosoever therefore shall humble himself as this little child, the same is greatest in the kingdom of heaven (Matt. 18:2–4).

The simple person is not to be childish but rather childlike. He is to be humble before God and His law, as a child is humble before his parents and their rules. He receives instruction in the basics of government. This instruction provides him with practical wisdom: the ability to make morally straight plans in a morally crooked world. Jesus said: "Behold, I send you forth as sheep in the midst of wolves: be ye therefore wise as serpents, and harmless as doves" (Matt. 10:16).

Similarly, instruction provides a young person with knowledge and discretion. Solomon presumes that these gifts are not normally associated with young people, who tend to be impetuous. The reader also presumes this. The fact that instruction according to wisdom can overcome the impetuosity of youth testifies to its transformational power.

So, the third implied benefit is that simple people, young people, and common people can master the rules of wisdom, which in turn produce success in life. This is an open book. It is available to all people. It is a manual of success that is available to mentally average people. Its implied promise: success for the wise. The wise need not be of above-average intelligence. They must be of above-average ethics.

The opening passage appeals to a person's positive self-image. Then it extends this appeal by asserting that this is not a matter of superior intelligence, but rather something open to all: ethics. It says, "You can do this."

D. The Power of Wise Instruction

Man is pictured in the opening words of Proverbs as being in need of instruction. A wise man receives instruction in wisdom, justice, judgment, and equity (fairness). The Hebrew words are revealing. The word for wisdom, *sakal*, means circumspect. It also means intelligent. There is the sense of prudence about the term. The word for justice, *tsedeq*, means rightness. It can also mean prosperity, which is worth noting. The word for judgment, *mishpat*, has the sense of rendering a verdict based on law. Finally, the word for equity, *meyshar*, refers to straightness. This reminds us of the Hebrews' instruction to Joshua before they entered the land of Canaan. "Only be thou strong and very courageous, that thou mayest observe to do according to all the law, which Moses my servant commanded thee: turn not from it to the right hand or to the left, that thou mayest prosper whithersoever thou goest" (Josh. 1:7). The Hebrew word for "prosper" here is *sakal*—wisdom. We see in this passage a relationship between faithful law-keeping and prosperity.

The text also says that such instruction provides subtlety for the simple and discretion to the young. The Hebrew word for subtlety can have the sense of guile: trickery. "But if a man come presumptuously upon his neighbour, to slay him with guile; thou shalt take him from mine altar, that he may die" (Ex. 21:14). The Gibeonites were subtle, tricking the Israelites into making a binding covenant with them to remain in the land as servants. They were wily. "They did work wilily, and went and made as if they had been ambassadors, and took old sacks upon their asses, and wine bottles, old, and rent, and bound up" (Josh. 9:4). In most instances, this word has the sense of devious plans, but not always. It can mean wisdom. Solomon says in this book, "O ye simple, understand wisdom: and, ye fools, be ye of an understanding heart" (8:5). It can mean prudence. "I wisdom dwell with prudence, and find out knowledge of witty inventions" (8:12).

The simple-minded person cannot rely on cleverness to achieve his ends. He lacks subtlety. Yet instruction can provide this missing ability. How is this possible? By providing the awareness of *social causation,* an awareness made possible by the lifelong experience of hearing the law of God in the context of real-world decision-making. This is what the Old Testament provided, in a way that no other ancient document did. It set forth the legal order of Moses in the context of the story of God's covenant people. That story was grounded in law. It was the manifestation of God's covenantal, law-bound dealings with a rebellious nation.

Conclusion

The Book of Proverbs begins by identifying the source of these proverbs: an internationally known ruler who possessed great wealth compiled them. This identification is sufficient to attract attention.

For those readers and listeners who recognize who Solomon was, the introduction offers three benefits: good judgment, personal success, and access for all. Through the information contained in this entire collection of proverbs, simple people can be made clever, and young people can be made discreet. Had these claims not come from a man of known integrity and widely known success, they would not be readily believed.

Early in this collection, Solomon sets forth the value of wisdom. He says that the kind of wisdom his instruction offers is something of great value. If it can make the simpleton subtle and the youth discreet, what can it do for the common man, who is neither simple nor young? What can it do for the clever person? Clearly, "A wise man will hear, and will increase learning; and a man of understanding shall attain unto wise counsels" (v. 5). This man is prudent.

Solomon invites the reader to consider the material in this collection. He says that wise people will do this. This implies that people who lack wisdom will not. He says, in effect, "If you are neither wise nor a person of understanding, you need not continue to read what I have to say." This is a form of screening: "Wise people only." This is a form of motivation. A reader presumably thinks he is wise, although not necessarily clever. He thinks: "This book is aimed at me." This is motivation to continue reading.

This promise of open access also implies that wisdom is not a matter of innate intelligence. If a simple person can be made subtle through a mastery of these proverbs, this is a great motivation for everyone to read and commit these proverbs to memory. It means that there is something beneficial here for everyone. Wisdom is presented here as a matter of ethics rather than a matter of innate intelligence.

A simple person can learn what is right. This information, when coupled with a willingness to apply biblical ethics in day-to-day decisions, leads to success. People want success. They want to believe that they can attain success. So, there is great motivation presented here for mastering and applying these proverbs: to become like Solomon.

For approximately three thousand years, millions of people have considered carefully what he had to say.

2

THE FEAR OF THE Lord

The fear of the Lord is the beginning of knowledge: but fools despise wisdom and instruction.

PROVERBS 1:7

Here is one of the fundamental verses in the Old Testament, on a par with "Hear, O Israel: The Lord our God is one Lord" (Deut. 6:4). This proverb establishes the fundamental principle of epistemology, which asks: "What can a man reliably know, and how can he know it?"

A. God the Judge

The proverb does not say that knowledge of the Lord *in general* precedes knowledge in general. It says that the *fear* of the Lord is the starting point for all accurate knowledge. We do not learn about the God of the Bible from a careful study of His incommunicable attributes—omnipotence, omniscience, omnipresence—let alone from any of medieval scholasticism's five proofs of God. Instead, we learn of God as the supreme cosmic judge who brings negative sanctions in both time and eternity. This is the God of the covenant: *God, the sanctions-bringer.*[1] Ignore this aspect of God's character, and you cannot possess accurate knowledge of either God or the cosmos. All such sanctions-denying knowledge, while potentially accurate in its observational details of specific cause and effect—drop the rock on your

---

1. Ray R. Sutton, *That You May Prosper: Dominion By Covenant*, 2nd ed. (Tyler, Texas: Institute for Christian Economics, [1987] 1992), ch. 4. Gary North, *Unconditional Surrender: God's Program for Victory*, 5th ed. (Powder Springs, Georgia: American Vision, 2010), ch. 4.

foot, and your foot hurts—keeps men ignorant of the cosmic drama: God vs. Satan, covenant-keeper vs. covenant-breaker.

The wise man accepts God as He says in the Bible that He is: the supreme agent of judgment. The fool does not. The wise man begins with the fear of God. The fool does not. The mark of the fool is that he despises wisdom and instruction.

This does not mean that he despises all instruction. Everyone learns about cause and effect in history. Everyone has a concept of the way the world works. But in the context of this passage, wisdom and instruction refer to applications of the principle that the God of the Bible should be feared. Wisdom and instruction refer to the Bible's theory of causation. Isaiah announced:

> I am the LORD, and there is none else, there is no God beside me: I girded thee, though thou hast not known me: That they may know from the rising of the sun, and from the west, that there is none beside me. I am the LORD, and there is none else. I form the light, and create darkness: I make peace, and create evil: I the LORD do all these things. Drop down, ye heavens, from above, and let the skies pour down righteousness: let the earth open, and let them bring forth salvation, and let righteousness spring up together; I the LORD have created it. Woe unto him that striveth with his Maker! Let the potsherd strive with the potsherds of the earth. Shall the clay say to him that fashioneth it, What makest thou? or thy work, He hath no hands? (Isa. 45:5–9)

The fool denies this. He believes that he operates in a world independent of the God of the Bible who brings judgment in history. The prophet Isaiah identified such a fool: the nation of Israel.

> Therefore hear now this, thou that art given to pleasures, that dwellest carelessly, that sayest in thine heart, I am, and none else beside me; I shall not sit as a widow, neither shall I know the loss of children: But these two things shall come to thee in a moment in one day, the loss of children, and widowhood: they shall come upon thee in their perfection for the multitude of thy sorceries, and for the great abundance of thine enchantments. For thou hast trusted in thy wickedness: thou hast said, None seeth me. Thy wisdom and thy knowledge, it hath perverted thee; and thou hast said in thine heart, I am, and none else beside me. Therefore shall evil come upon thee; thou shalt not know from whence it riseth: and mischief shall fall upon thee; thou shalt not be able to put if off: and desolation shall come upon thee suddenly, which thou shalt not know (Isaiah 47:8–11).

Isaiah brought a covenant lawsuit. Every covenant lawsuit threatens the listener with God's negative sanctions.

B. Avoiding Losses

Negative sanctions, not positive sanctions, are the focus of this proverb. The fear of the Lord is the beginning of knowledge. We do not fear His positive sanctions. We fear His negative sanctions. So, the beginning of knowledge points to the threat of loss. Jesus said to His disciples: "And fear not them which kill the body, but are not able to kill the soul: but rather fear him which is able to destroy both soul and body in hell" (Matt. 10:28).

A familiar theme in Western literature is the corrupt bargain with the devil. Someone seeks positive sanctions in history. In order to gain them, he makes a bargain—a contract—with Satan regarding the afterlife. He trades his soul in eternity for blessings in history. This theme is a variation of Satan's temptation of Jesus in the wilderness. "Again, the devil taketh him up into an exceeding high mountain, and sheweth him all the kingdoms of the world, and the glory of them; And saith unto him, All these things will I give thee, if thou wilt fall down and worship me" (Matt. 4:8–9).[2] Here, Satan offered positive sanctions. He did not mention negative sanctions. Neither did the serpent mention negative sanctions to Eve. He did not have to. Eve knew. "And the woman said unto the serpent, We may eat of the fruit of the trees of the garden: But of the fruit of the tree which is in the midst of the garden, God hath said, Ye shall not eat of it, neither shall ye touch it, lest ye die" (Gen. 3:2–3).

The fool denies that God brings negative sanctions in history. To turn to God as the source of positive sanctions in history would imply faith in God as the source of negative sanctions. So, the fool seeks positive sanctions elsewhere: from nature, from the strength of his own hands, or from a corrupt bargain with others. This is what Solomon warns against in the early section of the book.

Proverbs, along with the entire Bible, teaches that the positive sanctions offered by Satan or his covenant-breaking subordinates are not worth the price: the negative sanctions imposed by God. Proverbs affirms a value scale and a theory of causation that stand in opposition to Satan's. The wise man imputes great value to God's positive sanctions, but this is not the starting point for biblical wisdom. The starting point is man's imputation of negative value to covenant-breaking. *Covenant-keeping begins with the fear of God.* It is the avoidance of God's negative sanctions, not the promise of positive

---

2. Gary North, *Priorities and Dominion: An Economic Commentary on Matthew*, 2nd ed. (Dallas, Georgia: Point Five Press, [2000] 2012), ch. 3.

sanctions, that initially motivates the covenant-keeper. This fear of God is the first step to covenantal maturity.

Men trust something to provide positive sanctions. They also fear negative sanctions. If men fear God as the sanctions-bringer in history and eternity, they are less likely to fear any aspect of the creation, whose sanctions are both temporal and subordinate to God's sanctions. By trusting God and by obeying God, covenant-keepers have a sure way to deal with the negative sanctions threatened by the creation. They can exercise dominion over the creation precisely because they fear God more than they fear any aspect of the creation. In every social philosophy, the source of negative sanctions occupies the peak of the hierarchy. This proverb is clear: God occupies this place of supremacy.

We must seek to avoid the negative sanction of loss. The New Covenant affirms that the supreme positive sanction is God's removal of the threat of negative sanctions in eternity.

> Every man's work shall be made manifest: for the day shall declare it, because it shall be revealed by fire; and the fire shall try every man's work of what sort it is. If any man's work abide which he hath built thereupon, he shall receive a reward. If any man's work shall be burned, he shall suffer loss: but he himself shall be saved; yet so as by fire (I Cor. 3:13–15).[3]

The forfeiture of eternal salvation is the ultimate loss. In contrast, the loss of God's positive sanctions in eternity is tolerable. The imposition of God's negative eternal sanctions is not. They must be tolerated for eternity (Luke 16:19–31).[4]

Conclusion

The Book of Proverbs affirms God as the source of all sanctions, positive and negative. God has laid down His law in the Bible. This law is confirmed by sanctions, both positive and negative. Godly instruction affirms causality as governed by a sovereign God. The fool rejects such instruction.

The implication of this proverb is not intuitive, but it is crucial: *if you can avoid negative sanctions, positive sanctions will compound over time.* Success begins with a systematic program to avoid losses. The Book of Proverbs supplies this program.

---

3. Gary North, *Judgment and Dominion: An Economic Commentary on First Corinthians*, 2nd ed. (Dallas, Georgia: Point Five Press, [2001] 2012), ch. 3.

4. Gary North, *Treasure and Dominion: An Economic Commentary on Luke*, 2nd ed. (Dallas, Georgia: Point Five Press, [2000] 2012), ch. 40.

This implies that positive sanctions are more fundamental than negative sanctions. This in turn implies that dominion is more fundamental than linear history. It is not simply that time moves forward to final judgment. It is that there is progress in history, which is not limited to doctrinal precision. Covenant-keepers have legitimate hope for history. This begins with the fear of God.

Success begins with a systematic program to avoid losses.

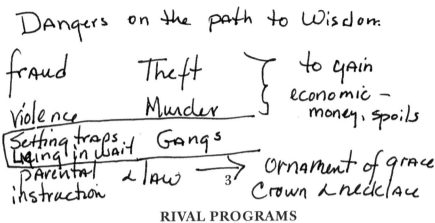

Dangers on the path to Wisdom:

fraud   Theft   ⎤ to gain
violence Murder ⎦ economic —
                        money, spoils

Setting traps, Gangs
Lying in wait
Parental   ∠ law →₃ Ornament of grace
instruction   Crown ∠ necklace

RIVAL PROGRAMS
OF INHERITANCE

My son, hear the instruction of thy father, and forsake not the law of thy mother:
For they shall be an ornament of grace unto thy head, and chains about thy neck.
My son, if sinners entice thee, consent thou not.

PROVERBS 1:8–10

A. Inheritance and Disinheritance

This passage deals with inheritance: point five of the biblical covenant.[1] A father tells his son that parental instruction and law are the equivalents of an ornament of grace—a crown—and a necklace. These are positive sanctions, clearly part of an inheritance: parents to son. The imagery here is of visible representations of power and wealth.

In contrast is disinheritance. The way of sinners is the way of death. Death comes in the form of temptation: to depart from the paths of righteousness. The father lists the enticements that sinners offer to righteous people in their effort to corrupt them. The list focuses on illegitimate ways to extract wealth from judicially innocent victims. These are crimes, for they involve either fraud or violence.

> If they say, Come with us, let us lay wait for blood, let us lurk privily for the innocent without cause: Let us swallow them up alive as the grave; and whole, as those that go down into the pit: We shall find all precious substance, we shall fill our houses with spoil (1:11–13).

---

1. Ray R. Sutton, *That You May Prosper: Dominion By Covenant*, 2nd ed. (Tyler, Texas: Institute for Christian Economics, [1987] 1992), ch. 5. Gary North, *Unconditional Surrender: God's Program for Victory*, 5th ed. (Powder Springs, Georgia: American Vision, [1988] 2010), ch. 5.

This is an exceptionally clear framing of the crime of theft. The language invokes the image of the grave. The victims are to be murdered. To "wait for blood" is to plot to commit murder. Life is in the blood.

> But flesh with the life thereof, which is the blood thereof, shall ye not eat. And surely your blood of your lives will I require; at the hand of every beast will I require it, and at the hand of man; at the hand of every man's brother will I require the life of man (Gen. 9:4–5).

> For the life of the flesh is in the blood: and I have given it to you upon the altar to make an atonement for your souls: for it is the blood that maketh an atonement for the soul (Lev. 17:11).

The goal is economic gain. "We shall find all precious substance, we shall fill our houses with spoil." This is disinheritance. The victims' heirs will someday deserve this wealth, but murderers plan to obtain it.

Then comes the proposed benefit. "Cast in thy lot among us; let us all have one purse" (1:14). The gang of murderers shares a common purse. The wealth of the innocent victims will fill this purse. Then the criminals will share the proceeds of the crime. Nothing is said regarding the proportional shares that will be eventually handed out to the participants. Nothing is said of the structure of organizational authority that decides who gets what and when. The target of this enticement is expected to trust the intent and judgment of those criminals who possess institutional authority. This assumption is known by the phrase, "honor among thieves."

B. A Criminal Conspiracy

The sinners entice a man into crime by offering him a share in the proceeds. But who is to police the thieves? Who is to monitor the purse? If it pays to spill innocent blood, why shouldn't it pay to spill the blood of one's partners in crime? The restraint of God's law is not part of the psychological makeup of criminals. There is not the same degree of *self-government* that we find in families that bring up their children to fear God and respect His law. Therefore, coercion within conspiracies must be far greater. Fear governs them.

Solomon is contrasting two ways of life: God-fearing and God-hating. He is contrasting the economic results of the two ways of life: prosperity and destruction. The righteous bring good judgment to their daily lives; the unrighteous bring bad judgment, violence, and destruction. The evil that men practice against the innocent becomes part of the psychological make-up of the evildoers. They cannot escape their habitual patterns of existence. They seek gain at the expense of those who possess wealth. Their colleagues in crime share the spoils. In so doing, they become each other's targets.

Solomon understood this. "For their feet run to evil, and make haste to shed blood. Surely in vain the net is spread in the sight of any bird, And they lay wait for their own blood; they lurk privily for their own lives. So are the ways of every one that is greedy of gain; which taketh away the life of the owners thereof" (1:16–19). What bird is he speaking about? Each member of the gang. They lay nets for each other, but not in plain sight. In the criminal conspiracy, the secret society, and the brotherhood of blood, the members are threatened by the inescapable results of their own ethics. They believe that non-members are fit for the slaughter. But this attitude cannot be restricted easily to the world outside the "household" of the brotherhood. It spreads into the inner circle.

C. Common Purse, Common Curse

The common purse guarantees their downfall. It becomes the supreme prize in an organization that imitates a family, but without the bond of love. As with a family's common purse, the gang's common purse is filled with money. What is the basis of the allocation of this money? In a family, the father allocates the family's wealth. In a criminal conspiracy, a pseudo-father does, or a council of would-be patriarchs. This raises the central organizational question: *Allocation by what standard?* Who imputes value to the individual efforts of the conspiracy's members?

Here is the central issue of all economic theory: *imputation*. Imputation is subjective. Value is therefore subjective. The epistemological question is this: How can men accurately impute economic value to the world around them? Specifically, how can they accurately assess the economic value of the contributions of other men?

The free market provides a constant assessment of each man's contribution to the production process. There is a gigantic *competitive auction* for labor, for capital goods, for raw materials, and for all other scarce economic resources. This auction process produces prices by which we can evaluate what we are worth to others in the market, as well as what they are worth to us. This competitive bidding process is based on a legal principle: open entry to a market, i.e., competition without coercion. Free pricing, the accountant's profit-and-loss report, and the legal right to transfer ownership are all essential to our knowledge of what different things really cost.[2] Economic freedom brings us accurate knowledge, and therefore more wealth.

In contrast to a free market, the criminal conspiracy is coercive. It is a collective. As in a socialist economy, it cannot permit open competition for men's services. Criminals cannot openly advertise their services to other "customers." Also, oath-bound brotherhoods are closed societies. Members cannot leave in response to higher bids from other criminal conspiracies. Thus, it becomes difficult—in fact, almost impossible—for the members of a criminal band to assess the economic contribution of each member.

Here is the curse of the common purse. The way that criminals decide who is to receive what portion is by coercion. The strongest get the largest portions. But this places a premium on ruthlessness. The bloodthirstiness of criminals is enhanced by the very nature of collective ownership. They all share one purse. The source of the capital in the purse is not economic production, but rather economic pillage and destruction. This is why criminal conspiracies and socialist governments are often allies. The concept of a common purse to be filled by stealing the wealth of productive people is common to both criminal conspiracies and socialist and communist political conspiracies. In both cases, to cite Hayek's famous tenth chapter in *The Road to Serfdom* (1944), the worst get on top.

Secrecy is basic to such societies. But this secrecy is not limited to those outside the brotherhood. "Surely in vain the net is spread in the sight of any bird" (1:17). *Those who are intent on snaring unsuspecting birds become masters of concealing nets.* Traps are sprung on those who least suspect them. For this reason, every member knows that he is a potential bird, and he must live a life of continual wariness. To escape traps and to set traps: this is on the minds of members of a criminal band. They snare the helpless as a way of life. These skills are not abandoned within the conspiracy.

Satanism exhibits certain recurring features: secret oaths, signs, and communications; death threats to any who would break the vow,

---

2. The classic statement of this principle is Ludwig von Mises, "Economic Calculation in the Socialist Commonwealth" (1920), reprinted in F. A. Hayek (ed.), *Collectivist Economic Planning* (London: Routledge & Kegan Paul, 1935), ch. 3. The academic community either ignored or actively denied the truth of Mises' insight until 1991, when the Soviet Union's socialist economy collapsed, and that enormous nation-empire ceased to exist.

of secrecy; malicious intent against those outside the secret order; the quest for wealth and power by means of coercion against the productive members of society; and the common purse. It was not an accident that Judas was a thief, that he secretly conspired against Christ, that he was possessed by Satan, and that he controlled the disciples' common purse (John 12:6). The temptations associated with the common purse are so great that the New Testament specifies that those who control church finances—deacons—must live otherwise blameless, public lives (I Tim. 3:8–13).[3] What goes into the common purse in a godly society is limited: the tithe for the church, and minimal revenues for the civil government. The society of Satan is the society of the universal common purse.

D. Faith in Violence

The intended targets of the conspiracy are judicially innocent. They also possess wealth. The conspirators devise a plan to reallocate this wealth into the common purse. They seek to substitute their goals for those of the innocent but economically successful victims. They seek to thwart the allocation of wealth that has been produced by society in a non-violent way. They propose to substitute violence for peace.

The teacher advises the listener to reject the offer and avoid the enticer. "My son, walk not thou in the way with them; refrain thy foot from their path: For their feet run to evil, and make haste to shed blood" (1:15–16). The mental image is of men moving in haste. They are not shuffling toward evil, nor walking at a brisk clip. They are running. This points to their self-conscious embrace of evil. There is no hesitation here. These conspirators are not ready to hear counsel from the righteous.

They know exactly what they are doing in the sense of self-conscious preparation. They do not know what they are doing in the sense of awareness of God's covenantal system of ethical cause and effect. Their understanding of causality is defective. They regard violence against the innocent as the basis of success in this life. They are power religionists.[4] This assessment undergirds the following passage.

> Surely in vain the net is spread in the sight of any bird. And they lay wait
> for their own blood; they lurk privily for their own lives. So are the ways

---

3. Gary North, *Hierarchy and Dominion: An Economic Commentary on First Timothy*, 2nd ed. (Dallas, Georgia: Point Five Press, [2001] 2012), ch. 4.

4. Gary North, *Authority and Dominion: An Economic Commentary on Exodus,* (Dallas, Georgia: Point Five Press, 2012) , Part 1, *Representation and Dominion* (1985).

of every one that is greedy of gain; which taketh away the life of the owners thereof (1:17–19)

If a bird can see the net, it will not venture into the trap. Success in the hunt rests on successful deception of the victim. The conspirators understand this, which is why their plan involves lurking. Thus, the innocent will fall into their trap. This passage points to the larger picture. God has set a trap for the conspirators.

This trap has a trigger: the conspirators' trap. *In setting a trap for the innocent, they will be snared themselves.* God's covenantal system of cause and effect governs men's plans. But covenant-breakers do not acknowledge that they operate in a larger system of causation. They do not understand that, in setting a trap for the innocent, they set a trap for themselves. "And they lay wait for their own blood; they lurk privily for their own lives."

The passage ends with a summation: "So are the ways of every one that is greedy of gain; which taketh away the life of the owners thereof" (1:19). The father warns his son that there is a pattern of criminality. The criminal seeks to gain at the expense of a proposed victim. The example of a band of murderous thieves serves as the model. The group seeks to get rich at someone else's expense. This involves murder. It is at bottom a transfer of inheritance.

The conspirators do not operate in a universe in which power is supreme. They operate in a universe in which *ethics is supreme*, for God is absolutely sovereign. He is a God of law and justice. There is power, but this power does not rest on the principle that might makes right. It rests on the principle that supreme right is enforced by supreme might. As the Creator, God possesses supreme right and supreme power. He delegates power and wealth in terms of His decree and the legal order He has established to govern mankind. The laws of inheritance, not the exercise of power, are to govern the transfer of property, generation to generation. All attempts to interfere with these Bible-revealed laws of inheritance are a form of theft.

Conclusion

The Book of Proverbs presents the story of competition for inheritance in history. Rival organizations compete for the allegiance of men. Each offers a program of inheritance.

The father's offer of inheritance is based on ethics: covenant-keeping. The first nine chapters of Proverbs present the father's testament

to his son: godly wisdom. The father's inheritance correlates righteousness and success.

In contrast is a rival program of inheritance. It leads to death. It is
based on an illegal attempt to steal the godly inheritance. Seduction
is basic to this program of disinheritance. So are deception, theft, and
murder. The archetype is the Fall of man in the garden. Its historical
extension is described here in the Book of Proverbs: a challenge to the
laws of righteousness by a conspiracy that promotes ethical rebellion.

Rival programs of inheritance

Godly wisdom   Death
    ↓   ↓
Righteousness &   deception
    Success   theft
                               murder

4

WISDOM AND WEALTH

Wisdom crieth without; she uttereth her voice in the streets: She crieth in the chief place of concourse, in the openings of the gates: in the city she uttereth her words, saying, How long, ye simple ones, will ye love simplicity? and the scorners delight in their scorning, and fools hate knowledge?

PROVERBS 1:20–22

A. The Lure of Two Women

Wisdom is personified as female in the Book of Proverbs. The first instance of this practice is here. There is no explanation for this in the proverb. My explanation is this: because covenant-breaking is pictured throughout the Old Testament as the equivalent of harlotry, and because the theme of the first nine chapters of Proverbs is the conflict between wisdom and foolishness, the personification of wisdom as female makes sense. *Wisdom is the faithful wife*.

Wisdom is pictured here as standing in the public square and calling men to return to her. There are three categories of listeners: simpletons, scorners, and fools. She goes into the streets, where people can be found. She goes into the concourse—the public square—which is where the streets come together: the center of the city. She also goes to the gates of the city, where civic judgment is rendered. *Biblical religion is a public faith for the public square.* It is not a religion confined to the hearth and home. It is therefore not the religion of classical Greece, where a wife tended the household's fire as a family priestess,[1]

---

1. Fustel de Coulanges, *The Ancient City: A Study on the Religion, Laws, and Institutions of Greece and Rome* (Garden City, New York: Doubleday Anchor, [1864] 1955), Book II, Chapter IX.

but had no influence in the courts.[2] In classical religion—Greece and Rome—women had no public role to play in the religion of the city. A woman served as a priestess at the Oracle of Delphi: the Pythia. Women served in Rome as vestal virgins who kept the city's fire burning. This was the only official religious role for Roman women. Women played no role in politics, since civic religion was the basis of politics.[3] The women who exercised influence in the corridors of power in classical Greece were courtesans—adulterous mistresses of powerful married men. In Israel, Deborah served as a judge. This would have been inconceivable in classical Greece.

Wisdom in this passage serves the same role as a prophet did in Mosaic Israel: someone who brings a covenant lawsuit against the nation. She publicly identifies the sources of Israel's covenant-breaking: simpletons, scorners, and fools. The people have gone astray. This is not a conspiracy against the people by covenant-breaking rulers. *This is a conspiracy against God by the whole nation.* Wisdom cries out: "Turn you at my reproof: behold, I will pour out my spirit unto you, I will make known my words unto you" (1:23).

Wisdom is personified. She offers to pour out her spirit on men. Wisdom here is presented as the personification of God. Wisdom is not pictured as impersonal, but rather as highly personal.

Wisdom is not the only woman in the public square. The harlot is there, too. She also seeks for those who will listen to her, and then follow her imprecations.

> For at the window of my house I looked through my casement, And beheld among the simple ones, I discerned among the youths, a young man void of understanding, Passing through the street near her corner; and he went the way to her house, In the twilight, in the evening, in the black and dark night: And, behold, there met him a woman with the attire of an harlot, and subtil of heart. (She is loud and stubborn; her feet abide not in her house: Now is she without, now in the streets, and lieth in wait at every corner.) So she caught him, and kissed him, and with an impudent face said unto him, I have peace offerings with me; this day have I payed my vows. Therefore came I forth to meet thee, diligently to seek thy face, and I have found thee (7:6–15).

B. The Correct Response

What is the correct response to these conflicting calls? "To know wisdom and instruction; to perceive the words of understanding; to re-

---

2. *Ibid.*, I:VIII:2, III.
3. *Ibid.*, III:VII:3, XII.

Richest Honor *long days*

ceive the instruction of wisdom, justice, and judgment, and equity; to give subtilty to the simple, to the young man knowledge and discretion" (1:2–4).

The early chapters of Proverbs are concerned with biblical wisdom: how to obtain it, cultivate it, and apply it. Proverbs also contrasts biblical wisdom with the false wisdom of this world, which lures the unsuspecting into the lusts of the flesh. It is stated repeatedly that wisdom is a valuable asset.

> Happy is the man that findeth wisdom, and the man that getteth understanding. For the merchandise of it is better than the merchandise of silver, and the gain thereof than fine gold. She is more precious than rubies: and all the things thou canst desire are not to be compared unto her. Length of days is in her right hand; and in her left hand riches and honour. Her ways are ways of pleasantness, and all her paths are peace (3:13–17).[4]

Of all capital assets, biblical wisdom has the highest rate of return.

The comparisons here are revealing. Gold, silver, precious gems, long life: wisdom is greater than all of these. Throughout the book, long life, riches, and honor are closely associated with biblical wisdom, indicating that wisdom leads to these external blessings. We are reminded of the words of Jesus concerning the kingdom of God: "But seek ye first the kingdom of God, and his righteousness; and all these things shall be added unto you" (Matt. 6:33).[5] The old hymn, "I'd rather have Jesus than silver and gold" really misses the point. Better to sing, "I'd rather have Jesus *and* silver and gold." There is a relationship between (1) the exercise of biblical wisdom, biblical justice, and biblical judgment and (2) outward signs of prosperity.

Solomon was noted both for his wisdom (I Kings 4:29–34) and his wealth (I Kings 10). In fact, the queen of Sheba's words linked the two. "And she said to the king, It was a true report that I heard in mine own land of thy acts and of thy wisdom. Howbeit I believed not the words, until I came, and mine eyes had seen it: and, behold, the half was not told me thy wisdom and prosperity exceedeth the fame which I heard" (I Kings 10:6–7).

C. What Is Wisdom?

The emphasis in Proverbs is not on the possession of knowledge as a mass of facts, including economic facts. Proverbs encourages the

---

4. Chapter 9.

5. Gary North, *Priorities and Dominion: An Economic Commentary on Matthew*, 2nd ed. (Dallas, Georgia: Point Five Press, [2000] 2012), ch. 15.

quest for wisdom, which is associated with honest judgment, justice, and fairness (equity). It is also important to have the ability to impart this wisdom to the naive ("simple") and the young, who are impressionable.[6] This indicates that knowledge of God's principles is not to be a monopoly of a priestly elite. "To understand a proverb, and the interpretation; the words of the wise, and their dark [puzzling] saying" (1:6). The translation of the mental puzzles of the wise into the language of the people is deemed by the public to be a sign of true wisdom. *Puzzle   Wisdom is applied ethics.*

Wisdom is not simply right knowledge, but also right action. *Wisdom is applied ethics.* There are cause-and-effect relationships in this world that must be respected if men are to prosper. The fundamental principle is this one: "The fear of the LORD is the beginning of knowledge: but fools despise wisdom and instruction" (1:7).[7] It is the awful (awe-full) *fear of God* that should begin a man's education. *This is the first principle of cause and effect.* The wise man is a competent judge of people, as well as situations. He relates God's principles of ethics to the concrete events of the day. Solomon's wisdom was demonstrated in the case of the two women who argued over whose baby was whose. He threatened to cut the child in half. He then saw which woman agreed to give up the child to the other (I Kings 31:28). This case is the biblical archetype of wise judgment by a civil ruler. Relating God's laws to men's lives is the essence of biblical wisdom. This is biblical *casuistry* in action.

The Book of Proverbs is an eminently practical book. The introductory section creates interest by the reader in what is to follow, thereby increasing the likelihood that he will take the proverbs seriously. The first nine chapters are devoted to a presentation of the importance of wisdom. Then 21 chapters follow, which give us the proverbs of Solomon (who had 3,000 of them, along with 1,005 songs: I Kings 4:32). Then the final chapter gives us the insights of King Lemuel's mother, whoever she was. These proverbs are supposed to be considered carefully and then acted upon.

These proverbs represent a form of capital. Adhering to the proverbs produces an increase in personal wealth. But an increase in personal wealth is not sufficient to guarantee success. This is one of the themes of the early section. What is needed to guarantee success is the wisdom to serve as a faithful steward of the wealth that is to come. To

---

6. Chapter 1.
7. Chapter 2.

present to men a handbook for increasing wealth is not enough; they need *moral capital* to make proper use of the forthcoming income.

Capital, in the Bible's perspective, comes from conformity to the laws of God (Deut. 28:1–14).[8] Increasing per capita wealth is part of God's program of "positive feedback," wherein conformity to God's law increases a man's wealth (and a society's wealth), which in turn is to serve as a confirmation of the reliability of the covenant. "But thou shalt remember the Lord thy God: for it is he that giveth thee power to get wealth, that he may establish his covenant which he sware unto thy fathers, as it is this day" (Deut. 8:18).[9] To establish His covenant, He gives faithful men their wealth. The progression is supposed to conform to this pattern: obedience...increase...greater obedience ...greater increase...dominion.

In order to integrate the laws of economics with the facts of economic life, men need a guide. This guide is the Bible. The special revelation of God gives men the interpretive framework for understanding economic cause and effect. Men are not to misuse their knowledge of economic cause and effect. This is why we are given the introductory chapters of Proverbs, to convince us that *the ultimate goal of personal wealth is the increase of capital necessary to implement biblical wisdom in a corporate public form: the kingdom of God*. To use the knowledge found in Proverbs for any purpose other than the extension of God's kingdom is a form of rebellion.

D. The Market for Wisdom

It was perhaps the greatest of Greek myths—a myth held mainly by Socrates, Plato, and their followers—that if men *understand* the truth and the good, they will *believe* the truth and *do* the morally upright thing. In the Greek philosophical tradition, knowledge is the pathway to salvation. *Knowledge saves.* In contrast, the Bible affirms that wisdom is the pathway to salvation. But it teaches that wisdom is not a matter of precise logic or intuitive insight. *Wisdom is the product of God's grace.* The natural man receives not the things of the Spirit (I Cor. 2:14).[10] Therefore, when wisdom is proclaimed in the streets, there may be few who respond favorably. The simpletons—moral sim-

---

8. Gary North, *Inheritance and Dominion: An Economic Commentary on Deuteronomy*, 2nd ed. (Dallas, Georgia: Point Five Press, [1999] 2012), ch. 69.

9. *Ibid.*, ch. 21.

10. Gary North, *Judgment and Dominion: An Economic Commentary on First Corinthians*, 2nd. ed. (Dallas, Georgia: Point Five Press, [2001] 2012), ch. 2.

pletons, not people with low intelligence—do not come and sit at the feet of the wise teacher. "But ye have set at nought all My counsel, and would [have] none of My reproof" (1:25). Simpletons do not take seriously the sin-restraining wisdom of God's law.

Solomon here equates wisdom with God. "Then shall they call upon me, but I will not answer; they shall seek me early, but they shall not find me: For that they hated knowledge, and did not choose the fear of the LORD: They would [have] none of my counsel: they despised all my reproof" (1:28–30). The simpletons had refused the counsel of God, whose word had been proclaimed in the streets. Now they face calamity all alone. Fear, desolation, and destruction are therefore inevitable (1:27).

1. No Market for Wisdom

The market for wisdom in Israel was nonexistent. Yet this was the era of Solomon, the wisest and richest of Israel's kings, at the peak of Israel's influence. Even at zero price, there was far more supply of wisdom than demand for wisdom. In short, *wisdom was a glut on the market*—not on the supply side, but on the demand side. So vast was this glut in relation to demand that the supply would eventually be removed by God. Wisdom would someday be sought, but none would be found. The father taught his son that God hides Himself from those who do not regard His word as valid and valuable in good times as well as bad. When bad times come, men seek answers, but wise answers are not to be found by those who are in rebellion against God. They seek, but they cannot find. God reserves the right to restrict the easy availability of wisdom in times of crisis whenever men have failed to take Him seriously during prosperous times.

Built into the creation is a cause-and-effect system based on adherence to, or rejection of, God's Bible-revealed law. Over and over, we are told that the response of a man to the law of God determines his external circumstances. *Prosperity is the product of men's outward adherence to biblical law*. Poverty is the result of outward adherence to another legal order, or an anti-legal order. "Therefore shall they eat of the fruit of their own way, and be filled with their own devices. For the turning away of the simple shall slay them, and the prosperity of fools shall destroy them. But whoso hearkeneth unto me shall dwell safely, and shall be quiet from fear of evil" (1:31–33). All societies that reject God's wisdom have self-destructive aspects.

When the Assyrians came to take Israel away, there was no mass repentance. When the Babylonians came to carry Judah away, there was no mass repentance. Men may have called upon some sort of god—a god of their own creation—but the God of the Bible did not hear them, judicially speaking. When the ways of the wicked finally result in the destruction of their prosperity, men are left without moral guidelines. The moral order that they had trusted now collapses before their eyes, and they do not know or understand the biblical alternative.

2. The Twentieth Century

After the First World War (1914–18), a wave of debauchery and "high living" swept the West. Weimar Germany's cabaret society, America's speakeasies, France's dada art movement, and the British elite's open rejection of Victorian morality were all aspects of men's rejection of pre-War morality, which had been at least Christian on the surface. In America, historians call this period "the Roaring Twenties." The roaring twenties turned into the disastrous thirties. Economic depression broke the public's confidence in the West's economic order. Socialists, redistributionists, and populists of all varieties came into power, or close to power. Germany and Italy went fascist-socialist. Britain and the United States went Keynesian, which was basically a form of statism, as Keynes admitted in his long-neglected introduction to the German language edition of his *General Theory* in 1936. The corporate state is still with us, struggling wildly in its death throes, desperately trying to find a way to achieve rapid economic growth without price inflation and massive indebtedness.

The crises of the 1930s and 1940s did not lead to widespread repentance in any Western nation. People chased after a number of superficially different economic and political solutions, but these all were variations of the Moloch state. The public's theology did not change, so their solutions were no better than the problems they were intended to solve. The debauchery of Weimar Germany—the pornography, homosexuality, occultism, and nihilism—has become today's universal subculture, and is increasingly being absorbed into the common culture of the day. So has Weimar Germany's policy of monetary inflation, though not nearly that severe. So has despair, though not nearly that severe. Weimar ended in the tyranny and war launched by the National Socialist Democratic Workers' Party (Nazis). The West must change direction if it is to avoid a similar outcome.

3. Reform Without Biblical Wisdom

There is a tendency on the part of deeply ideological groups to work for the destruction of the present world order, which is run by an Establishment. Anti-Establishment ideologues work for social revolution on the assumption that their group will pick up the pieces. Without the destruction of the present order, they say, there is no hope. Simultaneously, the current Establishment is desperate to consolidate its much-heralded new world order. It does so by means of its traditional strategies: political manipulation, control over money, control over education, international treaties, government-regulated trade agreements, government subsidies to big business and large voting blocs, and elitist initiation.

Christians should recognize that the market for wisdom is almost always minimal, except in historically rare periods, such as the late Roman Empire, Europe in the Middle Ages, the Protestant Reformation, and America's two religious revivals.[11] A revival of interest in God's wisdom is abnormal. When societies self-destruct, they are not often replaced by a Christian social order. Christians should work toward the reconstruction of the existing social order, but they had better recognize that the market for wisdom is limited today. Their message has not been taken seriously, any more than it was taken seriously in Solomon's day. The distressed masses run toward new, radical variations of today's Moloch state. There is nothing new under the sun.

> They would none of my counsel: they despised all my reproof. Therefore shall they eat of the fruit of their own way, and be filled with their own devices. For the turning away of the simple shall slay them, and the prosperity of fools shall destroy them (1:30–32).

Occasionally the market for wisdom increases. "But whoso hearkeneth unto me shall dwell safely, and shall be quiet from fear of evil" (v. 33). That is our hope today—our realistic but currently utopian hope.

Conclusion

The introductory remarks in Proverbs are an expansion of the closing remarks of Ecclesiastes: "Let us hear the conclusion of the whole matter. Fear God, and keep his commandments: for this is the whole duty of man. For God shall bring every work into judgment, with

---

11. The First Great Awakening (1730–50) and the Second Great Awakening (1801–50).

every secret thing, whether it be good, or whether it be evil" (Eccl. 12:13–14).[12] Wealth has a purpose. Wisdom tells us what this purpose is: a means of dominion. We are to think God's thoughts after Him, bringing all things into judgment, according to His standards of righteousness.

This is not an exclusively private faith with exclusively private consequences. It is a public faith with public consequences. It is covenantal faith. It involves the whole of society. This is why wisdom must be in the streets, calling covenant-breakers to turn back from their poverty-producing ways.

Wealth has a purpose — a means of dominion

They shall eat of the fruit of their own way —

---

12. Gary North, *Autonomy and Stagnation: An Economic Commentary on Ecclesiastes* (Dallas, Georgia: Point Five Press, 2012), ch. 45.

5

PATHS OF RIGHTEOUS JUDGMENT

For the LORD giveth wisdom: out of his mouth cometh knowledge and under-standing. He layeth up sound wisdom for the righteous: he is a buckler [shield] to them that walk uprightly. He keepeth the paths of judgment, and preserveth the way of his saints. Then shalt thou understand righteousness, and judgment, and equity; yea, every good path.

PROVERBS 2:6–9

The early sections of the Book of Proverbs deal with man's gaining wisdom from God: "To know wisdom and instruction; to perceive the words of understanding" (1:2). Wisdom is seen as the most valuable asset a person can possess. "If thou seekest her as silver, and searchest for her as for hid treasures; then thou shalt understand the fear of the LORD, and find the knowledge of God" (2:4–5). "The fear of the LORD is the beginning of knowledge: but fools despise wisdom and instruction" (1:7).[1]

The process begins with the word of God, this proverb says. "For the LORD giveth wisdom: out of his mouth cometh knowledge and understanding." This is *special revelation*. This is given uniquely to covenant-keepers. "He is a buckler [shield] to them that walk uprightly." That is, God defends His people in their walk before Him.

Here, as elsewhere in the Bible, wisdom is described as a pathway. Men walk down paths. A man walks on one path at a time. A pathway can head for destruction. This is the path of the unrighteous. In contrast is the path of righteousness. This proverb says that God preserves the way of the saints.

This preservation of their pathway is a gift of God. God grants to some people the wisdom to pursue judgment. The meaning here is

---

1. Chapter 2.

34

judicial, but judgment is a broader concept than civil law. It means the ability to assess the events of life in terms of God's holy law. *Judgment is ethical*.

"Then shalt thou understand righteousness, and judgment, and equity; yea, every good path." This proverb indicates that God directs men's steps down a particular path. Over time, the day-by-day obligation to make personal decisions creates understanding in the minds of the decision-makers. The indication here is that *the exercise of good judgment is cumulative*.

There are multiple paths of righteousness, according to Proverbs. These paths are revealed in the Bible. It is basic for long-term success that people walk in these paths. Those who leave these paths of righteousness thereby choose the ways of darkness (2:13), the paths to death (2:18). God calls the paths of righteousness, "the paths of life" (2:19).

To follow these righteous paths is to acknowledge and observe as morally and economically binding the biblically revealed foundations of long-term economic success: "For the upright shall dwell in the land, and the perfect shall remain in it. But the wicked shall be cut off from the earth, and the transgressors shall be rooted out of it" (2:21–22). The message here is this: in their respective pursuit of righteousness and unrighteousness, *covenant-keepers will displace covenant-breakers in history*. This comes as a result of the widespread exercise of righteous judgment. The positive sanctions of God's covenantal legal order overwhelm whatever positive benefits that are reaped by covenant-breakers through their adherence to the externals of biblical law. Over time, good gets better and bad gets worse, both ethically and culturally. *Covenant-keeping builds a permanent civilization. Covenant- breaking does not.*

As more people in society develop the skills associated with judging events and people's actions, the social order becomes more consistently biblical. Wisdom is not merely personal. It is corporate. This proverb says that God provides such wisdom. It is a form of grace, i.e., a *favor unmerited* by the person or society receiving the gift from God. This can be described accurately as *a subsidy from God*. He subsidizes His people. They in turn extend His dominion visibly in history.

This proverb provides insight into the process of dominion. This process is above all ethical. It is part of God's covenant with His people. Through the special revelation of biblical law, covenant-keepers extend the visible jurisdiction of God's kingdom. God then rewards them visibly, as members of His kingdom. The goal is the fulfillment of the dominion covenant (Gen. 1:27–28).[2] This is to take place in time and on earth.

Conclusion

The Book of Proverbs makes it clear that *the search for wisdom is the most important of all of men's investments*. We need a more complete wisdom than that which is innate to us (Rom. 2:14–15),[3] for sin has distorted our judgment and our ability to follow what we know to be morally binding (Rom. 1:18–22).[4] This wisdom must be paid for: search costs and self-discipline. This was Christ's point in His parable of the pearl of great price (Matt. 13:44–46).[5] While men are given some wisdom through common grace[6]—sufficient to keep them alive for a time on earth, and also sufficient to condemn them on judgment day (Rom. 1:18–22)—this *unmerited gift* (the meaning of the word "grace") is nevertheless incomplete. Men must search for wisdom. Men's knowledge of the paths of righteous judgment, and their subsequent willingness to walk in them—to become doers of the word and not hearers only (Rom. 2:13; James 1:22)—is the source of their long-term prosperity.

2. Gary North, *Sovereignty and Dominion: An Economic Commentary on Genesis* (Dallas, Georgia: Point Five Press, 2012), ch. 4.

3. Gary North, *Cooperation and Dominion: An Economic Commentary on Romans*, 2nd ed. (Dallas, Georgia: Point Five Press, [2001] 2012), ch. 3.

4. *Ibid.*, ch. 2.

5. Gary North, *Priorities and Dominion: An Economic Commentary on Matthew*, 2nd ed. (Dallas, Georgia: Point Five Press, [2000] 2012), ch. 31.

6. Gary North, *Dominion and Common Grace: The Biblical Basis of Progress* (Tyler, Texas: Institute for Christian Economics, 1987).

6

VISIBLE SUCCESS

law

My son, do not forget my teaching, but guard my commands in your heart; for long life and years in plenty will they bring you, and prosperity as well. Let your good faith and loyalty never fail, but bind them about your neck. Thus will you win favour and success in the sight of God and man.

PROVERBS 3:1–4 (NEB)

Normally, I use the King James Version to introduce each chapter, but in this case, the New English Bible brings out the substance of the passage far more graphically. The translation has a weakness, however: the translation of the Hebrew word, *torah*, as "teaching," rather than "law." It should read, "do not forget my law." The link between biblical law and visible prosperity is made clear by Solomon. It is the same link that is established by Deuteronomy 28:1–14.[1] Adherence to God's laws brings visible, external benefits. These benefits are long life and plenty.

A. Long Life

We have seen this before. The promise of long life is found in Exodus 20:12: "Honor thy father and thy mother: that thy days may be long upon the land which the LORD thy God giveth thee."[2] Paul wrote that this is the first commandment with a promise (Eph. 6:2). Long life is a universally recognized benefit. When a culture adheres to the tenets of biblical law, this proverb informs us, its inhabitants will be blessed by longer life spans. A biblical law-abiding civilization will be able

---

1. Gary North, *Inheritance and Dominion: An Economic Commentary on Deuteronomy*, 2nd ed. (Dallas, Georgia: Point Five Press, [1999] 2012), ch. 69.
2. Gary North, *Authority and Dominion: An Economic Commentary on Exodus* (Dallas, Georgia: Point Five Press, 2012), Part 2, *Decalogue and Dominion* (1986), ch. 25.

to be differentiated from biblical law-transgressing civilizations by means of statistically measurable life expectancies.

One economically relevant effect of this would be inexpensive life insurance policies. The risks associated with insuring the life of a person within a given age group will be lower than the risks of insuring the life of a person within the same age group in a law-transgressing culture. In other words, a company that attempted to charge the same annual premium (fee) for both societies would experience financial losses. In the law-abiding society, the attempt to charge a premium schedule appropriate in a law-transgressing society would result in loss-producing price competition from companies that charge lower fees. Similarly, any attempt to charge the lower premiums of the law-abiding society in a law-transgressing society would also produce losses. The premiums would not cover losses from the payment of death benefits to the heirs. There would be too many deaths per thousand, compared with the number of deaths per thousand within the same age group in the biblical law-abiding culture. This is what I mean by the phrase "statistically measurable." The differences would be statistically relevant, meaning financially relevant in this example.

Long life is a very specific promise. It is not something that can be relegated to the hypothetical realm of the exclusively spiritual. The Bible is not speaking merely of a "better outlook on life," or a "deeper spiritual life," but *statistically longer life expectancy* for members of any given age group. While good people can and do die young, more of them will survive into old age than in biblical law-transgressing societies. If the Bible is true, then certain predictions concerning life expectancy will be verifiable, and verifiable in economically relevant ways, namely, life insurance premium schedules. (I am speaking here of annual renewable term insurance—death-benefit insurance—rather than insurance policies that provide some sort of savings program.)

The life expectancy of those living in the West, and in nations that have adopted Western attitudes toward ethics, is higher than that which prevails in Third World cultures that are openly demonic or animistic, and also higher than in Third World cultures that have adopted Eastern monism as their philosophical foundation, which always includes mysticism as a way to escape the burdens of material existence. We have seen a steady increase in life expectancy in the West, especially since the Protestant Reformation. Western industrialism and Western agriculture combined with Western medical techniques to create a culture in which men have a legitimate hope for longer life. This culture was the product—though not exclusively—of the Protestant religion.[3]

B. Plenty

If the benefits of adhering to biblical law are visible in the area of life expectancy, as promised, then the economic benefits described in verse 2 should also be visible. The promise of "plenty" and "prosperity" is not to be understood as applying exclusively to the inner realm of the converted man's spirit. This promise must also apply to the external, measurable realm. *in history*

This is crucially important for a proper understanding of economic growth in the West, especially since about 1780, but also during the Middle Ages, as described by Prof. Lynn White, Jr. in his book, *Medieval Technology and Social Change* (1962). Biblical attitudes toward thrift, diligence in one's occupation, the legitimacy of wealth (antienvy), and faith in progress—in time and on earth (eschatological optimism/postmillennialism)—all combined to produce rapid economic growth, especially in the two societies most influenced by Puritanism, England and New England, and also in the Netherlands and Switzerland, which had been heavily influenced by Continental Calvinism. In Japan, an essentially Protestant attitude toward the future and toward the possibility of long-term progress has prevailed since the late nineteenth century.

Men will win favor in the eyes of other men and God if they show mercy and loyalty. They will be acknowledged as successful. This testifies to the existence of almost universally recognized signs of personal and national prosperity. There is sufficient revelation to men through nature and through their own minds to convince most men of the benefits of economic growth. Without this revelation, and without men's ability to respond to it, we could devise no statistically measurable indexes of wealth. We could not even define wealth. Men are made in the image of God; so, they recognize the external tokens of His favor when they see it. The economic success of a society governed by biblical law is, in fact, a means of international evangelism. "Keep therefore and do them [my commandments]: for this is your wisdom and your understanding in the sight of the nations, which

---

3. Max Weber was closer to the truth than his critics were. *His Protestant Ethic and the Spirit of Capitalism* (1905–6) presented the case. For my assessment, see Gary North, "The 'Protestant Ethic' Hypothesis," *The Journal of Christian Reconstruction*, III (Summer 1976).

shall hear all these statutes, and say, Surely this great nation is a wise and understanding people. For what nation is there so great, who hath God so nigh unto them, as the LORD our God is in all the things that we call upon him for?" (Deut. 4:6–7).[4] If men did not see before them the tokens of God's favor and success, and if there were no universally recognized standards of success, including economic success, then the testimony of God to pagan cultures would be drastically weakened. The common ground among men—the image of God—brings a degree of agreement concerning the general benefits of life that are worth pursuing. Such agreement is not perfect, for the image of God is twisted by sin, but there is at least a working agreement.

Conclusion

There should be no guilt associated with wealth gained through adherence to biblical law. Such wealth is, in fact, a legitimate reward for honoring God and a testimony of the faithfulness of God to His covenant promises, as the words of Proverbs explicitly state. Wealth earned in this fashion is a means of evangelism: not just money to finance missions, but wealth to display before pagans whose covenant-breaking economic philosophies—socialism, Marxism, Keynesianism—have produced either widespread poverty or slow economic growth.

The hostile attitude toward private, personal wealth—but not wealth controlled by state bureaucrats—that was displayed by Ronald Sider in his book, *Rich Christians in an Age of Hunger* (1977), was in flagrant opposition to these verses. David Chilton was correct in his 1981 critique of Sider: we were *Productive Christians in an Age of Guilt-Manipulators.*[5]

With Red China's abandonment of Communism after Deng Xiao Ping's reform of 1978, soon making China the fastest growing large economy in history, and with the collapse and then disappearance of the Soviet Union in 1991, the antipathy toward capitalism has grown

---

4. North, *Inheritance and Dominion*, ch. 8.

5. In the year Chilton died, 1997, Sider's 4th edition of *Rich Christians* was published. Here, he backed away from the hard-line anti-capitalist stance of the book's earlier editions. He even adopted several of Chilton's recommended anti-interventionist reforms of Keynesianism's state-regulated market, although without mentioning Chilton. The fifth edition appeared in 2005. In the four editions published after Chilton's book appeared, Sider never mentioned Chilton's book, which Chilton revised twice to deal with later editions of *Rich Christians*. For my review of Sider's 4th edition, see North, *Inheritance and Dominion*, Appendix F: "The Economic Re-Education of Ronald J. Sider."

muted, both within the humanist intelligentsia and Christian academia. In short, visible economic results eventually do persuade critics of the free market that the free market produces more rapid economic growth than any alternative system of ownership. Their criticisms then turn to other issues, which usually involve a critique of the tastes of the common man, who can buy more of what he wants under the free market social order.

THEOCENTRIC DECISION-MAKING

Trust in the LORD with all thine heart; and lean not unto thine own understand-
ing. In all thy ways acknowledge him, and he shall direct thy paths. Be not wise
in thine own eyes: fear the LORD, and depart from evil.

PROVERBS 3:5–7

A. God's Thoughts and Man's Thoughts

Solomon contrasts God with man's understanding. It should be clear
that the words, "thine own understanding," refer to man's thoughts
when they oppose God's thoughts—the failure of self-proclaimed autonomous man to think God's thoughts after Him. Solomon calls
men to conform their thoughts to God's thoughts in any given historical situation. The alternative? "Thou hast trusted in thy wickedness:
thou hast said, None seeth me. Thy wisdom and thy knowledge, it
hath perverted thee; and thou hast said in thine heart, I am, and none
else beside me. Therefore shall evil come upon thee; thou shalt not
know from whence it riseth: and mischief shall fall upon thee, and
thou shalt not be able to put it off: and desolation shall come upon
thee suddenly, which thou shalt not know" (Isa. 47:10–11).

The whole of man's confidence should be in God, the sovereign
Creator of the universe. None of man's confidence should be placed
in any aspect of the creation. The authority of the Creator over the
creation is thereby affirmed. God is trustworthy; the creation, including man, is not.

The *Creator-creature distinction* underlies Solomon's exhortation.
Man must put his trust either in God or in some aspect of the universe. There is no third option. When he makes a decision, it must

be in terms of information, personal evaluation of that information, and a concept of cause and effect. What undergirds cause and effect? What is the reliable source of knowledge regarding cause and effect? This is the great debate over epistemology: "What can man reliably know, and how can he know it?" The Bible's answer is clear: "Trust in the LORD, and do good; so shalt thou dwell in the land, and verily thou shalt be fed" (Ps. 37:3). Again, "Commit thy way unto the LORD; trust also in him; and he shall bring it to pass" (Ps. 37:5). "O, LORD, know that the way of man is not in himself; it is not in man that walketh to direct his steps" (Jer. 10:23). If a man humbles himself before God, acknowledging his position as a wholly dependent creature, then God will favor him and see to it that he does not pursue an evil, self-defeating course of action.

God directs the steps of all men, sinners and faithful. "The king's heart is in the hand of the LORD, as the rivers of water: he turneth it whithersoever he will" (Prov. 21:1). The path a man walks is laid out by God beforehand. "For we are his workmanship, created in Christ Jesus unto good works, which God hath before ordained that we should walk in them" (Eph. 2:10). The question is: Will a man admit his total dependence on God, seek God's will, and then follow it?

How can a man seek God's guidance? Does God whisper strategies in a man's ear? The Bible says that men must turn to the Bible-revealed law of God to gain access to His guidance. To find God's law is to find Him. "With my whole heart have I sought thee: O let me not wander from thy commandments. Thy word have I hid in mine heart, that I might not sin against thee" (Ps. 119:10–11). The mastery of God's commandments gives to men the access to the wisdom required to achieve success.

B. Efficient Sinning

The modern economist assumes a universe devoid of cosmic personalism. He speaks about economic efficiency without any consideration of God's law or the relationship between covenantal conformity to God's law and external economic successes. Only men and men's desires are relevant to him. If men want to gamble, or read pornography, or consort with prostitutes, or pursue homosexual experiences, then the free market will provide supplies to equal demand at market-clearing prices. Any civil law prohibiting such activities is discussed by free market economists in terms of such concepts as the resulting black markets, the increased costs of obtaining these consumer services and goods (including information costs), the misal-location of resources, and the structural inefficiencies created by the threat of coercion. Methodological individualism offers no justifica-tion for such civil laws—or any civil laws, for that matter.[1]

Without criminal charges from an injured party, economist and legal theorist F. A. Hayek argued, society cannot formulate rules against "victimless crimes," if rules regarding "actions toward other persons" arise only from court disputes, which Hayek favored. He assumed atheism, yet did not offer any evidence. "At least where it is not believed that the whole group may be punished by a supernatural power for the sins of individuals, there can arise no such rules from the limitation of conduct against others, and therefore from the set-tlement of disputes."[2] In short: *no God—no victimless crimes,* since there is no heavenly judgment against "innocent bystanders"—bystanders who refuse to press the claims of God's law in the legislatures and the courts.

Contrary to modern philosophy, ours is a world of cosmic person-alism.[3] God is totally sovereign over all things. Therefore, when men ignore Him, even when pursuing their goals "efficiently," they find in the end that they have achieved damnation at a cut-rate price. In fact, it is a sign of God's grace to them and also to godly people that He intervenes and restrains men in their quest for efficient sinning. If nuclear and biological weapons become available at discount prices for quantity purchases, then men will better understand the grace involved in the limits that God puts on certain free-market quests.

Does God require that every decision we make throughout the day be prayed about? Do we need to pray each time we decide to cross a street? No. The psychology of total dependence is to lead to *respon-sible decision-making,* not to endless self-doubts and hesitation about our familiar daily activities. We should hide God's word in our hearts, so that godly, careful behavior takes place instinctively, analogous to the way that a trained athlete does not think about each response, each move of his body. The athlete trains in advance; the Christian should do the same.

---

1. Murray N. Rothbard, *The Ethics of Liberty* (New York University Press, [1982] 1998).

2. F. A. Hayek, *Law, Legislation, and Liberty*, vol. 1, *Rules and Order* (Chicago: Univer-sity of Chicago Press, 1973), p. 101.

3. Gary North, *Sovereignty and Dominion: An Economic Commentary on Genesis* (Dallas, Georgia: Point Five Press, [1982] 2012), ch. 1.

Conclusion

Eastern religions call for men to "empty" themselves and let unknown forces take possession of their thoughts and actions. The Zen Buddhist trains for years in irrational "koans" ("What is the sound of one hand clapping?") and in physical deprivation, including unpredictable punishments from the master for seemingly harmless acts. God's way is different: a life of intellectual and moral discipline in terms of God's Bible-revealed word, which is the foundation of rationality, predictability, and control over internal human nature and external nature. God's chastisement is not irrational, nor is it to be despised (Prov. 3:11–12). It is the pathway to life and dominion, for it teaches us to master His Bible-revealed law and to rely on His grace in Jesus Christ, which is our way of acknowledging His sovereignty over our lives and His creation.

8

GOD'S RIGGED ECONOMY

Honour the LORD with thy substance; and with the firstfruits of all thine increase:
So shall thy barns be filled with plenty, and thy presses shall burst out with new
wine.

PROVERBS 3:9–10

A. Firstfruits and Blessings

This is a very brief recapitulation of Exodus 22:29 and 23:19, regarding the requirement of the firstfruits offering, and Deuteronomy 28:8: "The LORD shall command the blessing upon thee in thy storehouses, and in all that thou settest thine hand unto; and He shall bless thee in the land which the LORD thy God giveth thee." The Lord commands His blessing upon those faithful to His law.

First, this was not a suggestion under the Mosaic covenant. The passages in Exodus are very clear: giving God the firstfruits is not optional. Exodus 22:29 reads: "Thou shalt not delay to offer first of thy ripe fruits, and of thy liquors: the firstborn of thy sons shalt thou give to Me." The people of Israel had seen what happened to the firstborn sons of Egypt. They understood just how serious God is about collecting what is rightfully His. The Levites had been established as the representative firstborn sons of Israel (Num. 3:12–13). They were wholly God's, dedicated to full-time service in the tabernacle (Num. 3:7).[1]

Second, the firstfruits were a token offering. By far the greater expense was the lost time and long walk involved in journeying to the city where the tabernacle and then the temple were located. The

---

1. Gary North, *Sanctions and Dominion: An Economic Commentary on Numbers*, 2nd ed. (Dallas, Georgia: Point Five Press, [1997] 2012), ch. 3.

46

overwhelming economic success

firstfruits were part of Israel's system of annual festivals. These festivals are no longer operational, for they had to do with Israel as a sanctuary: a uniquely holy nation, which meant a nation set apart by God for His purposes.[2] The firstfruits were part of the Mosaic land laws and the priestly laws. These are annulled. This is not true of the tithe (Matt. 23:23). *economic growth*

Third, the command offers a profitable result: external blessings. Specifically, honoring God with the fruits of one's labor results in economic growth. Furthermore, the words "barns" and "presses" are plural. The covenantally faithful person should expect overwhelming economic success. The writer has directed his injunctions to his son (Prov. 3:1, 11), meaning a single individual. He is not speaking to a group. Thus, when the plural is used for barns and presses, it indicates wealth for an individual. *Grain & wine*

The relationship between blessing and firstfruits offerings is obvious. The firstfruits were grain and wine (Ex. 22:29). The blessings referred to in this proverb are full barns and full wine presses. In other words, *that with which men honor God is that with which God will honor men*. God says "them that honour me I will honour, and they that despise me shall be lightly esteemed" (I Sam. 2:30). God establishes with men a reciprocal relationship with respect to honor. Give God honor, and He will give you honor. Give God of your substance, and He will return the offering.

Full barns and full wine presses.

B. A Gambler's Delight

A gambler would be happy to play a game of chance that is rigged by "the house" to pay him more than he put "into the pot." If he could deduct one coin to pay to "the house" each time he won, in order to get the management to continue to rig the game in his favor, he would be happy to make this pay-off. Gambling casinos are well aware of this possibility. "Pit bosses" roam the floor, looking for signs that the casino's card dealers are favoring a particular player. If a player continues to receive winnings above what is statistically normal—that is, if a player continues to win at all—then management takes a close look at the dealer. The management assumes that the dealer could be being paid off by the winner.

God tells us that He, as the owner of the "house," has rigged "the game" in favor of those who honor Him. This proverb deals with

2. Gary North, *Authority and Dominion: An Economic Commentary on Exodus* (Dallas, Georgia: Point Five Press, 2012), Part 3, *Tools of Dominion* (1990), ch. 54.

Give God honor and He will honor you.

the firstfruits offering, which is no longer operational under the New
Covenant, since the firstfruits offering was tied to the holy land and
the holy place of the tabernacle-temple. It was paid to the Levites.
The tithe remains binding, even though the Levites are no more. Jesus said, "Woe unto you, scribes and Pharisees, hypocrites! for ye pay
tithe of mint and anise and cummin, and have omitted the weightier
matters of the law, judgment, mercy, and faith: these ought ye to have
done, and not to leave the other undone" (Matt. 23:23).[3] We are not
to leave the other—tithing—undone.

The general principle of honoring God, as the owner of creation
in general and each individual in particular, by paying a tithe on our
increase comes under the terms of this proverb. A person who pays a
mere 10% of his increase above the capital he put into the investment
will be permitted to "stay in the game" and collect his winnings. Just
as surely as there are statistical regularities wherever the law of large
numbers operates, God honors those who honor Him by giving their
firstfruits to Him.

Why is it that gamblers continue to play a game that they know is
rigged against them by the house, yet they refuse to work for a living
in a universe that is rigged in favor of those who pay a mere 10% of
their increase to the Management? Why is it that even God's people refuse to acknowledge the relationship between tithing and economic success? *Because they believe in a world of cosmic impersonalism.*[4]
The gambler believes in a world of chance, fate, and luck, which are
irreconcilable concepts. The serious gamblers also believe in statistical patterns, which is why they devote time to studying which cards
have been dealt earlier in the game. They try to "beat the odds" scientifically, yet they know that the odds are against them from the moment they sit down at the table. They prefer to believe in impersonal
"runs of luck" to overcome the impersonal "stacked deck" of statistical probability. In short, their faith is in cosmic impersonalism, not
God. They prefer playing a supposedly impersonal game to working
in a God-controlled personal universe.

These verses inform us of a universe that is totally personal. Its
laws are established in terms of persons: God and men. Those who
honor the person of God by paying a tithe on their increase will find

3. Gary North, *Priorities and Dominion: An Economic Commentary on Matthew*, 2nd ed.
(Dallas, Georgia: [2000] 2012), ch. 46.
4. Gary North, *Sovereignty and Dominion: An Economic Commentary on Genesis* (Dallas,
Georgia: Point Five Press, [1982] 2012), ch. 1.

that their works prosper in the sight of men. This cause-and-effect relationship is supposed to reinforce the faith of the faithful in the reliability of this covenant (Deut. 8:18).[5] It is also supposed to challenge the false religions of foreigners to the faith (Deut. 4:6).[6]

Such a universe warns men of their ultimate destiny. They are headed for judgment. The visible things of this world testify clearly to the invisible things (Rom. 1:20).[7] Thus, the predictable relationship between faithful giving and God's faithful returning challenges men's faith in the impersonal laws of probability. In an impersonal universe, there should be no predictable relationship of the kind proclaimed by Solomon. Between hard work and output, yes; between future-oriented thrift and income, yes; between bribing an official and rewards, yes; but not between giving money to God's earthly agency of tithe-collecting—the local church[8]—and subsequent prosperity. Should such a relationship exist, the whole foundation of rebellious man's epistemology would be shattered. This is why rebels prefer gambling to tithing. Better to lose to a man-rigged, probability-governed wheel or a deck of cards than to prosper in terms of a God-rigged universe. Better to honor with all of one's substance the corporations that control the gambling tables than to honor God with 10 percent of one's increase. The ethical rebel is a statistically predictable loser; he knows it, the "house" knows it, and God knows it.

Conclusion

By honoring God through the payment of a tithe, we place ourselves under the principle of reciprocal honor: "...them that honour me I will honour, and they that despise me shall be lightly esteemed" (I Sam. 2:30). This proverb, following the passages in Exodus governing the firstfruits offering, proclaims that a token economic honoring upward results in considerable economic honoring downward. This system of mutual honoring rested on a concept of cosmic personalism. *personal universe*

Gambling rests on incompatible concepts: impersonal chance, impersonal fate, impersonal luck, and impersonal laws of probabil-

---

5. Gary North, *Inheritance and Dominion: An Economic Commentary on Deuteronomy*, 2nd ed. (Dallas, Georgia: Point Five Press, [1999] 2012), ch. 22.

6. *Ibid.*, ch. 8.

7. Gary North, *Cooperation and Dominion: An Economic Commentary on Romans*, 2nd ed. (Dallas, Georgia: Point Five Press, [2000] 2012), ch. 2.

8. Gary North, *Tithing and the Church* (Tyler, Texas: Institute for Christian Economics, 1994).

ity. Men seek what is statistically improbable: prosperity by betting against the odds. They believe they are somehow personally special in a world of cosmic impersonalism. Lady luck may smile on them, assuming there is a lady who smiles, which they do not believe. So, they place at risk the goods that God has given to them. They honor the turn of a card or the spin of a wheel by giving back their wealth.

Sadly, those Christians who decry gambling but who do not believe in tithing have not understood the relationship between tithing and prosperity nearly so well as they have understood the relationship between gambling and poverty. They live in an epistemological no-man's land, caught between the impersonal laws of large numbers and the cosmic personalism of God's law. They cannot make up their minds about which kind of law really governs the day-to-day operations of the universe. They fail to believe in God's law as a tool of dominion. Until they make up their minds, they will remain neither big winners nor big losers.

Life is not a game. It is not governed by the law of large numbers. It is a brief period of testing in which men declare their faith publicly, both verbally and in terms of their actions, i.e., in word and deed. The firstfruits offering was a token public declaration of the Israelites' faith, both individually and corporately. God promised to reward those who made this token payment. While this annual festival is no longer required, the tithe is. The same principle applies: *a token payment to God yields a large reward*. The cause-and-effect system that governs investing reflects God's covenantal structure of sanctions. Economic law is rigged in favor of covenant-keepers who really do keep the terms of the covenant. This system of causation is neither impersonal nor random.

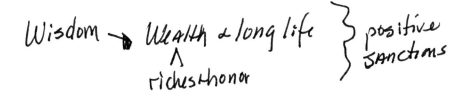

Wisdom → Wealth & long life } positive sanctions
        ∧
    riches+honor

9

THE VALUE OF WISDOM

Happy is the man that findeth wisdom, and the man that getteth understanding. For the merchandise of it is better than the merchandise of silver, and the gain thereof than fine gold. She is more precious than rubies: and all the things thou canst desire are not to be compared unto her. Length of days is in her right hand; and in her left hand riches and honour. Her ways are ways of pleasantness, and all her paths are peace. She is a tree of life to them that lay hold upon her: and happy is every one that retaineth her.

PROVERBS 3:13–18

Here, Solomon praises wisdom. Wisdom is the source of the two greatest measurable positive sanctions: wealth and long life. So, he insists that "the merchandise of it is better than the merchandise of silver, and the gain thereof than fine gold. She is more precious than rubies." These things can be used to purchase anything offered in the marketplace. But wisdom brings these things. You cannot buy wisdom with silver, gold, and rubies. You can obtain silver, gold, and rubies through wisdom. He repeats this advice:

> For wisdom is better than rubies; and all the things that may be desired are not to be compared to it (8:11).

> How much better is it to get wisdom than gold! and to get understanding rather to be chosen than silver! (16:16).

Speaking in the name of wisdom, he writes:

> Riches and honour are with me; yea, durable riches and righteousness. My fruit is better than gold, yea, than fine gold; and my revenue than choice silver. I lead in the way of righteousness, in the midst of the paths of judgment: That I may cause those that love me to inherit substance; and I will fill their treasures (8:18–21).

Wisdom — ways of righteousness & paths of judgment: — to inherit substance and full treasures.

Wisdom is the source of the goods that money can buy. Wisdom therefore ought to be higher than these goods on a wise man's scale of values. The fact that so few people place wisdom above silver, gold, and rubies indicates that wisdom is in even shorter supply than silver, gold, and rubies.

A. What Is Wisdom?

When God asked Solomon what he wanted in life, Solomon asked for wisdom.

> Give me now wisdom and knowledge, that I may go out and come in before this people: for who can judge this thy people, that is so great? And God said to Solomon, Because this was in thine heart, and thou hast not asked riches, wealth, or honour, nor the life of thine enemies, neither yet hast asked long life; but hast asked wisdom and knowledge for thyself, that thou mayest judge my people, over whom I have made thee king (II Chron. 1:10–11).

His reason for asking for wisdom? Wisdom would enable him to judge the nation. So, God granted him his request. Solomon gained this ability, which the people recognized. "And all Israel heard of the judgment which the king had judged; and they feared the king: for they saw that the wisdom of God was in him, to do judgment" (I Kings 3:28). Wisdom is the ability to make accurate judgments. How? By applying fixed ethical principles to specific situations. What are these fixed principles? Elsewhere, Solomon answered this question. "Let us hear the conclusion of the whole matter: Fear God, and keep his commandments: for this is the whole duty of man. For God shall bring every work into judgment, with every secret thing, whether it be good, or whether it be evil" (Eccl. 12:13–14).[1] Covenant-keepers should think representatively, on behalf of God.[2] They should think ethically, applying biblical law to circumstances.[3] They should think judicially, applying His Bible-mandated sanctions.[4] They should think about the consequences of their decisions and also people's actions in the future.[5]

---

1. Gary North, *Autonomy and Stagnation: An Economic Commentary on Ecclesiastes* (Dallas, Georgia: Point Five Press, 2012), ch. 45.

2. Point two of the biblical covenant model. Ray R. Sutton, *That You May Prosper: Dominion By Covenant*, 2nd ed. (Tyler, Texas: Institute for Christian Economics, [1987] 1992), ch. 2. Gary North, *Unconditional Surrender: God's Program for Victory*, 5th ed. (Powder Springs, Georgia: American Vision, [1980] 2010), ch. 2.

3. Point three: *ibid.*, ch. 3. North, ch. 3.

4. Point four: *ibid.*, ch. 4. North, ch. 4.

5. Point five: *ibid.*, ch. 5. North, ch. 5.

B. The Productivity of Wisdom

Wisdom brings to wise people the benefits that other people seek to purchase with gold and silver. Wisdom is the source of gold and silver, which in turn provide access to whatever is offered for sale. When a person can accurately assess the specifics of a situation, and then apply God's law to this situation, his decision will produce profit rather than loss. This world is governed by covenantal cause and effect. The wise person recognizes this and adheres to biblical law: the commandments of God.

It is possible to obtain gold and silver by defying God's law. The Psalmist recognized this (Ps. 73). But covenant-breakers face a world in which the system of inheritance is structured to transfer the wealth of the unjust to the just. "A good man leaveth an inheritance to his children's children: and the wealth of the sinner is laid up for the just" (13:22).[6] The economy is rigged in favor of the covenant-keeper. "Honour the LORD with thy substance; and with the firstfruits of all thine increase: So shall thy barns be filled with plenty, and thy presses shall burst out with new wine" (3:9–10).[7]

Conclusion

Biblical wisdom is a biblical law-based ability to make judgments, which in turn produce positive real-world results. This proverb's assertion of a connection between wisdom and wealth is based on God's covenant. So, it is wise to pursue wisdom rather than wealth. Wisdom can and does produce wealth. Wealth rarely produces wisdom.

Biblical wisdom — biblical law-based Ability to make judgments, which in turn produce real-world results

---

6. Chapter 41.
7. Chapter 8.

10

PAYING DEBTS PROMPTLY

Withhold not good from them to whom it is due, when it is in the power of thine hand to do it. Say not unto thy neighbor, Go, and come again, and tomorrow I will give; when thou hast it by thee. Devise not evil against thy neighbor, seeing he dwelleth securely by thee.

PROVERBS 3:27–29

A. Protecting the Weaker Party

The Mosaic law specified that wages must be paid at the end of the working day. "Thou shalt not defraud thy neighbour, neither rob him: the wages of him that is hired shall not abide with thee all night until the morning" (Lev. 19:13). The worker is in a weak position. He expects prompt payment because the law mandates this. An employer who delays payment upsets the plans of his employees. They have made decisions based on the legitimate expectation of payment at the end of the work day. To force them to scramble for money, or to delay payment to others, is to disrupt the chain of payments. It increases the level of uncertainty.[1]

The prompt payment of one's debts is a moral obligation. The neighbor who comes and requests whatever is owed to him deserves full consideration. The person who owes his neighbor anything is supposed to pay him upon request.

In a world of debt, it pays the debtor to delay repayment as long as possible if he is not paying any interest. Interest is an inescapable

---

1. Gary North, *Boundaries and Dominion: An Economic Commentary on Leviticus*, 2nd ed. (Dallas, Georgia: Point Five Press, [1994] 2012), ch. 13. See also Gary North, *Inheritance and Dominion: An Economic Commentary on Deuteronomy*, 2nd ed. (Dallas, Georgia: Point Five Press, [1999] 2012), ch. 61.

factor in human action. It is not a phenomenon limited to modern industrial economies. It stems from the time-preference factor of all human decision-making. Men prefer the present use of a scarce economic resource to the use of the same asset in the future, other things being equal. Thus, there is *a discount of future goods against present goods*. This discount is called the rate of interest.

We normally say that the debtor "has the use of the money." By this we mean that he has possession of scarce economic resources. These may be in the form of financial instruments, such as bank accounts, bonds, or other interest-producing assets. They may also be in the form of capital assets, such as tools. The point is, it is the debtor rather than the creditor who is able to use these assets in the present for his own personal benefit. He has control of the assets he borrowed.

B. Borrowed Gold

Consider the case of a monetary debt. A man owes his neighbor 20 ounces of gold. He has the gold on hand, but he believes that the paper money-denominated price of gold is likely to drop. He plans to sell the gold for a few days, take payment in paper money, and then repurchase the 20 ounces later at a lower price. He then pockets the difference between the original sales price in paper money and the later, lower repurchase price. This is what is known as "selling short." It involves economic uncertainty, since no one can be certain of the economic future.

During the time in which the debtor uses the gold for this purpose, the creditor cannot collect his property. He could make the same transaction. He could pocket the extra paper money that a successful "short" strategy would produce. Or he might want to loan the gold to someone else for an interest payment. Or he might want to buy a capital asset of some sort with the gold, especially at today's higher price for gold. If he cannot gain access to his gold, he loses the interest he might otherwise have received, or the opportunity to sell short, or the opportunity to buy the capital asset. Because the debtor has possession of the gold, he has an instrument of personal gain at his disposal.

The debtor wants the present use of the asset if he can avoid paying interest to the creditor. The creditor, on the other hand, has an economic incentive to repossess it on the agreed-upon date. Each man wants it in the present. There is a discount of future goods against identical present goods. Clearly, if you can retain possession of a more valuable asset (the asset in the present) and pay for its use by means of a less valuable asset (the discounted future value that you presently impute to the asset), you have an economic incentive to do so.

C. A Lying Debtor

Who should receive this asset? The Bible is clear: the owner, the one to whom it is due at a particular time. The existence of such a moral prohibition on retaining another man's property for an extra period of time is the result of God's awareness of a fundamental aspect of human action: *time-preference*, the foundation of the rate of interest.[2]

To keep possession of it when it is in one's hand is an "evil" (v. 29). It is a form of theft. The debtor, for whatever particular investment possibility, keeps it from the person who lawfully owns the asset. The rightful owner therefore forfeits whatever investment opportunities are available to him for the duration of the period of delay. This loss has been forced upon him by the debtor, who is profiting at the owner's expense.

The modern version of this evil is the familiar refrain, "Your check is in the mail." The creditor asks for prompt payment, and the debtor lies to him. Instead of saying "tomorrow I will give," the debtor says, "in a few days, you'll receive your money." This lie is even worse: it implies that the debtor has, in fact, already fulfilled his commitment. The creditor is not patiently foregoing payment, as in the case of the neighbor in Proverbs 3:28, who accepts the word of the debtor that he does not have the money, but will have it the next day. The creditor is led in this case to believe that the obligation has been met.

In the late medieval era, when all interest payments from loans to fellow Christians were prohibited, moneylenders developed a way to get around the prohibition by means of the ethics of this passage. Lenders would lend money, but only because the debtor made a verbal, unrecorded commitment to delay payment on the loan. Then the borrower would make a penalty payment—not technically an interest payment—to the lender because of the delay. The lender could go into a court of law or a church court, if necessary, and defend his acceptance of this extra money as a legitimate return for late payment (*more debitoris*). This was one of several legal technicalities (ethical subter-

---

2. Ludwig von Mises, *Human Action: A Treatise on Economics* (New Haven, Connecticut: Yale University Press, 1949), ch. 19.

fuges) by means of which a market for loanable funds was maintained
in spite of an official prohibition on all interest payments.[3]

The reason why men resorted to such subterfuges is that the eccle-
siastical authorities had misinterpreted the Old Testament passages
that prohibited interest from a charitable loan to an impoverished
fellow believer. They had interpreted these passages as universal con-
demnations of all interest, which they called "usury." Thus, they established a price control—a price ceiling of zero—on "the price of
money," meaning a price control on the inescapable discount of future
goods against present goods. The result, predictably, was a shortage
of funds—at the artificially low price—on the legal loan markets.

Conclusion

Delaying payment is described here as an act of theft. Solomon reminds his listeners of what the Mosaic law requires. Prompt payment
is mandatory.

The division of labor enables the vast majority to enjoy greater
productivity and therefore greater wealth. The fulfillment of contractual and traditional obligations extends the realm in which the
division of labor operates. Men cooperate with each other based on
their expectation of mutual benefit. The employee expects prompt
payment.

When men cannot trust each other to fulfill their obligations, they
search for more reliable partners in production. The range of contacts
is reduced. Output is reduced. Wealth is reduced.

---

3. Joseph A. Schumpeter, *History of Economic Analysis* (New York: Oxford University
Press, 1954), p. 103.

11

SURETYSHIP: TRANSFERRING LIABILITY

My son, if thou be surety for thy friend, if thou hast stricken thy hand with a stranger, thou art snared with the words of thy mouth, thou art taken with the words of thy mouth.

PROVERBS 6:1–2

Solomon is adamant about the necessity of avoiding surety. "Surety" is another word for co-signing for a loan. One man agrees to become responsible for the debts of another person, should that person default on his debt. The man who "strikes his hand" is obligated to honor the terms of the other man's contract. He has accepted personal liability for another man's economic performance.

Avoid such obligations, Proverbs teaches. "He that is surety for a stranger shall smart [know no peace, NEB] for it: and he that hateth suretyship is sure" (11:15). "A man void of understanding striketh his hands, and becometh surety in the presence of his friend" (17:18). "Be not thou one of them that strike hands, or of them that are sureties for debts" (22:26).

A. Collateralized Loans

There are rules for dealing with people who ignore this advice. A stranger is a person in the community who is not of the faith, and who therefore has no covenantal obligations either to the church or the wider covenanted community. If you lend to a stranger, be sure to take collateral from the person who has become the co-signer. The co-signer is now the "lender of last resort" for the stranger. The stranger may default. He may depart to a foreign land in the middle of the night. The person who has co-signed is therefore the most important individual in the transaction, as far as the creditor is concerned. Twice in Proverbs we find the following advice: "Take the garment that is surety for a stranger: and take a pledge [collateral] of him for a strange woman" (20:16; 27:13).

The "strange woman" is synonymous with religious apostasy, which Proverbs contrasts with wisdom, meaning the fear of the Lord (Prov. 2). The strange woman represents the culture of Babylon (Rev. 17:3–6), a Jezebel culture. Anyone who would co-sign for such a person lacks good judgment. He is all too likely to be cheated by the predictably faithless debtor for whom he has co-signed. Collect collateral in advance from such a person.

The motives for co-signing are varied. The obvious one is friendship. A person is approached by a friend, who asks him to "strike hands," or in modern terminology, to "put his name on the dotted line."[1] Why is this necessary? Why doesn't the friend simply put his own name on the dotted line? The fact is, he does, but the creditor is doubtful about the ability of the first debtor to make good on the debt. The creditor may not be willing to transfer assets to this person, or at least not at the prevailing rate of interest. The creditor may want to extract a higher rate of interest in order to compensate himself for the extra risk involved in loaning to a high-risk debtor.

B. A Co-Signer

If this higher rate of interest is so high that the debtor is even less likely to repay the loan, the creditor simply refuses to make the loan. In order to decrease the risk of loss on the loan, the creditor imposes a new restriction. He tells the debtor to locate a more solvent person who will agree to repay the loan, should the original debtor default. This lowers the risk premium involved in the market rate of interest. Because the risk of loss is lower, the risk premium is lower, and therefore the rate of interest can be set lower. The creditor is protected. By spreading the risk of default, the creditor believes that his loaned funds are more likely to be repaid.

The co-signer therefore increases his own financial exposure. He is being asked to co-sign because a lender is doubtful about the character of the debtor, or about his competence, or whatever. The co-signer is saying that friendship, or his own personal evaluation of the debtor's ability and willingness to repay, counts for more than

---

1. Contracts no longer have dotted lines. Perhaps they once did.

the evaluation of the potential creditor. He takes on the liability of repayment. He says, in effect, "the evaluation of my friend by the creditor is incorrect, and I will demonstrate my confidence in my own superior judgment by co-signing."

There is another possible motivation: charity. The co-signer expects his friend to default, but he co-signs anyway, in order to enable the first man to achieve his life's goals. Co-signing such a loan is an act of grace—an unmerited gift. This was Christ's motivation in laying down His life for His friends (John 15:13). He became surety for them (Heb. 7:22).

Insurance contracts were developed in the late Middle Ages that involved co-signing by risk-takers. Insurers would guarantee investors in a trading venture. If a merchant's ship sank, they would repay the investors. For this, the insurers were guaranteed an insurance "premium": a fixed percentage of the original investment. This was called "bottomry." Because they bore the risk of failure, insurers made the venture possible, for investors would then put money into the project. But insurers ("co-signers") were paid for taking this risk. They spread their risk by insuring numerous ventures.

Modern civil governments have taken on many responsibilities that private, voluntary co-signers might otherwise be asked to bear— and which they would decline to accept. But, unlike private insurers, the state does not enter the loan market in quest of financial profit. The state is buying political support and expanding state power by means of its ability to "sign the taxpayers' names on the dotted line." For example, the state creates guarantees for the repayment to lenders of private, profit-seeking loans to private companies or foreign nations, should the debtors default, thereby subsidizing both the lenders and the recipient companies or foreign governments. These state-subsidized debtors therefore obtain loans at below-market interest rates, since the risk premium in the private loans' interest rates falls sharply.

The state also creates guarantees for depositors who put their money into government-insured banks and other lending agencies. This subsidizes these lending institutions and all those who borrow from them, since they can do business at lower interest rates. Higher-risk debtors can now obtain loans, because taxpayers are implicitly compelled by their rulers to co-sign for the government-insured lending institutions. Farmers receive guarantees for crop prices; they also gain access to below-market interest rates for home loans. The housing market especially has been subsidized ever since the 1930s in the United States by various loan-guarantee programs. An important political goal for any special-interest group is to become eligible for the subsidy of government co-signed loans.

Because all loan markets are now linked directly to currency systems, domestic and international, the whole fabric of Western trade is threatened by default. The world has loaned to "strange women"; in fact, the whole system of modern political economy is operated by "strangers" to the faith. And because the co-signing is political and compulsory, few of the faithful can escape.

Modern interventionist civil governments have produced compulsory co-signing on a scale never dreamed of by Solomon. In effect, all tax-financed welfare programs are a form of surety. Citizens have become financially liable for each other's mistakes, tragedies, and incompetence. The results are becoming clear: the threat of massive bankruptcies, either openly or through the concealed bankruptcy that is produced by monetary inflation.

When Jesus Christ died on the cross for the sins of His people, He became surety for them (Heb. 7:22). The enormous cost involved in His becoming personally liable for His people's eternal debts to God provides the most graphic example in all of history of the potential costs of one's voluntary assumption of other men's personal inabilities. *Christ bore unlimited liability.* Only a man fully willing to bear a great deal of risk—and who has the capital to repay the debt completely—should contemplate becoming surety for a friend. He must limit his liability.

Conclusion

Debt is always risky. The debtor can lose whatever collateral he possesses. Debt is more risky when a co-signing debtor does not know the economic position of someone he has co-signed for. Such debt places the preservation his wealth into the hands of someone who could not qualify for a loan, based on his own signature and assets. A co-signer's plans can be disrupted by the failure of the primary debtor to pay his debt on time.

It is unwise to co-sign a note for anyone. It places your assets on the line. A person who does not have sufficient capital, including a good credit rating, to be granted a loan is a high-risk debtor. Creditors seek to protect their loans. They demand that a poor credit risk find someone else to put his name on the debt, meaning his wealth.

12

ANTS AND SLUGGARDS

Go to the ant, thou sluggard; consider her ways, and be wise: which having no guide, overseer, or ruler, provideth her meat in the summer, and gathereth her food in the harvest.

PROVERBS 6:6-8

In Western folklore, the story of the grasshopper and the ant has been a familiar one for millennia. *Aesop's Fables* includes it. The diligent ant works through the summer, gathering food for the winter, while the carefree and careless grasshopper ignores the threat of winter. The grasshopper takes advantage of the summer weather to dance and sing, as if the good weather would last forever. He assumes that there are no future crises to prepare for by sacrificing today. When winter comes, he faces starvation. He then comes to the ant and begs for food. The ant refuses; there is insufficient food for both of them.

A. Survival and Success

This passage in Proverbs forces us to consider the requirements of survival and success. The New English Bible translates the passage as follows: "...but in the summer she prepares her store of food and lays in her supplies at harvest." To imitate the ant, we must become future-oriented. We must begin to count the costs of our activities (Luke 14:28–30).[1] If we are unwilling to work hard today, we will come to poverty. "How long wilt thou sleep, O sluggard? When wilt thou arise out of thy sleep? Yet a little sleep, a little slumber, a little folding of the hands to sleep: so shall thy poverty come as one

---

1. Gary North, *Treasure and Dominion: An Economic Commentary on Luke*, 2nd ed. (Dallas, Georgia: Point Five Press, [2000] 2012), ch. 35.

that travaileth [as a robber, NEB], and thy want as an armed man" (vv. 9–11).

Sluggards resent the lifestyle of ants. The activities of ants testify to a world-and-life view different from that held by sluggards. The sluggard is content to sleep. He allows the events of life to pass him by. He assumes that the peacefulness of sleep and the enjoyment of leisure can be purchased at zero cost or minimal cost. There is no crisis ahead, or if there is, nothing can be done to prepare for it successfully. There is no need to prepare for the future.

B. Class and Time Perspective

Edward Banfield, the Harvard political scientist, described this outlook as lower class. He said that class divisions in society are not based on the size of individual bank accounts or occupational status; they are based on a person's time perspective. Upper-class people are future-oriented. Lower-class people are present-oriented.[2] What characterizes the upper-class person is his diligence in sacrificing present pleasures for future productivity and achievement.[3] Ludwig von Mises would say that upper-class people, as described by Banfield, have very low time-preference; they save for the future in response to very low interest rates. The upper-class society therefore enjoys relatively low rates of interest. Upper-class investors respond to low rates of interest, whereas the lower-class investor demands very high rates of interest in order to persuade him to forfeit the present use of his economic resources.[4]

Upper-class societies—future-oriented, high-thrift societies—tend to experience higher rates of economic growth. People buy what they want: future consumption rather than present consumption. In contrast, lower-class societies put a high premium on present consumption. They sacrifice future consumption in order to achieve this goal. Ants and sluggards have different goals and different time perspectives.

C. Pietism and Poverty

Pietism (e.g., certain types of fundamentalism and monasticism) and quietism (e.g., mysticism) focus their interest on "spiritual" goals, which are contrasted with material or "earthly" goals. Members of

---

2. Edward C. Banfield, *The Unheavenly City: The Nature and Future of Our Urban Crisis* (Boston: Little, Brown, 1970), pp. 53–54.

3. *Ibid.*, pp. 48–53.

4. Ludwig von Mises, *Human Action: A Treatise on Economics* (New Haven, Connecticut: Yale University Press, 1949), ch. 18.

both groups believe that the proper perspective of New Testament believers is passivity toward the earthly future. They misinterpret Paul's words, "Be careful for nothing" (Phil. 4:6a), which can also be translated "be full of care for nothing," or better yet, "have no anxiety" (NEB). They argue that Paul meant that we should not devote lots of resources to planning for the future and investing in terms of our plans. Christ's warning in the Sermon on the Mount, "Take therefore no thought for tomorrow: for the morrow shall take thought for the things of itself. Sufficient unto the day is the evil thereof" (Matt. 6:34), is interpreted to mean that all planning is unwise. Yet what Christ taught was the illegitimacy of a paralyzing worry about the future—a paralysis that leads to little planning, or planning to meet crises that never come. Such worry is wasteful. "But Seek ye first the kingdom of God, and his righteousness, and all these things shall be added unto you" (Matt. 6:33).[5] The material blessings will follow when men concern themselves with establishing God's kingdom.

The pietist interprets "kingdom of God" to mean the *kingdom of the internal*. He insists: "When men concern themselves with the details of prayer, church worship, and personal piety, then God will take care of them." This belief is basic to the faith of the pietist. He believes that the practical, down-to-earth future-orientation represented by the behavior of the ant is a now-superseded Old Testament standard. With respect to material things, the pietist claims to be as unconcerned as the sluggard is. The pietist folds his hands for hours in prayer; the sluggard folds his hands for hours in slumber. In both cases, the approach is outwardly the same: folded hands. So is the outward result: poverty.

The biblical view is expressed by the actions of the ant: diligence concerning that which sustains life. "He becometh poor that dealeth with a slack hand: but the hand of the diligent maketh rich" (10:4).[6] Slack hands, folded hands: the result is poverty. "The soul of the sluggard desireth, and hath nothing: but the soul of the diligent shall be made fat" (13:4).[7] A fat soul and wealth can be compatible, although they can sometimes be incompatible (Ps. 106:15). Hard work, future orientation, thrift, attention to details, high income, and contentment under God: here is the Bible's "wealth formula."

---

5. Gary North, *Priorities and Dominion: An Economic Commentary on Matthew*, 2nd ed. (Dallas, Georgia: Point Five Press, [2000] 2012), ch. 15.

6. Chapter 21.

7. Chapter 38.

D. Word and Bread

Man does not live by bread alone, but by every word that proceeds out of the mouth of God (Deut. 8:3b; Matt. 4:4[8]). Yet man does not live by the word of God alone, either, if by "word of God," we mean an "internalized" word—reading only, prayer only, handing out tracts only, or preaching only. What is forbidden is the concept of separation of word and bread. We see this in 40 years of manna in the wilderness (Deut. 8:3a), and in Christ's resumption of eating after the completion of His 40-day wilderness experience (Matt. 4:2). We also see it in the celebration of the Passover and the Lord's Supper. What produced bread in the promised land of Canaan, when the manna ceased (Josh. 5:12), was not a program of strictly internal religious exercises, but attention to the whole of God's word, including biblical law, and also including a thoughtful consideration of the ant, not to mention the sluggard.

Some American fundamentalists react in self-righteous outrage to Christians who spend money on dehydrated food storage programs, gold and silver coins—the economic equivalent of the construction of a tornado shelter. They say that such preparations for the future are a sign of a lack of faith in God, a humanistic concern with earthly cares of the world. Their shibboleth of shibboleths: "God will take care of me!" This really means that when a crisis comes, they will wind up on the doorsteps of those who did prepare, calling on them to show charity to them, which supposedly is their Christian duty. "God will take care of me" really boils down to "You ants will take care of me." This is also the sluggard's cry.

Jesus' answer to these hand-folding critics is found in the parable of the 10 virgins, who awaited the return of the bridegroom. Five were wise and took oil in their lamps. Five were foolish and took no oil. "And all the foolish said unto the wise, Give us of your oil; for our lamps are gone out. But the wise answered, Not so, lest there be not enough for us and you: but go ye rather to them that sell, and buy for yourselves" (Matt. 25:8–9). The result: "And while they went to buy, the bridegroom came; and they that were ready went in with him to the marriage: and the door was shut" (v. 10). Such is the fate of foolish virgins, sluggards, and pietists. God takes care of them, for sure, but not in the way they had hoped for.

---

8. North, *Priorities and Dominion*, ch. 1.

Conclusion

The ant is pictured here as future-oriented. She stores up food in summer. She sacrifices present consumption for the sake of future consumption.

The ant takes steps in summer to solve the problem of winter, when nature will produce no crops. The annual cycle of feast and famine is overcome by the actions of ants in laying up food in advance for the winter season.

No one tells the ant what to do. The ant does it naturally. Solomon tells the lazy person to imitate the ant, i.e., to become self-motivated. This is a feature of the free market. No government agency issues orders concerning what should be produced, yet self-motivated producers systematically provide goods and services that customers desire. This requires future-orientation and careful planning by producers.

A worthless person, a wicked man.
— has false mouth.
He winks with his eye, speaks with his feet, and teaches with his fingers
Perversity in his heart. He devises mischief continues. He sows discord.

FALSE SIGNALS AND UNRELIABILITY

Deceitful person

A naughty [worthless] person, a wicked man, walketh with a froward [false] mouth. He winketh with his eyes, he speaketh with his feet, he teacheth with his fingers. Frowardness [perversity] is in his heart, he deviseth mischief continually; he soweth discord. Therefore shall his calamity come suddenly; suddenly shall he be broken without remedy.

PROVERBS 6:12–15

Moral worthlessness eventually translates into economic poverty. The person described here is someone who continually deals falsely with others. The wink, the crossed fingers, the special signals to partners in deceit: all are part of a pattern of unreliability. The person says one thing, but he communicates a different message to others who are part of the "inner circle" who understand the secret signs.

A. Deception and Discoordination *Secret signs*

Secret signs and communications establish a psychological distinction between "them"—the suckers—and "us," meaning those "in the know." The deceiver is in fellowship with others who understand the meaning of the special signs. They see themselves as adversaries of those who do business with them. Others may adhere to their words and contracts, but the insiders do not feel bound by their own words. A promise is not seen as binding, and a contract is not to be fulfilled, unless it is immediately beneficial to the one who has made the promise.

The spread of such an outlook is disastrous for any society. Men must make decisions in life concerning the future. They are inescapably *interdependent* with other people. They attempt to achieve their

67

Evil gangs

goals through the voluntary cooperation of others, who are simultaneously pursuing their own goals. This *dovetailing of personal plans* is made possible by voluntary contracts. One man relies on another to assist him in completing his plans.

Deception increases the costs for everyone who is relying on the deceiver to fulfill the terms of his contract. The man is unreliable, yet other people have made plans in terms of his word. Even if they are not being defrauded deliberately, their plans will go awry. It will take extra time or capital to complete those plans because of the nonperformance of the deceiver.

This person actively spreads strife. He divides people from each other. Again, this increases other people's costs of cooperation. They find it more difficult to deal with each other because of mutual suspicions. One evil person is capable of disrupting the plans of many others. The dominion covenant is thwarted because the strife undermines the productivity that is the product of the division of labor. It takes longer and becomes more expensive to subdue the earth.

What is significant is the suddenness of his downfall. Normally, men receive warnings. They see other people grow wary of them. Their business revenues decline. They find it difficult to gain cooperation with other individuals, who fear they will go bankrupt and not perform their contractual obligations. In other words, as men conduct their daily affairs unwisely, other men call attention to their shortcomings, directly or indirectly. Unreliable people either learn from experience or else they see their income declining steadily.

There is another important factor to consider. The free market economy creates incentives to correct antisocial behavior. A man may learn directly from his profit-and-loss statements that he must restructure his business dealings. If he fails to repent (turn around), then some other person may be able to step in and offer to help the faltering business—for a fee, of course. Finally, competitors may step in and offer to buy up the business. Step by step, the free market economy allows other men to confront an inefficient man with the reality of his failures.

In contrast, this deceiver falls overnight. Whatever negative signals he receives are either ignored by him—he trusts no signals, being a misuser of signals—or else misinterpreted. Perhaps his partners in deception are now setting him up. They are doing to him what he did to others. Because he trusts the signals of his accomplices, he becomes vulnerable to them. Because he thinks fraud can overcome the pressures of the free market, he ignores signals from honest men. After all, they are the suckers. A cunning man never gives a sucker an even break.

B. Price Controls

Government-enforced price controls are a form of false signals. The government tells the voters that they will be able to buy goods and services at below-market prices. But the bureaucrats are winking: at economic law, or at black market operators, or at insiders. Price controls misinform the public about the supposed availability of goods and services at prices that are artificially low (price ceilings). Those "on the inside" know better. They can arrange their economic affairs accordingly. Those who are not in the know—the majority of voters—become the suckers. The result: economic shortages (from price ceilings) or gluts (from price floors),[1] and the eventual disruption of the whole economy.

Price ceilings are especially insidious. The voters are deceived into believing that they can count on other citizens (sellers) when working out their respective plans. But sellers resist selling at a loss; they want unrecorded payoffs, or special barter deals, or other inducements to trade. This creates resentment and strife. It subsidizes envy. The controls generate improper responses to the true conditions of supply and demand. Eventually, the whole economy collapses or becomes stagnant. The more the false signals, the more devastating the collapse.

Calamity comes swiftly and without remedy. Nobody trusts the deceiver. He cannot gain cooperation of others because of the pattern of deception he has established. His "capital reserve"—a good reputation—is depleted. Without it, he finds it difficult to rebound from disaster. He needs cooperation, but he cannot find people who will sell it to him. He has priced himself out of the market. Dealing with him is too risky. Until the very end, he believes himself to be immune to false signals. This is his undoing: he fails to respond to accurate signals—signals that tell him to change his ways or else be judged.

Conclusion

Deception can be indulged in by individuals and civil governments. Individual deception has limited consequences, both to the deceiver

---

1. Murray N. Rothbard, *Man, Economy, and State: A Treatise on Economic Principles*, 2nd ed. (Auburn, Alabama: Mises Institute, [1962] 2009), ch. 12:5.

and those deceived. Word gets out regarding a person's lack of trustworthiness. Government deception is more insidious, for it relies on people's trust in authority.

Price controls are forms of institutionalized deception. Government officials announce that an item must not be sold above a specific price. If free market conditions would produce a higher price, the item begins to go off the official, visible markets. Sellers refuse to sell for less than what the item is really worth, according to buyers' bids.

Deception increases the cost of doing business. It therefore reduces the amount of cooperation in the market. This reduces the division of labor and therefore productivity. A society's wealth is reduced from what it otherwise might have been.

In a free market, the penalties against deception reduce the quantity of deception at the margin: little by little. Negative feedback steadily pressures the deceiver to change his ways or else suffer more losses. In contrast, deception by governments continues, because the public's negative feedback rarely falls on the faceless officials who are enforcing the programs that rely on deception. There is not comparable pressure to change course.

14

THE LIGHT OF GOD'S LAW

My son, keep thy father's commandment, and forsake not the law of thy mother. Bind them continually upon thine heart, and tie them about thy neck. When thou goest, it shall lead thee; and when thou awakest, it shall talk with thee. For the commandment is a lamp; and the law is light; and reproofs of instruction are the way of life.

A. Parents Represent God Judicially

Solomon identifies his own judgment with wisdom and the law. The early sections of Proverbs are focused on this theme: the importance of biblical wisdom, which is personified as female (Prov. 8) and equated with God, the source of life: "But he that sinneth against me wrongeth his own soul: all they that hate me love death" (8:36).

By making this identification, and also by including a mother's advice, Solomon asserts that it is possible for men to act as the legal representatives of God to their children. Parents come in the name of God, imparting His wisdom to their children. They bear lawful authority, and they have access to God's standards of righteous living.

It is a constant complaint against Christianity in our age that "No one knows the will of God." This is used by relativists as a justification of opposing all civil law (anarchism), especially in sexual matters, or as a justification of the rejection of all Bible-based opposition to a particular civil law (statism). There is supposedly no law of God to infringe on man, either as an autonomous individual (anarchism) or as an autonomous collective species (statism). Because God is

71

"wholly other,"[1] He cannot communicate with man; therefore, no man is morally or legally bound to impose the terms of God's law on anyone else. God is so high that He cannot lift man up from sin. God is so pure that men need not strive to match the standards set by God. In short, the relativistic rebel asks, "Hath God said, 'Be ye holy, for I am holy' (Lev. 11:44)?" Then he answers his own question: "No; God says, 'Be ye unholy, for I alone am holy.'"

Solomon categorically rejects such argumentation. A parent who has personally mastered biblical law *does* have access to part of the mind of God. Paul wrote: "For who hath known the mind of the Lord, that he may instruct him? But we have the mind of Christ" (I Cor. 2:16).[2] This law is a revelation that is not the special wisdom of a closed priesthood. It is to be proclaimed to every citizen. In Israel, it was to be read every seventh year to the assembly of the people (Deut. 31:10–13).[3] Because God holds men responsible for the performance of the terms of this law, He has revealed this aspect of Himself to men. Man is made in the image of God and can therefore receive God's law. The argument that God's mind is too far removed from man's mind is an attempt to deny man's nature as God's image-bearer. *It is an assertion of man's autonomy.*

As a best friend

B. Internalizing Biblical Law

Solomon tells his son that the law is to be mastered to such an extent that it is always with him. Its terms are to be indelibly etched into his heart, meaning the deepest recesses of his mind. The law is personified as a constant companion. "When thou goest, it shall go with thee; when thou sleepest, it shall keep thee; and when thou awakest, it shall talk with thee" (v. 22). When men ask mental questions, their answers should be structured by the very words of God. The mind is to encounter the law of God at all times. God's law is to guide men's thoughts.

When biblical guides men's thoughts, it should also guide their steps. *Without biblical law, men walk in darkness.* Like a blind man is

---

1. The phrase is Karl Barth's, the most influential heretical Protestant theologian of the twentieth century. For critiques of Barth's theology, see Cornelius Van Til, *The New Modernism* (1947) and *Christianity and Barthianism* (1962), both published by P&R. Barth tried to shove God out of history and into Kant's unknowable noumenal realm.

2. Gary North, *Judgment and Dominion: An Economic Commentary on First Corinthians*, 2nd ed. (Dallas, Georgia: Point Five Press, [2001] 2012), ch. 2.

3. Gary North, *Inheritance and Dominion: An Economic Commentary on Deuteronomy*, 2nd ed. (Dallas, Georgia: Point Five Press, [1999] 2012), ch. 75.

he who departs from biblical law. He wanders aimlessly. Worse, he wanders into the pit of death. The reproofs of the law are "the way of life" (v. 23b). In other words, to be without biblical law's correction is to be in the pathway of death.

C. Alive With God's Law

Is this different from New Testament teaching? Paul wrote: "For I was alive without the law once: but when the commandment came, sin revived, and I died. And the commandment, which was ordained to life, I found to be unto death" (Rom. 7:9–10). What does this mean? It means exactly what Proverbs teaches. Sin deceives men; the law allows us to see what we are and where we are headed. The law points to our need for regeneration; without it, we perish. The law serves as our guide. If we did not have its testimony, we would not understand our fallen ethical condition.

To be "alive without the law" means to be ignorantly dead in our sins. It means that we do not understand our true spiritual condition. Paul was not saying that he was ethically pure, and therefore the possessor of eternal life, before he read the Mosaic law, for "death reigned from Adam to Moses, even over them that had not sinned after the similitude [likeness] of Adam's transgression" (Rom. 5:14). The Mosaic law "killed" him in the sense that it showed him that he was already spiritually dead, as a son of Adam. Thus, the law pointed him toward the pathway of life, Jesus Christ.

Biblical law should be as basic to our decision-making as a flashlight's beam is on a dark night. A man who shines a light on the ground "naturally" steps only into the circle of light. He "naturally" avoids stepping into the darkness. He does not know what dangers lurk in the darkness, so in order to avoid possible dangers, he steps only on the lighted portion of the path.

We know that the very essence of the sin of man is to prefer spiritual darkness to light. "And this is the condemnation, that light is come into the world, and men loved darkness rather than light, because their deeds were evil" (John 3:19). *What is really "natural" to fallen man is to avoid the Bible's lighted ethical pathway.* Solomon therefore counsels his son to regard the ethical light cast by the law as he would regard the visible light cast by a lamp. The law is a "lamp unto our feet." But it takes training to learn to trust the light of the law. This trust is not instinctive in fallen man, which is why Solomon has given his son the Proverbs.

Conclusion

To keep from getting "tripped up" in life, men must adhere to the terms of biblical law. To have God's law as your companion is to have a counselor who is looking out for your best interests. To act in terms of this law's counsel is to walk in the pathway of life. Conforming instinctively to the law's directing counsel should be like walking instinctively in the circle of light. It is our ethical responsibility to become instinctive conformers to the law.

15

RESTITUTION AND IMPARTIALITY

Men do not despise a thief, if he steals to satisfy his soul when he is hungry. But if he be found, he shall restore seven fold; he shall give all the substance of his house.

PROVERBS 6:30–31

A. Crime Against God and Man

Theft is a crime against God, the victim, and society. We should not argue that a "crime against property" is ethically subordinate to a "crime against mankind," for property is simply "a bundle of rights of ownership," and these rights are possessed by men under God. *A crime against property is therefore a crime against mankind.* Theft transfers wealth to law-breakers and away from those who have not broken a civil law. It transfers wealth from those who have served customers efficiently in a competitive market. It reduces the capital of those who have demonstrated their ability to meet the needs and wants of customers at prices the customers have been willing and able to pay. Theft therefore reduces the present wealth of individual victims, and it may reduce the future wealth of customers, who will not be equally well-served by those who had benefited them before—the productive victims of theft who have been decapitalized by the thieves. Theft also increases everyone's uncertainty about his economic future, which in turn tends to raise the costs of protecting property, thereby lowering per capita wealth.

Another proverb announces: "Remove far from me vanity and lies; give me neither poverty nor riches; feed me with food convenient for me: lest I be full, and deny thee, and say, Who is the LORD? Or lest I be poor, and steal, and take the name of my God in vain" (30:8–9).[1]

---

1. Chapter 85.

Middle-class comfort is normally preferable to both poverty and great wealth, for both extremes involve temptations for sinning against God. Neither grinding poverty nor great wealth is generally beneficial to the majority of men.

The poor man in this example has succumbed to the temptation. He has stolen bread, a staple of life. He is not a professional thief. He was hungry, and he took bread to satisfy his hunger. Who can blame him? *God blames him.* The law enforcement system blames him. He must pay "sevenfold" to the victim. Restitution is legally inescapable. Because he is poor, the extent of the restitution payment will hurt him greatly. He has so little that he stole bread. Any extra expense will disrupt his household. Nevertheless, he must pay up to "all the substance of his house."

If he has no economic reserves at all, he will be sold into slavery to raise the money to pay his victim. This is great incentive for him to find the restitution payment money somewhere.

B. Restitution in the Mosaic Law

We should understand that the details of this incident are not to be taken literally. The law of God requires double restitution for all theft (Ex. 22:4),[2] except the theft and subsequent slaughter or sale of sheep (four-fold) and oxen (five-fold) (Ex. 22:1).[3] Anyone familiar with biblical law knows that seven-fold restitution is a figurative term, like the seven-fold judgment of God on anyone who persecuted Cain (Gen. 4:15), and Lamech's prideful boast of his ability to revenge himself 77-fold (Gen. 4:24), meaning eleven times greater than the God's metaphorical restitution payment. Sometimes a number in the Bible is to be interpreted figuratively, not literally. Solomon knew that his audience would know the details of biblical law. What was his point in exaggerating? To make a point.

Few poor men would really be bankrupted by double restitution for a loaf of bread. The point is, the economic burden of the restitution payment would be proportionately greater for him than for a rich man who stole a loaf of bread. *The required restitution payment has nothing to do with the criminal's ability to pay.* The law does not play favorites. God is not a respecter of persons (II Sam. 14:14). Both rich and poor must make restitution, which is based on the market price

---

2. Gary North, *Authority and Dominion: An Economic Commentary on Exodus* (Dallas, Georgia: Point Five Press, 2012), Part 3, Tools of Dominion (1990), ch. 43.

3. *Idem.*

of the item stolen. Income, whether of the thief or his victim, has nothing to do with the extent of restitution. "Ye shall do no unrighteousness in judgment: thou shalt not respect the person of the poor, nor honour the person of the mighty but in righteousness shalt thou judge thy neighbour" (Lev. 19:15).[4] Restitution also has nothing to do with the victim's feelings about the criminal. The criminal's motivation is equally irrelevant. Rich or poor, hungry or fat, thieves must make restitution in terms of the value of the stolen property. The Bible condemns both deeper-pocket jurisprudence (deciding against the rich because they can afford the loss) and shallow-pocket jurisprudence (deciding in favor of the poor only because they are poor).

Solomon is warning us that if the Bible specifies punishment for a "trivial crime against property," how much more is the punishment against adulterers, which is anything but trivial (vv. 32–35)? If a victim demands repayment from one whom he does not despise, will he allow his wife's seducer to go free? If he refuses to show mercy to his wife, when biblical law is enforced, then the punishment must involve the death of both of adulterers (Lev. 20:10). The judicial issue here is victim's rights.[5]

The predictability and impartiality of biblical law are to undergird the social order. All those who break the law are subject to its penalties. This points to the final judgment. God does not "grade on a curve." Paul wrote: "All have sinned and come short of the glory of God" (Rom. 3:23). It may cost a convicted impoverished thief all that he owns to pay his debt to the victim. The debt must be paid. It will cost every ethical rebel an eternity in hell. The debt must be paid. The point is clear: *the debt must be paid.* There is no escape, no appeal to "circumstances," no plea bargaining, and no suspended sentences. The law is rigorous, for the law's Author is rigorous.

Conclusion

All men are equally protected when biblical law is enforced. Rich men are defended from poverty-stricken thieves; poverty-stricken owners are defended from rich thieves. *Economic uncertainty is reduced by the very certainty of the law's penalties.* This benefits customers and producers, who can meet together and make exchanges, confident that

---

4. Gary North, *Boundaries and Dominion: An Economic Commentary on Leviticus*, 2nd ed. (Dallas, Georgia: Point Five Press, [1994] 2012), ch. 14.

5. North, *Authority and Dominion*, ch. 33. Cf. Gary North, *Victim's Rights: The Biblical View of Civil Justice* (Tyler, Texas: Institute for Christian Economics, 1990).

all parties will be protected by law from fraud and theft. It leads to greater output through a more extensive division of labor—a division of labor based on voluntary exchange and the protection of private property.

16

LAW: NATURAL VS. CREATIONAL

Counsel is mine, and sound wisdom: I am understanding; I have strength. By me kings reign, and princes decree justice. By me princes rule, and nobles, even all the judges of the earth.

PROVERBS 8:14–16

A. Biblical law: A Tool of Dominion

God speaks in this chapter anthropomorphically as wisdom, a female source of power and blessings. "She crieth at the gates" (v. 3). Wisdom contrasts her ethics with Satan's, also feminine (7:10–23). (This feminine identification is found only in Proverbs.) The conclusion: all those who hate me, says wisdom, love death (8:36b).

The link between understanding and strength is made explicit (v. 14). *Wisdom is a tool of dominion.* By following the counsel of wisdom, men attain power over external events. It is in terms of wisdom that kings reign, judges rule, and the nobility retains power. All the judges of the earth hold office by means of wisdom.

By identifying wisdom with God, the Bible proclaims the cosmic personalism of existence.[1] God is sovereign over all kings and rulers. He is not a manipulator behind the thrones of men. He is sovereign (Isa. 45). They are not.

Does this mean that all powerful rulers are God-fearing, or at least biblical law-abiding? No; Canaanite kings were reprobate and had to be destroyed. Does it mean that kings consciously understand that God is sovereign over them? Again, no; only after seven years

---

1. Gary North, *Sovereignty and Dominion: An Economic Commentary on Genesis* (Dallas, Georgia: Point Five Press, [1982] 2012), ch. 1.

of madness did Nebuchadnezzar acknowledge his dependence on God (Dan. 4). The Pharaoh of the exodus never did. Does it mean that there are universally understandable principles of natural law to which all rational men have access through human reason? No.

B. Rival Legal Theories

The Bible teaches a creational version of natural law theory. This stands in contrast to humanism's natural law theories. Humanistic natural law theory asserts that there are universally valid governing principles in the world that can be discovered through the use of reason, meaning a neutral reasoning process unaided by God's special revelation in the Bible. Sometimes this reasoning capacity is called "right reason" —"wrong reason" being the process by which other natural law advocates reach conclusions that the defender of "right reason" disagrees with. The natural man studies logic and facts, and if he reasons correctly, the natural law theorist believes, this natural man can come to understand the governing principles of the universe. This reasoning process is inductive. A gathering of facts, when coupled with a study of logic, can result in the attainment of wisdom.

In contrast, the Bible teaches that all of creation is revelational. Ethically rebellious men hold down (or hold back) the truth in their unrighteousness (Rom. 1:18–22).[2] Because all creation reveals God, it testifies to the existence of governing principles. Men choose to worship other gods and other principles. Whatever is creational, and therefore revelational, has been twisted by the natural man, who refuses to receive the things of the spirit (I Cor. 2:14).[3] Whatever is creational is regarded by the natural man as unnatural—unnatural to his ethics and goals.

Nevertheless, this proverb insists that all kings and judges rule by means of biblical wisdom. This is what God testifies about Himself. There can be no rule by the authorities apart from wisdom. What can this mean? Clearly, rulers do evil things, and evil rulers do evil things continually. How can they be said to rule in terms of wisdom?

---

2. Gary North, *Cooperation and Dominion: An Economic Commentary on Romans*, 2nd ed. (Dallas, Georgia: Point Five Press, [2000] 2012), pp. 20–21. Cf. John Murray, *The Epistle to the Romans*, 2 vols. (Grand Rapids, Michigan: Eerdmans, 1965) II, p. 37.

3. Gary North, *Judgment and Dominion: An Economic Commentary on First Corinthians*, 2nd ed. (Dallas, Georgia: Point Five Press, [2001] 2012), ch. 2.

C. Obedience and Power

It means that, insofar as rulers wish to maintain their power, they must honor certain fundamental aspects of the creation. Satan does this. When he sought to curse Job, he came before God for permission to exercise power (Job 1:6–12; 2:1–7). He possesses no power apart from his understanding of God. When he tempted Eve, he cited God's instructions to Adam (Gen. 3:1). When he tempted Christ, he cited God's words in the law (Luke 4:3–12).[4] Christ, unlike Eve, cited the applicable passages of the Mosaic law to answer Satan, and then abided by them in order to overcome him. Eve cited the relevant law to Satan (Gen. 3:3), but then failed to act in terms of its requirements. Specially revealed law offered her guidance to overcome Satan, just as it offered to Christ, but she spurned the law and its guidance, and therefore she went into bondage to her adversary.

Power therefore is a product of ethical actions that are in conformity to biblical law. Weakness therefore is the product of ethical action not in conformity to biblical law. As men seek power, they discover regularities: by following the terms of biblical law, they increase their power. *Biblical law is a tool of dominion.*[5] Inductively, power-seeking men learn to honor those regularities of creation that bring them power. *Biblical law is a tool of dominion.*

The revelation of God's law in the Bible speeds up the process of discovery. Without biblical revelation and special grace, men eventually refuse to follow the logic of creational law. Because men are perverse, and because God's mercy delays His wrath, rulers fail to discern the comprehensive legal-order that undergirds human power. They abandon biblical law. They are not immediately destroyed. They teach themselves a false lesson, namely, that ethical rebellion pays high dividends. They misinterpret the creational law-order.

The "trial and error" method of discovery leads men to an understanding of some of the principles of power, and so they rule in terms of them. But men's willful rebellion, when coupled with God's temporal mercy to His people, eventually brings weakness and external defeat, as in the case of Egypt in Moses' day. Without the restraint of special grace—personal regeneration and the Bible's revelation of God's law—rulers cannot perpetually maintain their control over

---

4. Gary North, *Treasure and Dominion: An Economic Commentary on Luke*, 2nd ed. (Dallas, Georgia: Point Five Press, [2000] 2012), ch. 2.

5. Gary North, *Authority and Dominion: An Economic Commentary on Exodus* (Dallas, Georgia: Point Five Press, 2012), Part 3, Tools of Dominion (1990).

external reality. Wisdom is ultimately presuppositional: men are to begin with wisdom; they cannot come to understand all of its rules and then conform themselves to these rules by means of inductive, trial-and-error reasoning. *Therefore, natural law theory leads to natural weakness and defeat.* It elevates the powers of unaided human reason, which is at war with wisdom's understanding.

Conclusion

The two forms of natural law theory—creational and natural—are applications of the two forms of knowledge: covenant-keeping and covenant-breaking, saved and lost. The mind of man was distorted by Adam's Fall. Only through God's special grace, which includes knowledge of the Bible, is the covenant-breaker able to escape the burden imposed by original sin.

The natural man does not receive the things of the spirit. Among these things not received is a correct understanding of the covenantal structure of the universe. Cause and effect in the universe are ethical. Obedience to biblical law produces outward success, including the attainment of power over the creation. This power includes authority over other people. There are regularities in society. These regularities are covenantal.

To attain success and then to keep it, the covenant-breaker must obey biblical law. He can do this in a preliminary sense by adhering to basic moral rules of behavior that have their origin in God's covenants. But he holds back the truth because of his anti-covenantal heart. Eventually, he breaks away from God's law. The more consistent he is with his anti-covenantal presuppositions, the sooner and the more radical this break will be. Without special grace, no society can indefinitely adhere to the principles underlying biblical law, even the legal order corrupted by the Fall.

All natural law theories that do not begin with the covenants of God and the Fall of man will produce a covenant-breaking legal order. They cannot produce a covenant-keeping legal order. They therefore cannot produce justice. All of them are unwise.

17

THE POSSIBLE DREAM

I love them that love me; and those that seek me early shall find me. Riches are honourable with me; yea, durable riches and righteousness. My fruit is better than gold, yea, than fine gold; and my revenue than choice silver.

PROVERBS 8:17–19

The Bible does not promise all men riches, fame, or power. It does not promise health or wealth to all men. But it does promise wisdom to all those who will seek it. This is one quest that will always be rewarded, and rewarded with treasures greater than gold or silver.

Wisdom in Proverbs is an anthropomorphic representation of God. We do not discover wisdom, meaning God, by means of some trial-and-error inductive reasoning process. We must therefore begin with God (wisdom) as our operating first principle. The New Testament proclaims: "But without faith it is impossible to please him: for he that cometh to God must believe that he is, and that he is a rewarder of them that diligently seek him" (Heb. 11:6). To *get* wisdom, we must first *have* wisdom. We must believe in order to exercise faith. We must be regenerate in order to seek salvation, for the natural man does not receive the things of the spirit; they are foolishness (anti-wisdom) to him (I Cor. 2:14).[1]

Solomon is famous for his request of God. Like the pagan stories of the man who is offered a wish by a genie who lives in a metal lamp, Solomon asked in a dream for a gift from God: the greatest of all gifts, wisdom. Because he asked for wisdom rather than long life, riches, or victory in war, God granted him his request (I Kings 3:6–14). But

---

1. Gary North, *Judgment and Dominion: An Economic Commentary on First Corinthians*, 2nd ed. (Dallas, Georgia: Point Five Press, [2001] 2012), ch. 2.

the lure of idol-worshipping women—wisdom's feminine antithesis, described in Proverbs 7—finally overcame his wisdom (I Kings 11). Which feminine principle of life will men worship: the harlot's invitation or God's wisdom?

Men pursue economic long-shots. They gamble rather than work. They pan for gold rather than set up stores to sell miners the pans. They hope for the miracle and neglect the productive. They seek out the big deal and forfeit numerous little deals that would equal the pay-off of the big one, given enough time. They chase rainbows and ignore the sunshine. They "bet against the house" and pass by a sure thing. *lady luck*

God's wisdom is personified as a woman who loves those who seek her. The pagan's "lady luck" is also female, but she loves no one. She "smiles" on some men, but she is as capricious as her name implies. She cannot be safely trusted. God is not an impersonal, capricious force in the universe; His words can be trusted. Seeking after Him is not an exercise in futility. The universe is not impersonal or "rigged" against mankind. It is rigged against ethical rebels, but it is simultaneously rigged in favor of those who seek God.[2]

Proverbs 7 and 8 personify the two masters, God and Satan, by means of anthropomorphic language: the two women. The great harlot of Babylon—the antichrist's world order—is female (Rev. 18). The universe is not impersonal, but radically personal.[3] Men serve one of two masters, not impersonal forces, whether inevitable (fate) or random (luck). Men inescapably seek after one woman or the other, the harlot or wisdom. Both call to men: the harlot from the twilight (7:9), and wisdom from the high places and the gates of the city (8:2–3).

How soon should men seek wisdom? Early. By seeking wisdom early, men are guaranteed success. The harlot calls to men in the twilight, to spend the night illicitly. Wisdom calls early, as at daybreak. The day is to be given over to seeking wisdom. He who is diligent in the quest will be rewarded.

By comparing the treasures of wisdom with the precious metals, Proverbs drives the point into the minds of men: *the most valuable asset of all is wisdom.* Solomon was already wise when he asked for wisdom; he recognized that he was asking for the most valuable of all assets. Wealth subsequently flowed to his kingdom (I Kings 10:14–21). The

---

2. Chapter 8.

3. Gary North, *Sovereignty and Dominion: An Economic Commentary on Genesis* (Dallas, Georgia: Point Five Press, [1982] 2012), ch. 1.

fame of this rule spread everywhere (I Kings 4:3–11). The powerful and wealthy came to him for counsel (I Kings 10:11–13). In short, he achieved indirectly, through wisdom, the goals that other men seek directly through intrigue, magic, and violence.

God speaks clearly to men. They can understand His words because they are made in His image. He communicates to them by means of analogies and metaphors. When He compares the value of wisdom with gold, He speaks a universal language. Like the pocket-book parables of Jesus, the economic language of *wisdom personified* can be grasped by anyone, in the day of Solomon or in the twenty-first century.

The universality of gold and silver as desirable assets to lay up in one's treasury reinforces the words of wisdom. When men think about the universal forms of wealth, they think of gold and silver. Across the globe, men understand the value of the precious metals. Abraham's wealth was counted in these metals (Gen. 13:2). When men speak out against the economic importance of gold and silver, they speak nonsense. When John Maynard Keynes spoke of gold in 1923 as a barbarous relic,[4] and when Lenin suggested in 1921 that the victorious Bolsheviks would someday use gold for public lavatories,[5] they proclaimed utopianism ("utopia": no place). These two spokesman of their era spoke for both sides of the Iron Curtain. Both men had contempt for Christian society. Keynes the atheistic homosexual and Lenin the atheistic revolutionary knew enough about Christianity to prefer the harlot of the twilight.

Conclusion

The quest for wisdom is man's only sure thing. Gaining wisdom is better than gaining gold and silver. Thus, the pay-off is very high, and the risk of failure is zero, if men continue to seek wisdom's face. Solomon ceased the quest and went to the harlot in his later years. He died, and his son—the son to whom the Proverbs were presumably addressed—rebelled and lost the northern kingdom. The quest must be begun early, and it must not end as twilight approaches.

---

4. John Maynard Keynes, "A Tract on Monetary Reform" (1923), in Keynes, *Essays in Persuasion* (London: Macmillan, 1931), p. 208.

5. V. I. Lenin, "The Importance of Gold Now and After the Complete Victory of Socialism" (1921). Reprinted in *The Lenin Anthology*, ed. Robert C. Tucker (New York: Norton, 1975), p. 515.

18

PUBLIC PATHS OR PRIVATE CORNERS

I lead in the way of righteousness in the midst of the paths of judgment: That I may cause those that love me to inherit substance; and I will fill their treasures.

PROVERBS 8:20–21

A. Rival Paths

The first nine chapters of the Book of Proverbs serve as an introduction to the practical, concrete applications of God's proverbial wisdom to the affairs of life. These introductory remarks cover the fundamental principles of life. They lay the foundation. The main theme is this: *attaining and applying biblical wisdom are the chief end of life* (4:5–7). Everything that follows in Proverbs rests on this basic presupposition.

There are practical aspects of these early remarks. The themes of power, wealth, fame, and long life are not absent. The overriding themes are not these, however. Things that matter most are righteous judgment, covenantal faithfulness, avoiding the harlot, honest dealing, and the commandments of God. Above all, the commandments of God.

Wisdom is a guide for the way of righteousness—not an impersonal guide, but a living guide. *Wisdom in Proverbs is an anthropomorphic representation of God*. God guides men along the way of righteousness, as an experienced traveller guides a newcomer. Step by step, the traveler advances behind wisdom, who in this case is the original pathbreaker. There is no possibility that the guide will lose her way.

The imagery of the pathway is explicit in Proverbs 8:20. This same imagery is used to describe the requirement of the people of Israel to follow strictly all rulings imposed by the priestly judges. "According to the sentence of the law which they shall teach thee, and according to the judgment which they shall tell thee, thou shalt do: thou shalt not decline from the sentence which they shall show thee, to the right hand, nor to the left" (Deut. 17:11). The path is obviously narrow; no deviation is permitted.[1] Christ reaffirmed this in His Sermon on the Mount: "Enter ye at the strait [narrow] gate: for wide is the gate, and broad is the way, that leadeth to destruction, and many there be which go in thereat: Because strait is the gate, and narrow is the way, which leadeth unto life, and few there be that find it" (Matt. 7:13–14).[2]

The concept of the path of righteousness refers to personal righteousness. The focus of concern for the father is the moral righteousness of his son. Nevertheless, this path also refers to public righteousness, including law enforcement. Self-government first; then comes the application of biblical law to areas of life under the jurisdiction of the righteous man. How could it be otherwise? Because self-government under biblical law produces wealth and influence, the extension of the rule of biblical law proceeds outward, from self-governed individuals to others under their lawful jurisdiction.

B. Obedience and Wealth

Does self-government under biblical law produce wealth and influence? Proverbs 8:21 affirms that it does. More than this: wisdom leads men along the path of judgment in order to cause those behind her to become prosperous. Those who love wisdom will inherit substance; those who love wisdom will have their treasuries filled.

This does not mean that all wise men will get rich. The true wealth is wisdom herself (God Himself): durable riches, fruit that is more valuable than gold (vv. 18–19). But because men who follow wisdom are promised *better forms of wealth*, one testimony of God to the reliability of His word is that covenant-keeping men will inherit inferior forms of wealth: earthly wealth. This is an affirmation of God's ability and willingness to deliver even greater riches in eternity.

We see an analogous example of this principle—God's delivery of lesser earthly riches, which testifies to God's ability to deliver greater, heavenly riches—in Jesus' healing of the palsied man. First, He said

---

1. Gary North, *Inheritance and Dominion: An Economic Commentary on Deuteronomy*, 2nd ed. (Dallas, Georgia: [1999] 2012), ch. 41.

2. Gary North, *Priorities and Dominion: An Economic Commentary on Matthew*, 2nd ed. (Dallas, Georgia: [2000] 2012), ch. 17.

to the man, "Son, be of good cheer; thy sins be forgiven thee" (Matt. 9:2b). Certain scribes murmured within themselves, "This man blasphemeth" (v. 3). "And Jesus knowing their thoughts said, Wherefore think ye evil in your hearts? For whether is easier, to say, Thy sins be forgiven thee; or to say, Arise, and walk? But that ye may know that the Son of man hath power on earth to forgive sins (then saith he to the sick of the palsy), Arise, take up thy bed, and go unto thy house. And he arose, and departed to his house" (vv. 5–7).

Men can see the results of righteousness. Christ healed the palsied man. "But when the multitudes saw it, they marvelled, and glorified God, which had given such power unto men" (v. 8). *Visible success strengthens the public authority of the righteous man.* In Christ's case, it led to even greater resentment on the part of the religious leaders of His day, who saw the transfer of political power involved in Jesus' demonstration of His lawful authority under God.

God wants to honor publicly those who honor Him publicly: "...for them that honour me I will honour..." (I Sam. 2:20). One way is to grant them riches and honor (Prov. 8:18).[3] To internalize these references to external economic success is to minimize the power of God to manifest His reliability and sovereignty, in time and on earth. Such a "spiritualizing" interpretation is too often governed by an impulse that is related to the hostility displayed by the religious leaders of Israel against Jesus. They deeply resented Jesus' ability to heal men before the gaze of the multitudes. He was manifesting His power in public. They would have preferred Him to work His miracles privately, or not at all. They would have preferred to face a religion of strictly "internal" blessings. Such a religion would not have resulted in a public confrontation—the kind of confrontation that the Pharaoh of Moses' day so deeply resented.

Paul understood the impact of a religion of publicly manifested power. He announced to a civil magistrate, "I am not mad, most noble Festus; but speak forth the words of truth and soberness. For the king knoweth of these things, before whom also I speak freely for I am persuaded that none of these things are hidden from him; for this thing was not done in a corner" (Acts 26:25–26).

Pietists, like atheists and Satanists, prefer a version of Christianity that sits in a corner, not drawing attention to itself or to the God of might and power who controls all of life in terms of His decree. They prefer durable riches alone to durable riches with wealth and public

---

3. Chapter 17.

honor. They sing, "I'd rather have Jesus than silver and gold," while we sing, "I'd rather have Jesus *and* silver and gold." They prefer a world of reduced public confrontation and minimal dominion. They prefer to pray in a corner and avoid the paths of civic judgment. They prefer cultural impotence to cultural responsibility.

Men generally achieve their goals in the long run when they are willing to pay the price; pietists are no exception. They have already achieved their goal of public irrelevance. While they continue to specialize in cultural irrelevance, dominion-oriented Christians can begin to specialize in occupying the paths of righteous public judgment. Pietists get what they want; they should stop complaining because dominionists expect to get what they want.

Conclusion

The Book of Proverbs teaches that wisdom is the chief goal of life. External, visible success is a mark of this wisdom. Obedience to God's laws produces blessings. These blessings are both external and internal.

Wisdom produces righteousness. This indicates that wisdom is an outworking of redemption, for the Bible is clear: fallen man does not work his way into salvation, either with the works of his hands or the works of his mind. Wisdom is a gift of God. Solomon understood this.

Wisdom so defined produces prosperity. This is an aspect of covenantal inheritance. *God visibly honors the righteous.* This visible honor testifies to the holiness of God and His law. He is not a failure in history. This message is rejected by the vast majority of Christians in my day, who are pietists: internal salvation (spiritual healing) only. The world at large is not seen as being affected by this internal transformation. The local church, yes. The family, yes. But not civil government. Not the civilization. Covenant-keepers with a pietistic outlook believe they have no responsibilities for the social order. This is not what Solomon's proverbs taught.

19

TREASURES OF WICKEDNESS

Treasures of wickedness profit nothing: but righteousness delivereth from death.

PROVERBS 10:2

There are two truths taught by this proverb: (1) there are measurable treasures that are the result of wickedness; (2) righteousness delivers men from death. Both of these truths demand an explanation derived from the texts of the Bible.

A. Choose Wealth

1. Wealthy wicked: The problem of the covenant-breaking wealthy plagued Asaph. "For I was envious at the foolish, when I saw the prosperity of the wicked. For there are no bands in their death: but their strength is firm. They are not in trouble as other men; neither are they plagued like other men" (Ps. 73:3–5). But Asaph then asserted that their success is the basis of their subsequent downfall: "Therefore pride compasseth them about as a chain; violence covereth them as a garment. Their eyes stand out with fatness: they have more than their heart could wish. They are corrupt, and speak wickedly concerning oppression: they speak loftily" (Ps. 73:6–8). They do not believe that God sees their deeds: "And they say, How doth God know? And, Is there knowledge in the most high? Behold, these are the ungodly, who prosper in the world; they increase in riches" (Ps. 73:11–12). The message is clear: ungodly men prosper. The exegetical challenge is to make sense of this principle in light of the outline of Deuteronomy 28, which proclaims that godly societies prosper, and rebellious societies are destroyed by the judgment of God. Does this principle not also apply to individuals? Is there a disconnect between economic causation for individuals and society?

The outline in Deuteronomy 8 provides the key. It presents a stage theory of development. First, God gives covenant-keepers His Bible-revealed law, so that they might preserve and expand their wealth. Then He gives them a capital base to work with (8:1).[1] Second, they begin to prosper. This prosperity is supposed to confirm their faith in the reliability of God's covenant: "...for it is he that giveth thee the power to get wealth, that he may establish his covenant which he sware unto thy fathers, as it is this day" (8:18).[2] The external blessings are to serve as spiritual reinforcement. Third, people are tempted to forget God, and to assert their autonomy. God warns men against this sin: "And thou say in thine heart, My power and the might of mine hand hath gotten me this wealth" (8:17).[3] Fourth, there is a period of judgment against those who rebel against God in this fashion (8:19–20).[4]

There is a fifth possible stage: restoration (Isa. 2). There are two kinds of negative judgment: judgment unto restoration and judgment unto oblivion. Whether a society experiences restoration depends upon the ethical response of the society to God's judgment.

The Bible is clear: there are covenantal blessings and cursings that involve the whole society. The Bible is equally clear about the possibility of wealthy wicked people. They may be wealthy in any of the five stages, but wealth in the hands of wicked people as a class is characteristic of the third stage: autonomy and rebellion, which is the prelude to stage four, i.e., the comprehensive judgment of God.

The point made by this proverb is that the treasure held by the ungodly person profits him nothing. In other words, he has made *an entrepreneurial error* by thinking that the pay-off was worth the corruption necessary to obtain it. The wicked man's efforts produce a personal loss.

Does this mean that wealth as such is unprofitable? No; it means that wealth is unprofitable for the wicked individual. There is *objective value* in a treasure—objective in the sense that God imputes value to it—but the wicked man does not appropriate this value without also gaining the vengeance of God. He sees only the value of the treasure and the ethical cost of attaining it; he does not see the hidden costs of rebellion. Thus, the subjective value of this treasure to the wicked is

---

1. Gary North, *Inheritance and Dominion: An Economic Commentary on Deuteronomy*, 2nd ed. (Dallas, Georgia: Point Five Press, [1999] 2012), ch. 17.
2. *Ibid.*, ch. 22.
3. *Ibid.*, ch. 21.
4. *Ibid.*, ch. 23.

ultimately negative, what Proverbs 25:22 describes as "coals of fire" on the heads of the unrighteous.[5]

B. Choose Life

2. *Mortality tables*: Long life is characteristic of covenant-keeping men. Men who honor their parents have long lives (Ex. 20:12).[6] Long life is a universally agreed-upon blessing. Thus, all people can see this beneficial biological result of godliness in society as a whole (Deut. 4:6–8),[7] and they are thereby encouraged to enter into a covenant with God.

Righteous men, in the aggregate, are delivered from death for a longer period of time than unrighteous men are. Individual righteous men may die young, and individual wicked men may die old, but in the aggregate, long life goes to the righteous. Because all have sinned and come short of the glory of God (Rom. 3:23), all men eventually die, in time and on earth.[8] Nevertheless, long life points to eternal life. Men to whom the righteousness of Christ is imputed by God's grace can expect eternal life and therefore long lives on earth. The gift of eternal life, which is publicly manifested at the final judgment, is preceded by an earthly parallel—not for every righteous man, but for men in general who adhere in general to the provisions of biblical law.

People in Third World nations have shorter life expectancies than people in Western, industrial countries. Why? Because Third World nations are characterized by such afflictions as animism, Hinduism, Buddhism, Islam, and imported Western socialism. Socialism came early to these nations during their period of Westernization, not a century after free market economics created a massive capital base, as was the case in the industrial West. The oil-rich Muslim nations are exceptions to the rule regarding paganism, but their wealth is dependent upon the productivity of the West, which has discovered valuable uses for oil. Japan also has escaped the economic curses of paganism by imitating Western law and western technology. The Japanese have also adopted a Western, linear view of time, as well as Western doctrines of thrift and hard, smart work. Japan has adopted

---

5. Chapter 76.

6. Gary North, *Authority and Dominion: An Economic Commentary on Exodus* (Dallas, Georgia: Point Five Press, 2012), Part 2, *Decalogue and Dominion* (1986), ch. 25.

7. North, *Inheritance and Dominion*, ch. 8.

8. The only exceptions: those alive at the time of the Second Coming (I Thess. 4:17).

a Protestant ethic without adopting Protestant theology. The result has been rising per capita wealth. China after 1978 imitated Japan, with similar economic results.

Humanism is steadily eroding the capital base of the West, and if state regulation of the economy continues to be enforced by Western civil governments, then the West will eventually become poor by comparison to Asia. But, in terms of external law, the legal codes of Western nations are still closer to biblical law than the law codes of Third World nations are. So is Western humanism's view of linear time. The difference can be seen by comparing mortality tables of various societies.

Conclusion

Why do we see the wicked prosper? This question bothered Asaph. It bothers most covenant-keeping people at some point in their lives. There has to be an explanation that is consistent with what the Bible teaches about historical cause and effect.

Deuteronomy 8 presents a five-stage theory of history: from poverty to wealth to either poverty or greater wealth. Some wicked people prosper in every stage, but the third stage—wealth unto autonomy—offers the great threat to the continued success of society. Autonomy brings the historical wrath of God.

There are visible signs of a society that adheres to the principles of biblical law. One example is longer life. The West has enjoyed this since the at least mid-nineteenth century, when the social order more fully adopted biblical principles of private ownership and independence from the state. This longer life span is seen in lower life insurance rates.

20

FAMISHED SOULS AND EMPTY PURSES

The LORD will not suffer the soul of the righteous to famish: but he casteth away the substance [cravings] of the wicked.

PROVERBS 10:3

The tenth chapter of Proverbs begins with a series of contrasts: wise sons vs. foolish sons (v. 1), ill-gotten wealth vs. righteousness (v. 2), righteous people vs. wicked people (v. 3), lazy people vs. industrious people (v. 4). These are not contrasts between people's capacities for work, or obtaining capital, or their basic intelligence. These contrasts are ethical.

This proverb is difficult to translate. Older versions (King James, American Standard) refer to the *soul* of the righteous; later versions (Revised Standard, New American Standard, New English Bible) refer to *hunger*. "The LORD does not let the righteous go hungry" (NEB). Is the focus of the passage primarily spiritual or primarily physical?

Psalm 106 offers parallel ideas and parallel problems of translation. Speaking of the Israelites in the wilderness, the psalmist says, "They soon forgot his works; they waited not for his counsel: But lusted exceedingly in the wilderness and tempted God in the desert And he gave them their request, but sent leanness into their soul" (vv. 13–15). The contrast in the language of the King James is between physical or biological lusts (probably their demand for meat: Num. 11) and spiritual maturity. Problem: the New English Bible translates verse 15 as follows: "He gave them what they asked, but sent a wasting sickness among them" [margin reading: "in their throats"].

A. A Lack of Meat

The Israelites had complained in the wilderness about their lack of meat. The King James Version reads as though their request was spiritual: "…but now our soul is dried away." The New English Bible translates it as: "Now our throats are parched" (Num. 11:6). In other words, the Hebrew language so closely links the human soul and physical attributes (e.g., throat) that the translators are not agreed concerning the proper focus of concern of the writers.

What presents a difficulty in translation also presents a lesson in biblical theology. The language of Old Testament so intertwined the spiritual and the physical that we are not always certain which aspect an author had in mind, or even if he clearly distinguished the two. But we do know this much: there was a close link in the authors' minds between spiritual conditions and external conditions. The Israelites in the wilderness were given the physical meat that they had requested, yet they remained spiritually blind. They received meat in the form of the birds (Num. 11). They continued to grumble against God. Only Joshua and Caleb were allowed to enter the promised land (Num. 14). The contrast is clearly between righteousness and unrighteousness, between trusting in God and complaining to God. Yet the language of the original request, which was unquestionably a demand for physical meat, can be translated so as to make the request appear to be a spiritual quest, "our soul is dried away" (King James).

Once we understand how closely they linked body and soul, we begin to understand the contrasts in Proverbs. Righteousness is linked with prosperity, while unrighteousness is linked with poverty. A man's spiritual condition is understood as having predictable (statistically significant) consequences for his external economic situation. Few biblical doctrines are more resented by humanists and socialists than this one. It means that *men are responsible before God and other men for their overall success or failure*.

God will not starve a man who is ethically subordinate to Him. The hunger that godly men experience, both spiritual and physical, will be satisfied by God. Covenant-keepers can be confident in God. They can go about their daily tasks knowing that God will sustain them. This confidence encourages them to organize their lives according to biblical law, since they need not fear that temporary setbacks will bury them or destroy the long-term effects of their work.

B. Wealth Transfer

In contrast, the unrighteous are told that God will thwart their desires and plans. Either they will fail, in time and on earth, or else the capital they accumulate will eventually be transferred to the righteous (Prov. 13:22). They may work hard, build a capital base, and attempt to extend their dominion across the face of the earth, but they and their heirs will not achieve their covenant-breaking goals.

It is not that God casts away their substance—their capital base—as implied by the translation of the King James. He *transfers* it, putting it to uses different from those planned by the original developers. What is cast away is their *desires*. They may well achieve their goals in terms of building up a capital base; what is promised here is that their desires will not be achieved.

The Bible affirms the temporal efficacy of hard work, thrift, and the other personal disciplines that we associate with the phrase, "the Protestant ethic." But these virtues are not sufficient to produce the results hoped for by the wicked. In the language of the economist, the Protestant ethic is "necessary but not sufficient" for long-term economic growth. This ethic must be sustained by the theology that created it. It is not an autonomous ethic that can be effectively adopted, long term, by any and all cultures, because covenant-breaking cultures cannot sustain this ethic indefinitely. They will either abandon it or else adopt the confession of faith that undergirds it.[2]

This proverb therefore gives confidence to the righteous and hopelessness for the wicked. By affirming hope for the righteous, God provides His people with the *attitude of victory* that is so necessary in any long-term program of dominion. By affirming despair for the unrighteous, God also strengthens His people. There is both a positive and a negative aspect to the dominion covenant: "we win; they lose." We are "programmed" for victory. God's enemies are "programmed" for defeat.

Conclusion

The righteous man receives a two-fold feeding: spiritual and physical. The Hebrews did not separate the two realms. The wicked man also is dealt with in a two-fold manner. Both his soul and his purse become lean (Hag. 1:6). *Two-fold feeding and two-fold starving*: this is the underlying theory of economic development in the Proverbs.

---

1. Chapter 41.
2. Gary North, *Dominion and Common Grace: The Biblical Basis of Progress* (Tyler, Texas: Institute for Christian Economics, 1987), ch. 6.

21

SLACK HANDS AND
EMPTY PURSES

He becometh poor that dealeth with a slack hand: but the hand of the diligent maketh rich.

PROVERBS 10:4

A. Work and Wealth

The Bible is quite clear about a major cause of personal poverty: a person's unwillingness to work. Proverbs returns to this theme repeatedly. The cause-and-effect relationship between slack hands[1] or folded hands and poverty is real, the Bible says. He who would avoid poverty must work diligently.

The Bible does not teach that poor people are always lazy. The Book of Ruth makes it plain that Ruth was a righteous woman, but she was poor. She had to glean for a living, indicating that she was extremely poor (Ruth 2).[2] Gleaning was hard, low-paying work. No one did it who had a regular job. Gleaning was a form of welfare, but it required hard work (Lev. 19:10; Deut. 24:21).[3] She was faithful—so committed to her mother-in-law that she was willing to leave her nation and journey to Israel to live. But it should be noted that Ruth did

---

1. Sometimes the Hebrew word is translated as "deceit" (Job 13:7; Job 27:4; Psalms 32:2; 52:2).

2. Gary North, *Disobedience and Defeat: An Economic Commentary on the Historical Books* (Dallas, Georgia: Point Five Press, 2012), ch. 9.

3. Gary North, *Inheritance and Dominion: An Economic Commentary on Deuteronomy*, 2nd ed. (Dallas, Georgia: Point Five Press, [1999] 2012), ch. 62; cf. North, *Boundaries and Dominion: An Economic Commentary on Leviticus*, 2nd ed. (Dallas, Georgia: Point Five Press, [1994] 2012), ch. 11.

not remain poor. God delivered her into wealth through marriage to a generous wealthy man, Boaz (Ruth 4).[4]

Similarly, the Book of Job teaches that poverty can come upon a man despite his high moral character. The mistake of the first three of Job's four "comforters" was in concluding that God must have been visiting judgment upon him because of some sin on his part (Job 4:7–9). They understood the usual relationship between immorality and personal poverty; they failed to understand the sovereignty of God in His departure from this normal pattern in unusual circumstances. Again, it must be borne in mind that Job was subsequently delivered by God and elevated to an even higher position of wealth and status (42:12).[5] He was not called upon to remain in poverty, although God made it clear to Job that it was well within God's sovereign right to cast Job down and keep him down, had it suited Him.

The slack hand reflects a moral weakness on the part of the lazy person. God calls men to work hard in order to exercise dominion. Man's work has been cursed ever since Adam's Fall, but it is still man's moral responsibility to labor, to attempt to overcome progressively the external effects of the curse. How? Through moral behavior, which includes hard work. *A man's character is reflected in his attitude toward work.* A man who is unwilling to work long and hard is not to be regarded as a paragon of biblical virtue.

Slack hands produce poverty. The cause-and-effect relationship between slack hands and poverty mirrors the relationship between diligence and riches. *This proverb appeals directly to men's economic self-interest.* The moral virtue of hard work is an underlying theme in the Bible, but the appeal here (and in most other passages) is not to morality as such, but rather to *the economic fruits of morality.* It is the universal (or nearly universal) desire of men to improve their economic circumstances. This is the underlying presupposition of this proverb. Only because there are God-created cause-and-effect relationships between morality and hard work, and between hard work and wealth, are large numbers of otherwise unconcerned and

---

4. North, *Disobedience and Defeat*, ch. 11.

5. He lost his 10 children (Job 1:2, 19). The text in Job 42 does not mention this, but it hints at it. "He had also seven sons and three daughters. And he called the name of the first, Jemima; and the name of the second, Kezia; and the name of the third, Keren-happuch. And in all the land were no women found so fair as the daughters of Job: and their father gave them inheritance among their brethren" (Job 42:13–15). Numerically, there was no difference. These daughters were special. But the other 10 children were dead. He did not have 20 children. Gary North, *Predictability and Dominion: An Economic Commentary on Job* (Dallas, Georgia: Point Five Press, 2012), ch. 6:D.

immoral men motivated to discipline themselves by means of hard labor. Their production blesses themselves and their families, and it also blesses those who benefit through peaceful trade with them. Per capita wealth of many people is thereby increased.

In sharp contrast to the thesis of socialistic "liberation theology," God is not on the side of the poor as such. He is on the side of the righteous, including the righteous poor. Most of all, He is on the side of His own word, which sets forth the moral and occupational criteria for escaping poverty. Poverty is to be shunned, just as immorality is to be shunned. Wealth is a legitimate goal and a reward for shunning immorality in one's occupation. More than any other specified cause of poverty, the Bible singles out *morally dissipated living*, whose chief occupational manifestation is slack hands.

B. Manual Labor

The contrast between lazy and diligent is not a contrast between manual labor and intellectual labor. Solomon, who compiled these proverbs (10:1), and who spoke 3,000 proverbs altogether (I Kings 10:32), was obviously not a manual laborer, nor did God or men expect him to be. His reputation as a wise judge was world renowned, even among kings (I Kings 4:34). This brought glory to God, for by upholding the law of God, a nation builds a foundation of long-term prosperity, and this in turn elevates God's reputation throughout the world (Deut. 4:5–8).[6] Rendering godly judgment in any occupation is as important a job as manual labor.

Nevertheless, God has called most men throughout history to be manual laborers. Not until the advent of the later phases of the Industrial Revolution, in the mid-twentieth century, was the capital base of northern Europe and the United States able to sustain a majority of working people in occupations that did not require hard physical labor. Until this period, the social division of labor between manual labor and intellectual labor had always been weighted heavily on the side of manual labor.

Output had always been low for most manual laborers because of the lack of capital, including intellectual and entrepreneurial capital. Per capita productivity did not permit the average family to store up a large quantity of surplus products beyond basic survival needs. So, there was little to offer in trade. Pre-industrial society was not suffi-

---

6. North, *Inheritance and Dominion*, ch. 8.

ciently productive to permit large numbers of intellectual workers
and professional tradesmen to exercise their callings. Low output per
capita kept supplies of surplus goods low, so the division of labor was
retarded.

C. Tools in Hand

Of course, we can also look at per capita productivity from the demand side. Until the laws and ethics of the West sanctioned non-manual, non-agricultural labor as a legitimate calling for the masses, and
until the West's favorable outlook toward trade, money-lending, and
entrepreneurship encouraged the development of a large number of
non-manual laborers, the per capita productivity of the masses remained low. Because most workers could afford to buy only simple
tools, and could sell into only minimally developed markets, only
a few of them could increase their per capita productivity over the
long haul. Until they had an opportunity to buy the mass-produced,
price-competitive consumer and capital goods and services of urban,
industrial civilization, they had only mere survival as their primary incentive to sacrifice present income for the sake of increasing their capital base of tools and education. Tools and education are the primary
means of increasing productivity in a society already marked by long
hours of hard work. In non-industrialized societies, once agricultural
laborers have produced a sufficient number of goods to insure their
survival for one more season, they generally reduce their work hours
and their rate of savings, thereby reducing their ability to trade with
non-agricultural workers. They prefer leisure to greater wealth. They
count leisure as wealth, which it is. But it does not compound.

It was the so-called "Protestant ethic" of the West that enabled
society to build up its capital base and simultaneously encourage the
development of an extensive division of labor. The effects of this new
world-and-life view were comprehensive. The entire civilization of
Protestantism was transformed. This is what the Bible teaches men to
expect. A shift in a civilization's theology has implications far beyond
the confines of the sanctuary and the study.

Several of the medieval monastic orders displayed this same work
ethic. The Cistercians and Benedictines are good examples. Monks
took individual vows of poverty, worked long hours, consumed very
little, invented new agricultural tools, increased output, and sold
at low prices. The monasteries made great profits, which they re-in-
vested. These orders grew rich. Then, every few centuries, they had to

be reformed to restore them to their original spirituality, which rested on vows of poverty and celibacy.

Under Protestantism, especially Calvinism, but also Methodism, a new ethical outlook spread to the general population of Northern Europe. It affirmed that what the medieval sacerdotal orders had experienced—economic growth—is legitimate for all God-fearing, God-obeying people and societies.

Conclusion

Laziness produces poverty. This is a continuing theme in the Book of Proverbs. *Laziness is a manifestation of moral weakness.*

This proverb appeals to personal self-interest: visible success. This is a positive sanction. But more fundamental is the means of success: righteousness. God is on the side of the righteous. He shows this by blessing them for obedience.

Manual labor is rigorous. Mental labor can be rigorous. The contrast is not between categories of labor but rather qualities of labor.

What we call the Protestant ethic was basic to the coming of the Industrial Revolution and its high output. Max Weber was correct in 1905.[7] This view has been denied by many scholars. Their bias against covenant-breaking religion as a cause of poverty is balanced only by their hostility to the idea of covenant-keeping religion as a cause of wealth. Either result indicates that religion has consequences economically. This thought is offensive to modern scholars, who begin with the assumption of the irrelevance of God except as a social delusion.

[handwritten note:] Covenant-breaking religion is a cause of poverty.

Covenant-Keeping religion is a cause of wealth.

---

7. Gary North, "The 'Protestant Ethic' Hypothesis," *The Journal of Christian Reconstruction*, III (Summer 1976).

22

HARVESTING IN DUE SEASON

He that gathereth in summer is a wise son: but he that sleepeth in harvest is a son that causeth shame.

PROVERBS 10:5

A. A Time for Everything

Timing is practically everything. This is a continuing message in the Bible. "To every thing there is a season, and a time to every purpose under the heaven" (Eccl. 3:1).[1] An overriding concern of the godly man should be his lack of time. The strength of youth is not to be wasted. "Remember now thy Creator in the days of thy youth, while the evil days come not, nor the years draw nigh, when thou shalt say, I have no pleasure in them; while the sun, or the light, or the moon, or the stars, be not darkened, nor the clouds return after the rain" (Eccl. 12:1–2). Jesus' words reflect this same concern: "I must work the works of him that sent me, while it is day: the night cometh when no man can work" (John 9:4).

Solomon does not say that sleeping is wrong. What he says is that sleeping late during the days of harvest is wrong. The sleeper has failed to understand the relationship between timing and success. He has assumed that he can rest at his discretion. The Bible says no. People are to work for six days; they are to rest on the seventh (Ex. 20:10).[2] The sabbath rest comes at the end of time, when the ethical

---

1. Gary North, *Autonomy and Stagnation: An Economic Commentary on Ecclesiastes* (Dallas, Georgia: Point Five Press, 2012), ch. 7.

2. Gary North, *Authority and Dominion: An Economic Commentary on Exodus* (Dallas, Georgia: Point Five Press, 2012), Part 2, *Decalogue and Dominion* (1986), ch. 24.

battles of life are over. We celebrate the sabbath before the final day of judgment because we honor ritually what God has promised definitively. But Paul's image of the athletic event, especially the race, points to the necessity of running fast and hard while the race is in progress (I Cor. 9:24;[3] Phil. 3:14;[4] see also Heb. 12:1).

The image of the harvest was used by Jesus to motivate His disciples. "Thus saith he unto his disciples, The harvest truly is plenteous, but the labourers are few; pray ye therefore the Lord of the harvest, that he will send forth labourers into the harvest" (Matt. 9:37–38). The wealth potential of the harvest is enormous. It is so great that the few harvesters available to do the work are insufficient, compared to the extent of the crop. In other words, the value of the laborer's output is high because of the extensive crop. But time is short. The burden on the existing harvesters is very heavy, not because there is an insufficient potential return on their labor, but the opposite: there is a huge potential return, but also huge potential waste if the crop is not gathered in due season.

B. Pacing Ourselves

This proverb testifies to the existence of rhythms in life. A man must pace himself according to the conditions of the market. No successful distance runner runs equally fast throughout a long race, irrespective of the conditions of the course, the distance remaining, his energy reserves, and the speed of his competitors. Similarly, the farmer must pace himself in terms of the seasons. There are times during the year when the pay-off for hard labor is relatively low. There are times to sit and sharpen scythes, and there are times for working intensely from dawn to dusk, in order to take advantage of the brief period of the harvest. A dull scythe will wait another day in the dead of winter; in due season, the harvest will not. Whatever is not harvested on time will rot.

The imagery of the harvest points to an all-or-nothing situation. It comes once a year. All the work and capital that has been invested in order to produce a crop is "on the line" during the harvest season. *The labor theory of value is incorrect*. So is every other cost-of-production theory. Just because the labor or capital inputs were valuable at

---

3. Gary North, *Judgment and Dominion: An Economic Commentary on First Corinthians*, 2nd ed. (Dallas, Georgia: Point Five Press, [2001] 2012), ch. 12.

4. Gary North, *Ethics and Dominion: An Economic Commentary on the Epistles*, (Dallas, Georgia: Point Five Press, 2012), ch. 21.

the time of planting in no way guarantees a profitable return on the investment. The unharvested crop is worth only what mulch is worth, no matter how much capital and labor was invested at the planting. The person who indulges himself and rests during the harvest throws away the potential value of the crop. If he sleeps, then he has placed a very high price tag on his slumber—not the value of the capital and labor over time that he invested, which is gone whether he sleeps or not, but the value of the crop. He has calculated foolishly, and he brings shame on his father, who is expected to have instructed him in wisdom.

Maximum production is achieved by proper pacing. The person who treats the whole year as if it were the harvest will deplete his resources without gaining a continually high return on his investment. He will waste his emotional and physical reserves, as well as his stock of capital. Life does not offer equally high rates of return every day. *What is important is performance over an entire life span.* There is a sort of "average rate of return" for an entire life. This is what men are responsible for.

C. Neglecting the Harvest

The man who neglects the harvest is a fool. His investment's rate of return is totally dependent on his ability and willingness to harvest his crop in due season. The higher the value of the harvested crop, the higher his average rate of return on his investments over the whole year. If he fails to gather the crop during the harvest season, his total rate of return drops to zero, and so does his average rate of return. If the value of the harvest is zero, then the value of the investment is also zero. This is an agricultural application of the universally applicable economic doctrine of "sunk costs."[5] In the ground, the present value of the seeds, the fertilizer, and the worn-out equipment is utterly dependent on the *expected future value* of the crop. If the crop cannot be harvested, then the invested resources are of zero value. This investment is required if there is to be a harvest, but once in the ground, it is gone forever.

An analogy is the college student who works hard throughout the year, but who sleeps through the final exam. He has just lost a semester's tuition payments for that course, and he may have lost his opportunity to return again for the next semester if this pulls down

---

5. Gary North, *An Introduction to Christian Economics* (Nutley, New Jersey: Craig Press, 1973), ch. 26.

his grade point average. The failing grade is awarded irrespective of the amount of effort that the student put into his preparation for the exam, however important his preparation might have been, had he not slept through the exam. But the analogy of the harvest is even more stark, for the sleeping student at least retains some of the information he learned, even if he fails the final exam. The sleeping harvester has nothing left except perhaps some tax-reducing written receipts for labor and capital expended in a missed opportunity.

Once the harvest season is over, the formerly sleepy harvester can do nothing to reap his return. This, of course, is analogous to the sleep of death. There is an irreversible aspect of time: "...it is appointed unto men once to die but after this the judgment" (Heb. 9:27). Eastern religions often teach the doctrine of reincarnation, a theology of nearly infinite opportunities over nearly eternal cyclical time. But the Bible teaches the doctrine of linear time. A lost harvest is forever lost. A lost life is forever lost. There is "only one life per customer," just as there is only one harvest per crop.

This explicitly biblical perspective concerning time has made the West industrious and hard-working. *The concept of linear time made possible the concept of economic development.* Prior to the Protestant Reformation, and especially the seventeenth-century Puritans, neither theologians nor social philosophers, East or West, believed that long-term economic growth is possible. Long-term economic growth was not characteristic of Western culture before Christianity. The rapid economic growth of modern times began in Protestant Britain and spread to Protestant America. It has become an imported phenomenon in pagan Third World nations, made possible initially by an alien imported worldview and imported capital.

Conclusion

Work requires a sense of timing. There is a time to work hard. There is a time to work at a more leisurely pace. In times of harvest, long, hard work is required. He who ignores this will not have success. Each person needs to pace himself according to the season.

Time is linear. This outlook is uniquely biblical in origin. The ideas of creation, Fall, and redemption are presented in a linear fashion. This outlook made possible the concept of compound economic growth, but only when coupled with the eschatological optimism of postmillennialism, the view of some seventeenth-century Dutchmen and many seventeenth-century Puritans. Prior to the Puritans, the concept of linear history did not include the concept of permanent expansion.

The harvest is an all-or-nothing period. The investments made during the planting season come to fruition or failure in the harvest. This indicates that the value of the inputs at the time they are put to use depends on the *expected final value of their output*. The harvest is the output. Thus, to slumber during the harvest is economically suicidal. The labor theory of value, like every cost-of-production theory, is refuted by this proverb. The result of slumber at harvest time is poverty, no matter what expenses were borne during planting.

23

VISIBLE BLESSINGS

Blessings are upon the head of the just: but violence covereth the mouth of the wicked.

PROVERBS 10:6

A. Two Sets of Sanctions

When we see the word "blessing" or "blessed," we are often dealing with a beatitude. There are numerous beatitudes in the Book of Proverbs.[1]

The second half of this proverb is obscure. The King James translators contrast violence and blessings: both are visible. Violence "covers" the mouth of the wicked, while blessings "cover" the head of the righteous. But the New American Standard Bible translates the Hebrew word translated "cover" as "conceals." The New English Bible translates it as "choked."

The meaning of the verb is debated, but there can be no doubt that violence is associated with the mouth of the wicked, whether his mouth conceals it, is choked by it, or is covered by it. *The mouth is the place where violence lurks.* The schemes of the wicked man are set forth verbally. Eventually, his plans become plain. The tongue is compared to an untamed beast that requires a bridle to control it (Ps. 39:1; James 1:26; 3:2).

The righteous man controls his tongue; the unrighteous man does not. It eventually reveals what he is. The righteous man can be iden-

---

1. They are: 3:13, 18, 33; 5:18; 8:32, 34; 11:26; 14:21; 16:20; 20:7; 22:9; 24:25; 28:14, 20; 29:18. Gary Brady, *Heavenly Wisdom: Proverbs simply explained* (Webster, New York: Evangelical Press, 2003), p. 252.

107

tified, this proverb tells us. He is known by the blessings on his head. Obviously, there is some literary reference here. Unless someone goes around wearing a crown of jurisdiction—and only kings, bishops, military officers, and police officers are identified in this way—blessings are not literally worn on a person's head. What is the frame of reference? Most likely, it is the oil of anointing. The words of Psalm 23 come to mind: "Thou anointest my head with oil; my cup runneth over" (5b). It was God who anointed David. The effects of this anointing become ever-more visible to his enemies.

The contrast between the righteous man and the unrighteous man, between the wise man and the fool, is the underlying theme of Proverbs. There is a way of wisdom and a way of destruction. Those who travel down each path are eventually distinguishable, in time and on earth, according to Proverbs. *Whatever dwells in the heart of a man eventually manifests itself.* But this does not answer these questions: (1) Why should there be visible blessings and visible cursings? (2) Why are the differences not limited to visible differences in people's personal behavior? This is the question of covenantal sanctions: point four of the biblical covenant.[2]

B. The Dominion Covenant

The garden of Eden was to have served as a training ground for man. It was a place where Adam could have developed competent judgment. His skills as a keeper (protector) and dresser (gardener) of the garden were to have become visible. Eventually, he was supposed to have taken these judgmental skills into the world outside the garden, in order to subdue it to the glory of God.

The dominion covenant involves visible blessings. The beauty of the garden was to have been aesthetically more pleasing to man and God than the natural beauty of the untamed earth. A man's success in exercising dominion was originally planned by God to have outward manifestations. The very process of developing godly judgment was a process of understanding and applying God's standards to every area of life. When applied, these standards were to have been visible, analogous to the visible goodness of the creation in response to God's perfect application of His own standards of performance. This is why

2. Ray R. Sutton, *That You May Prosper: Dominion By Covenant*, 2nd ed. (Tyler, Texas; Institute for Christian Economics, [1987] 1992), ch. 4. Gary North, *Unconditional Surrender: God's Program for Victory*, 5th ed. (Powder Springs, Georgia: American Vision, 2010), ch. 4.

He could evaluate his own workmanship and pronounce it very good (Gen. 1:31).[3]

There are principles of cause and effect in the creation. Righteousness leads to blessings in history, both spiritual (inward) and dominical (outward). The works of the righteous man's hands are intended to shine before men, just as his personal behavior is to shine. The works of a righteous nation (Deut. 4:5–8)[4] and the church (Matt. 5:14–16)[5] are also to shine before men, calling attention to the superiority of the Bible's principles of administration (garden keeping) to all other principles. God did not do sloppy work in His own name when He created all things. Neither individuals nor nations are to do sloppy work in the name of God.

How are we to judge performance? By the stated principles of the worker, and also by the results. *The righteous plant bears good fruit.* By their fruits ye shall know them, Christ said (Matt. 7:20).[6] But the analogy of the garden should point to the need for visible blessings: successful performance of the gardening assignment was itself a reward, namely, a more beautiful environment.

The cause-and-effect universe created by God enables us to judge the quality of a person's performance by the results he achieves. God sees to it that righteousness receives blessings. These blessings are to serve as visible signs of the covenant, which call forth even more faithful adherence to that covenant: "…for it is he that giveth thee power to get wealth, that he may establish his covenant which he sware unto thy fathers, as it is this day" (Deut. 8:18).[7] *Blessings are given by God to reinforce men's good behavior.* Visible blessings are to remind men of the reality of the covenantal foundation of society. Good behavior is visible; so are God's blessings for good behavior.

C. Ethical Consistency

It may take time for these visible blessings to appear. If the mouth of the unrighteous eventually reveals the kind of character that lies behind it, why shouldn't the blessings of the righteous reveal the char-

---

3. Gary North, *Sovereignty and Dominion: An Economic Commentary on Genesis* (Dallas, Georgia: Point Five Press, [1982] 2012), ch. 5.

4. Gary North, *Inheritance and Dominion: An Economic Commentary on Deuteronomy*, 2nd ed. (Dallas, Georgia: Point Five Press, [1999] 2012), ch. 8.

5. Gary North, *Priorities and Dominion: An Economic Commentary on Matthew*, 2nd ed. (Dallas, Georgia: Point Five Press, [2000] 2012), ch. 6.

6. *Ibid.*, ch. 18.

7. North, *Inheritance and Dominion,* ch. 22.

acter of both the individual and the God who sovereignly controls the universe? Why should the power of God not be made manifest to all, just as the weakness of the unrighteous should be manifested? Why should we regard it as odd that the rival cause-and-effect principles, righteousness vs. unrighteousness, should produce visibly different results?

In the short run, evil men can be blessed externally, as a prelude to their destruction (Deut. 8:11–20).[8] In the short run, righteous men can experience poverty and external cursings (Job). In the long run, and in the aggregate (society as such), unrighteousness produces destruction (Deut. 28:15–68) and righteousness produces visible blessings (Deut. 28:1–14).[9]

There is a tendency for Christian pietists to recoil in horror to the idea that righteous behavior produces visible blessings. Pietists resent the biblical teaching that righteousness produces long-term affluence and power, and that ethical rebellion produces long-term poverty and weakness. They see widespread visible blessings of God as either random or else as a prelude to God's coming judgment.

The biblical doctrine of visible blessings teaches that redeemed men are given external blessings in order to confirm them in their faith, *so that they may take on additional responsibilities*. Pietists resent the whole idea of the dominion covenant, of which the doctrine of visible blessings is a part. They prefer to believe that faithful Christians will be burdened by *internal responsibilities only*, and therefore any blessings that God pours out on His people will be limited to the internal, psychological realm of man's spirit. They reject the idea that righteous behavior produces external blessings. They are even further away from an understanding of God's dominion covenant than a reprobate like Ben Franklin was, for he was still influenced by the Puritan thought, as he admitted in his autobiography.[10] He could write that "honesty is the best policy," not because he believed in the God of the Bible, but because he had seen the external results of such a God-ordained principle. Modern pietists look at the wealth that the Protestant ethic has produced, and they hide their eyes in disbelief, hoping to find another explanation. So do humanists.

---

8. *Ibid.*, chaps. 21–23.

9. *Ibid.*, ch. 69.

10. He read Cotton Mather's *Essay to Do Good* at the age of 11, he said in his autobiography. In a letter to Samuel Mather, 1773, he recounted a meeting he had with Mather's forebear when Franklin was 23.

Conclusion

The undisciplined tongue tends toward violence. A righteous person must exercise discipline over what he says. This is another application of the general theme in Proverbs: wisdom vs. foolishness.

There are two covenantal paths. One is righteous. The other is not. One leads toward dominion. The other leads toward death. Each path is visible. Each has visible consequences.

This proverb opposes sloppy work. *A man's work should reflect his confession.* A covenant-keeper's work should testify to the reliability of the God of the covenant. This means that there are visible results of confessions, and these results must reflect the lords of the rival covenants. If they do not, then one or both of the representatives are not acting consistently with his professed covenant's standards.

24

THE STRENGTH OF CAPITAL

The rich man's wealth is his strong city: the destruction of the poor is their poverty.

PROVERBS 10:15

The structure of each proverb in the tenth chapter presents a positive-negative contrast. First, a benefit or desirable goal is presented. This benefit is linked to wisdom and righteousness. Then a negative is presented. This undesirable outcome is said to be the product of foolishness or wickedness.

When Solomon speaks here of the rich man, there is no suggestion that the rich man is in any way morally compromised. The reference to him is in the first half of this proverb. Thus, it would be misleading to conclude that there is anything innately objectionable either to riches or to the idea that the rich man's wealth does serve as a means of safety for him.

Conversely, there is nothing said in favor of poverty. The poor man's condition is not desirable. His poverty constitutes his destruction. He is unable to place much confidence in his external condition. He has no high wall.

The question then arises: Why are riches referred to elsewhere in the Bible as a snare, a temptation? And why are poor people singled out repeatedly as being blessed by God? If this proverb is true, then what information are we missing in order to make sense out of all the other verses that seem to teach the opposite?

Man's premier temptation is to be as God (Gen. 3:5). Successful men look at their condition in life, and they make a false conclusion, namely, that the work of their hands is responsible for all that they possess. This temptation clearly is greater in the life and experience of a rich man. The poor man may prefer not to take credit for his impoverished condition. The rich man is proud of what his efforts supposedly have produced (Deut. 8:17).[1]

The danger for the successful person is that he begins to regard his "wall" as an autonomous source of protection for him. Like the walls that surrounded ancient cities, the rich man's wall may appear to be nearly impervious to attack. His enemies are outside the gates; they cannot bring him down.

In contrast, the poor man sees his poverty and recognizes that he is already destroyed. What the rich man fears, the poor man is experiencing. He is less tempted to place his trust in his environment. His environment has already proven to be a weak source of defense. He is unlikely to place much confidence in it.

Is it an advantage to have a protecting wall? Most certainly. The fact that Jericho's wall did not withstand the blast of God did not mean that Israel was to build cities without walls or to tear down the walls that existed when the Canaanites were destroyed. The people of Jerusalem were supposed to keep the walls in repair. Under Nehemiah, the people of Jerusalem began the reconstruction of the wall, which had been broken by Babylon (Neh. 2:17–18).

What good does a wall do? It forces an enemy to think twice about the cost of attacking a stronghold. The defenders have time to prepare a defense against the onslaught of enemy forces. The capital investment in the wall serves as a source of security later on, when troubles and dangers appear. *A wall is a standing testimony to the future-orientation of the builders.* They cared enough to sacrifice present consumption expenditures in order to defend themselves and their heirs from attack.

A wall is an admission that an unexpected event can overturn a city's plans. It is a testimony to the power of the unexpected. The same is true of riches. Capital in the form of cash or other readily negotiable assets can be used to defend a business during hard times, or to buy legal advice, or to establish a new business when conditions change. The "high wall" of wealth is a barricade against hard times. It protects the rich man from disasters that would bankrupt a poor man, causing him to sell himself into slavery or to go deeply into debt.

The truly rich man is a man with net assets. He has little or no debt. His capital is his own. It is not a wall with a hole in it, as heav-

---

1. Gary North, *Inheritance and Dominion: An Economic Commentary on Deuteronomy,* 2nd ed. (Dallas, Georgia: Point Five Press, [1999] 2012), ch. 21.

ily indebted capital is. He is not on the verge of poverty. The market normally cannot bring him to his knees, making him destitute.

Walls can be breached. Destruction can come to all men, including the rich. But the rich man has a barrier that the poor man does not possess. The higher the wall, the more difficult it is for enemies to scale it. The rich man has a high wall. He is not easily overrun by his enemies.

Conclusion

This is the description of a desirable condition. All men want safety. All men fear the coming of destruction—the defenseless condition of the poor man. Thus, one of the blessings of covenantal faithfulness is wealth: capital resources that reflect economically the spiritually protected status of the redeemed man. The outward condition of the man who is blessed by God ideally reflects his inward, eternal condition.

Need 601 payments
MC payments due
Tru contract

The visible is evidence
of the invisible.

25

JUST WAGES

The labour of the righteous tendeth to life: the fruit of the wicked to sin [punishment].

PROVERBS 10:16

The contrast between righteousness and wickedness continues. This proverb informs us of two types of wages: life and punishment. The righteous man sells his labor services for a wage: life. This proverb confirms the teaching of the commandment to honor parents in order to attain long life (Ex. 20:12).[1] Long life is a universally pursued earthly goal. In contrast, the wicked man's income is punishment ("sin" in the KJV). There is a predictable correspondence between each type of behavior and its appropriate reward.

The relationship between ethics and economics is obvious. God declares certain actions righteous and others wicked. There is life for those who act righteously, but people who defy God and pursue wickedness are punished. The context of this proverb does not suggest an exclusively heavenly reward. *The preliminary manifestation of eternal wages is temporal.*

Paul's words parallel this proverb: "The wages of sin is death; but the gift of God is eternal life through Jesus Christ our Lord" (Rom. 6:23). His focus was more clearly that of the final judgment. But numerous proverbs make it plain that earthly affairs are indicative of the eternal condition that each person can expect. There is a *preliminary reward system* that reveals, however imperfectly, the spiritual status of society's members.

---

1. Gary North, *Authority and Dominion: An Economic Commentary on Exodus* (Dallas, Georgia: Point Five Press, 2012, Part 2, *Decalogue and Dominion* (1986), ch. 25.

This contrast between the two forms of wages refutes what was once known as the labor theory of value. The classical economists from Adam Smith through John Stuart Mill, including Karl Marx, relied on some version of this theory of value. They assumed that human labor expended in production is the basis of market value. The more labor that is used to manufacture a product, the higher its market price.

Many unsolvable problems were produced by the intellectual labor of those who held this theory. Why is it more profitable to invest in capital in a leisure-oriented industrial nation than in sub-Sahara Africa, where there is so much human labor available at cheap wages to add to the production process? Why is a randomly discovered diamond mine or gold mine so valuable, compared to years of labor devoted to the development of a perpetual motion machine? Eventually, no matter how much time and effort its defenders spent on it—and Marx's second and third volumes of *Das Kapital* (published posthumously) are lasting monuments to just how much labor they expended—the market value of this idea continued to fall.

Beginning in the early 1870s, there appeared an unconnected trio of economists, subsequently called neoclassical economists,[2] who argued that the market value of labor is dependent upon the market value of labor's output. The production of a heavily demanded product or service that requires a highly specialized type of labor (e.g., brain surgery) will highly reward those who possess the particular skill or resources involved. The high price that customers are willing and able to pay will tend to lure other laborers into the labor market for this particular service. It is therefore not labor that gives value to the product, neoclassical economists argued, but market demand by customers. In other words, *customers' subjective preferences and objective purchases are economically authoritative in the marketplace.* Their preferences, revealed through market competition, create an objectively determined market value (price) for products and therefore for both labor and land (resource) inputs that produce these products.

Two forms of labor may be expended on a particular task by two different people. Their physically measurable labor may be close to identical. The righteous man in some instances may receive the same money wage as the wicked man, yet God rewards them differently in eternity. But can their earthly wages differ? The Bible says yes. So does economic theory.

---

2. Carl Menger (Austria), Léon Walras (Switzerland), and William Stanley Jevons (England).

How can this be? Doesn't the free market pay equal wages for equal work? No. It pays *equal wages for equal net value, after costs*, produced by the workers. A lawless man is a higher-risk employee. The employer wants hard-working people who are honest and predictable on the job. He wants people with good reputations in the community. He wants people who will stay with the company for many years. The physically measurable daily labor output of two workers may be the same, but the net value of each man's output to the employer (and therefore to the consumer) may be very different in the long run. Their wages today may reflect this difference.

The Bible's perspective is even more subtle. There is more to economic rewards than the market's rewards. There is also the sovereignty of God. Ours is a personal universe created and sustained by a personal God. He brings glory to Himself by rewarding those who abide by His commandments and who thereby bring honor to Him. In the aggregate, righteous men buy themselves longer life spans (Prov. 10:2).[3] It is God, not the market, who enables them to exercise dominion, on average, longer than the wicked can.

Conclusion

Earthly rewards reflect the spiritual kingdom for which a person labors: two different kingdoms, two types of reward. Thus, there are limits to the market as an institutional source of rewards for productive service. God sees men's hearts, and He rewards them accordingly, although the market is one factor in the distribution of these rewards, since God does not bless or punish men in an historical or institutional vacuum.

Men who work hard for the kingdom of God, honoring God's laws and proclaiming His righteousness, receive more valuable rewards than drunkards who rob, pillage, and die young. The external earthly rewards of most citizens will reflect, in the long run, their ethical condition, because their ethical condition regulates their economic performance. The more closely the social institutions of a society conform to those specified in the Bible, the more predictable the visible relationship will be between ethics and income.

---

3. Chapter 19.

26

LEGITIMATE RICHES

The blessing of the LORD, it maketh rich, and he addeth no sorrow with it.

A. Riches and Stewardship

To begin, the Hebrew word translated here as "rich" means exactly what it means in English *accumulation*. The context in earlier passages where the word appears is clear: wealth.

> That I will not take from a thread even to a shoelatchet, and that I will not take any thing that is thine, lest thou shouldest say, I have made Abram rich (Gen. 14:23).

> The LORD maketh poor, and maketh rich: he bringeth low, and lifteth up (I Sam. 2:7).

> Be not thou afraid when one is made rich, when the glory of his house is increased; For when he dieth he shall carry nothing away: his glory shall not descend after him (Ps. 49:16–17).

> He becometh poor that dealeth with a slack hand: but the hand of the diligent maketh rich (Prov. 10:4).[1]

It would be incorrect to interpret this proverb as dealing with spiritual riches in contrast to assets easily exchanged in a market. The kinds of riches here are marketable riches. A person could put a "for sale" sign on them.

The tip-off is the second part of the promise: "...he addeth no sorrow with it." Why should Solomon have added this? Because in

---

1. Chapter 21.

118

many passages in the Bible, riches are associated with negative sanctions and sorrow. Solomon here distinguishes riches as blessings from riches as cursings. This is an important passage. It makes clear that *riches as covenantal blessings are not to be regarded as a liability*. They are not Trojan horses with sorrow hidden inside.

The spiritually wise man understands that riches increase one's personal responsibility. Jesus taught this clearly.

> And that servant, which knew his lord's will, and prepared not himself, neither did according to his will, shall be beaten with many stripes. But he that knew not, and did commit things worthy of stripes, shall be beaten with few stripes. For unto whomsoever much is given, of him shall be much required: and to whom men have committed much, of him they will ask the more (Luke 12:47–48).[2]

There is an inescapable burden associated with riches: stewardship. Every asset's owner is legally God's agent and is therefore responsible to God for its administration (Luke 19:12–15).[3]

Solomon says that when riches come from God in the form of a *blessing*—a positive covenantal sanction—there is no negative sanction attached to it, i.e., sorrow, but there is added responsibility. This is an inescapable aspect of stewardship. This responsibility is not a threat to the covenant-keeper. The covenant-keeper sees an increase in his responsibility as a motivation to extend God's dominion in history. This is an honor, not a curse. It is a reason to rejoice, not shed tears. To use a military example, it is the equivalent of a promotion. The threat to a military career is a reduction of rank due to incompetence or disobedience to lawful authority. Yet a reduction in rank is a reduction in responsibility.

B. Covenant Sanctions

The Mosaic law affirmed the existence of a predictable relationship between covenantal faithfulness and external blessings.

> And it shall come to pass, if thou shalt hearken diligently unto the voice of the LORD thy God, to observe and to do all his commandments which I command thee this day, that the LORD thy God will set thee on high above all nations of the earth: And all these blessings shall come on thee, and overtake thee, if thou shalt hearken unto the voice of the LORD thy God (Deut. 28:1–2).[4]

---

2. Gary North, *Treasure and Dominion: An Economic Commentary on Luke*, 2nd ed. (Dallas, Georgia: Point Five Press, [2000] 2012), ch. 28.

3. *Ibid.*, ch. 46.

4. Gary North, *Inheritance and Dominion: An Economic Commentary on Deuteronomy*, 2nd ed. (Dallas, Georgia: Point Five Press, [1999] 2012), ch. 69.

These are covenantal blessings. They are evidence of God's faithfulness to His covenant people. He extends their dominion through blessings of various kinds, which are listed in the passage. These are visible blessings. The Hebrew word translated as "blessings" in Deuteronomy 28:2 is the same Hebrew word in Proverbs 10:22.

This passage makes it inescapably clear that wealth is a covenantal blessing of God. This does not mean that it cannot be used by God as a lure into personal disaster. In Proverbs, there are numerous passages that say specifically that God uses wealth as a snare to trap covenant-breakers.

So, the presence of wealth in a person's possession is not, in and of itself, a sign that God looks favorably on the owner's efforts. When wealth is accompanied with a public profession of faith in the God of the Bible and also by outward conformity to God's Bible-revealed law, wealth can safely be presumed by the owner and those around him to be a legitimate blessing from God.

C. Hostility to Wealth

Within every civilization, there are people who pursue wealth fanatically. There are other people who scorn wealth universally. Both outlooks are marks of covenant-breaking. This proverb tells us that wealth is not random. God directs the flow of wealth. He does so within the context of *binding covenant oaths* under His authority. "But thou shalt remember the LORD thy God: for it is he that giveth thee power to get wealth, that he may establish his covenant which he sware unto thy fathers, as it is this day" (Deut. 8:18).[5] He does so outside His covenant.

> Thus saith the LORD to his anointed, to Cyrus, whose right hand I have holden, to subdue nations before him; and I will loose the loins of kings, to open before him the two leaved gates; and the gates shall not be shut; I will go before thee, and make the crooked places straight: I will break in pieces the gates of brass, and cut in sunder the bars of iron: And I will give thee the treasures of darkness, and hidden riches of secret places, that thou mayest know that I, the LORD, which call thee by thy name, am the God of Israel. For Jacob my servant's sake, and Israel mine elect, I have even called thee by thy name: I have surnamed thee, though thou hast not known me (Isa. 45:1–4).

Solomon also warns: "Riches profit not in the day of wrath: but righteousness delivereth from death" (11:4).[6] "The rich man's wealth is

---

5. *Ibid.*, ch. 22.
6. Chapter 30.

his strong city, and as an high wall in his own conceit" (18:11).[7]

So, wealth must be seen within the context of the biblical covenant: confession and obedience. When it is the product of covenantal obedience, it is legitimate.

Conclusion

Riches can come without sorrow. They are tools of dominion. They enable the steward-owner to accomplish more for God's kingdom, which is why he is held responsible for exercising greater responsibility (Luke 12:47–48). To imagine that wealth necessarily produces sorrow and should therefore be avoided is the equivalent of arguing that responsibility produces sorrow and should therefore be avoided. This is the belief of pietists everywhere. They resent any suggestion that the domain of responsibility is as broad and deep as the domain of Satan, the squatter. They seek to limit their responsibility. One manifestation of this attempt is to decry wealth as universally unholy. Solomon thought otherwise.

---

7. Chapter 54.

27

A MATTER OF INHERITANCE

The fear of the wicked, it shall come upon him: but the desire of the righteous shall be granted. As the whirlwind passeth, so is the wicked no more: but the righteous is an everlasting foundation.

PROVERBS 10:24–25

Here is the familiar contrast between the covenant-breaker and the covenant-keeper. Here also is a discussion of sanctions. Each covenantal agent has his appropriate sanctions: point four of the biblical covenant.[1]

A. A Matter of Vulnerability

We begin with the main fear that burdens the wicked. The wicked person has a dominant fear. Of course, he has more than one, but this proverb speaks of fear in the singular. This fear is a constant concern in his life. This proverb says that this dominant fear will come upon him. That which he has feared most will arrive in his life. That with which he has been obsessed will overtake him. He has hoped to avoid it somehow, but he will fail. God will thwart his plans to escape his fear.

This proverb does not mention the fact that most fears of most people never materialize. They worry, yet this emotional drain is wasted. Jesus said: "But seek ye first the kingdom of God, and his righteousness; and all these things shall be added unto you. Take therefore no thought for the morrow: for the morrow shall take thought for the things of itself. Sufficient unto the day is the evil thereof" (Matt. 6:33–34).[2]

---

1. Ray R. Sutton, *That You May Prosper: Dominion By Covenant*, 2nd ed. (Tyler, Texas: Institute for Christian Economics, [1987] 1992), ch. 4. Gary North, *Unconditional Surrender: God's Program for Victory*, 5th ed. (Powder Springs, Georgia: American Vision, 2010), ch. 4.

2. Gary North, *Priorities and Dominion: An Economic Commentary on Matthew*, 2nd ed. (Dallas, Georgia: Point Five Press, [2000] 2012), ch. 15.

It is with this fact of life as a backdrop that this proverb's warning gains its sharpness. The covenant-breaker is not living in an impersonal universe operating in terms of a dialectical conflict between statistical randomness and unbreakable natural law. He is living in a universe governed by cosmic personalism.[3]

> I am the LORD, and there is none else, there is no God beside me: I girded thee, though thou hast not known me: That they may know from the rising of the sun, and from the west, that there is none beside me. I am the LORD, and there is none else. I form the light, and create darkness: I make peace, and create evil: I the LORD do all these things. Drop down, ye heavens, from above, and let the skies pour down righteousness: let the earth open, and let them bring forth salvation, and let righteousness spring up together; I the LORD have created it (Isa. 45:5–8).

The sinner is known by God and identified accurately as an enemy of God. God has structured His universe to operate in terms of a covenantal, ethics-based system of causation. The sinner will be found out. His constant fear will eventually come upon him.

This condition of vulnerability is contrasted with the condition of the covenant-keeper. The covenant-keeper also lives in a world of cosmic personalism. The covenantal structure of cause and effect imposes sanctions in history. The sanctions for covenant-keeping are positive. So, the desire of the righteous shall be granted. Again, this proverb identifies a single concern: *desire*, in contrast to fear. This is the defining desire of the covenant-keeper, in contrast to the defining fear of the covenant-breaker. Jesus identified what should be the defining desire of the covenant-keeper: to seek first the kingdom of God and his righteousness. "Ask, and it shall be given you; seek, and ye shall find; knock, and it shall be opened unto you" (Matt. 7:7).[4] This had been Solomon's experience. He had a desire. He asked God to fulfill it. "Give me now wisdom and knowledge, that I may go out and come in before this people: for who can judge this thy people, that is so great?" (II Chron. 1:10).

> And God said to Solomon, Because this was in thine heart, and thou hast not asked riches, wealth, or honour, nor the life of thine enemies, neither yet hast asked long life; but hast asked wisdom and knowledge for thyself, that thou mayest judge my people, over whom I have made thee king: Wisdom and knowledge is granted unto thee; and I will give thee riches,

---

3. Gary North, *Sovereignty and Dominion: An Economic Commentary on Genesis* (Dallas, Georgia: Point Five Press, [1982] 2012), ch. 1.

4. North, *Priorities and Dominion*, ch. 16.

and wealth, and honour, such as none of the kings have had that have been before thee, neither shall there any after thee have the like (II Chron. 1:11–12).

B. Time and Eternity

The second, connected, proverb contrasts the respective conditions of the covenant-breaker and covenant-keeper. "As the whirlwind passeth, so is the wicked no more: but the righteous is an everlasting foundation."

The image of the whirlwind is graphic. A tornado or its equivalent rolls through a community, leaving devastation in its wake. A few minutes before, there were homes, orchards, and storage buildings. In a brief period, these are all gone. The labor of many people's hands over long periods was invested for the sake of future gains. They invested time and raw materials. They sacrificed. Then, in a few minutes, the whirlwind levels all of these dreams. The investments are now of greatly reduced value. They may be negative: the cost of hauling away the debris. This is the condition of the covenant-breaker. His future is little more than a pile of rubble. Whatever he built will be blown away. His efforts will leave no trace.

In contrast is the covenant-keeper. He is said to be a foundation. This foundation is anchored in eternity. The word can be translated "bottom." It means what it does in English. "So will I break down the wall that ye have daubed with untempered morter, and bring it down to the ground, so that the **foundation** thereof shall be discovered, and it shall fall, and ye shall be consumed in the midst thereof: and ye shall know that I am the LORD" (Ezek. 13:14). In God's wrath, nothing remains of a structure, but a covenant-keeper's foundation is eternal. The image here is of a collapsed wall. So, the passage is pointing, not to a person, but to *a person's efforts in history*. The covenant-keeper's efforts are secure. He will leave more than a trace. His work will serve as the starting point for successors.

This work will be everlasting. This is the same word that is used in a passage describing God's covenant with mankind through Noah. "And the bow shall be in the cloud; and I will look upon it, that I may remember the everlasting covenant between God and every living creature of all flesh that is upon the earth" (Gen. 9:16). It will extend down through the ages.

Conclusion

The sanctions are imposed by God in history. These sanctions are positive and negative. Positive sanctions are the fulfillment of a person's desire and the guaranteed extension of his legacy through time. Negative sanctions are the advent of a person's greatest fear in life and the obliteration of his work down through time. It is the difference between establishing and cutting off.

Ultimately, the distinction is a matter of inheritance, the fifth point of the biblical covenant.[5] The sanctions have opposite effects: the destruction of a person's inheritance and the extension of inheritance through time.

---

5. Sutton, *That You May Prosper*, ch. 5. North, *Unconditional Surrender*, ch. 5.

28

UNRELIABLE SUBORDINATES

As vinegar to the teeth, and as smoke to the eyes, so is the sluggard to them that send him.

PROVERBS 10:26

This proverb deals with the issue of the delegation of authority. There is hierarchy in human institutions. Hierarchy is part of the structure of God's covenant.[1]

The division of labor is mandatory for the extension of God's kingdom in history. "Two are better than one; because they have a good reward for their labour" (Eccl. 4:9). This division of labor is both horizontal and vertical. We rely on those around us to provide what we want when we want it at a price we are able to pay. These people are outside our control. We must persuade them because we cannot command them. We also rely on people who are under us if we work in a hierarchical organization. These people to some degree are under our control. Economic progress is accompanied by the growth in the number of such organizations.

A. Neither Omniscience Nor Omnipotence

Men are not omniscient. We cannot see what is going on beyond a very limited view. We must trust others to provide them with accurate information. We can buy information from outside the organization. We can also obtain information from within the organization. This

---

1. Ray R. Sutton, *That You May Prosper: Dominion By Covenant*, 2nd ed. (Tyler, Texas: Institute for Christian Economics, [1987] 1992), ch. 2. Gary North, *Unconditional Surrender: God's Program for Victory*, 5th ed. (Dallas, Georgia: Point Five Press, [1980] 2012), ch. 2.

126

involves the classifying, identifying, collecting, selecting, evaluating, and packaging of information, so that those above and below in the chain of command can make effective decisions that enable the organization to fulfill its goals.

Beyond the assembling of information there is execution. Men are not omnipotent. They cannot force people to do exactly what they say. In every organization, there are tasks assigned to specific people by those who are higher in the chain of command. In a government bureaucracy, the funding is collected by legal force at the top of the pyramid. The money and authority are allocated downward. It is a top-down system. In contrast is the profit-seeking privately owned organization. Here, top decision-making is confined to budgeting, developing general guidelines, and establishing success indicators, i.e., standards of performance. Initiative in executing the plan lies at the bottom. It is a bottom-up system with respect to execution of the plan.[2]

B. Relying on Subordinates

Those higher in the chain of command become dependent on individuals at lower levels. Everyone in the middle has two sets of dependents: those higher and those lower. Those high in the operation rely on subordinates to execute plans: applying general plans to specific situations, i.e., a reconciliation of the one and the many. This in turn requires a degree of initiative by the plan's implementers. It involves personal responsibility. Others in the organization are dependent in the organization of the smooth, integrated, predictable fulfillment of assignments.

Those who are lower in the chain of command require guidance from those above them. Those above them are in charge of explaining the general rules to those below. Lower-level employees also require budgeted assets in order to fulfill their assignments. This demands attention to details and also leadership abilities. It is not enough to give orders. There must be follow-up.

In every organization there are go-getters and sluggards. The goal of the organization's directors is to hire more of the former and fewer of the latter. The sluggards require nagging in order to persuade them to do three things: (1) do what they said they would do; (2) do it with the assets allocated; (3) do it on time. They may also require other forms of negative sanctions.

---

2. On the differences between these two organizational models, see Ludwig von Mises, *Bureaucracy* (New Haven, Connecticut: Yale University Press, 1944).

Sluggards reduce the efficiency of the organization that employs them. Too much time and energy must be expended to get sluggards to perform at minimal standards. Those high in the chain of command who become dependent on sluggards must constantly intervene to get the sluggards to do their jobs well. Those higher up have their own operations at risk at all times. Sluggards increase this risk. They are like fools. "He that sendeth a message by the hand of a fool cutteth off the feet, and drinketh damage" (Prov. 26:6).

Conclusion

The sluggard is an annoyance both to those above and below him. This proverb mentions only those above him. They are in charge. They will take the blame if the sluggard fails to deliver the specified goods or services on time and within his budget. Those below him will also suffer from his lack of attention to his assignment. They are dependent on the hierarchy to deliver the guidelines, interpretations, and assets necessary to complete their assignments. A sluggard threatens them, too.

Economics — Christian worldview

29

MEASURING OUT JUSTICE

A false balance is abomination to the LORD: but a just weight is his delight.

PROVERBS 11:1

A. Weights and Measures

This is a comment on the Mosaic law: "Ye shall do no unrighteousness in judgment, in meteyard, in weight, or in measure. Just balances, just weights, a just ephah, and a just hin, shall ye have: I am the LORD your God, which brought you out of the land of Egypt" (Lev. 19:35–36).[1]

Here, we are told how God responds to dishonest weights and measures, as well as to honest ones. The former angers Him; the latter delights Him. This message is repeated in Proverbs.

A just weight and balance are the LORD's: all the weights of the bag are his work (16:11).[2]

Divers weights, and divers measures, both of them are alike abomination to the LORD (20:10).[3]

Just weights are identified as God's *work* (16:11). The same Hebrew word is found in the commandment to honor the sabbath, which is contrasted with work. "Six days thou shalt do thy work, and on the seventh day thou shalt rest: that thine ox and thine ass may rest, and the son of thy handmaid, and the stranger, may be refreshed" (Ex. 23:12).

---

1. Gary North, *Boundaries and Dominion: An Economic Commentary on Leviticus*, 2nd ed. (Dallas, Georgia: Point Five Press, [1994] 2012), ch. 19.
2. Chapter 52.
3. Chapter 57.

129

By identifying just weights as God's work, this proverb implies that God took an active role in creating standards. They were not an afterthought, let alone the product of would-be autonomous men's would-be autonomous minds.

In Deuteronomy, this point is driven home.

> Thou shalt not have in thy bag divers weights, a great and a small. Thou shalt not have in thine house divers measures, a great and a small. But thou shalt have a perfect and just weight, a perfect and just measure shalt thou have: that thy days may be lengthened in the land which the LORD thy God giveth thee. For all that do such things, and all that do unrighteously, are an abomination unto the LORD thy God (Deut. 25:13–16).[4]

Notice that there is a blessing attached to this law: long life. This same blessing is associated with the commandment to love one's parents (Ex. 20:12).[5] While this proverb does not specifically say that the use of unjust weights will shorten men's lives, the idea is implied by the contrast.

Why should just weights have such importance that God would promise long life to those who honor this law? This is a major positive sanction—indeed, it is a universally sought-after sanction. Wherever this sanction is invoked by a text—and it is invoked only twice in connection with a Mosaic law—we should take the law seriously. The law is a life-and-death matter.

B. Representative Infractions

Weights and measures are representative of justice in general, as Leviticus 19:35 indicates: "unrighteousness in judgment." Leviticus 19:37 brings the reader back to the chapter's overall topic. "Therefore shall ye observe all my statutes, and all my judgments, and do them: I am the LORD."

Tampering with weights is a form of deception. It is a form of theft. The seller, who is a specialist in his field, uses his specialized knowledge to defraud a buyer, who presumably is less well informed. The social division of labor, which is a blessing to society as a whole because of specialized production, is being misused by a person who possesses specialized knowledge. This kind of fraud is easy to perpetrate because so few people will recognize it. The seller makes a small

4. Gary North, *Inheritance and Dominion: An Economic Commentary on Deuteronomy*, 2nd ed. (Dallas, Georgia: Point Five Press, [1999] 2012), ch. 65.

5. Gary North, *Authority and Dominion: An Economic Commentary on Exodus* (Dallas, Georgia: Point Five Press, 2012), Part 2, *Decalogue and Dominion* (1986), ch. 25.

profit on every transaction—so small that few people will ever notice it. The fraud is widespread in the sense of multiple victims.

The Bible singles out this crime as representing crime in general. The perpetrator thinks he will not be caught. He thinks that God will not see or will not care or will not intervene on behalf of the victims. This is characteristic of criminals.

> The wicked, through the pride of his countenance, will not seek after God: God is not in all his thoughts. His ways are always grievous; thy judgments are far above out of his sight: as for all his enemies, he puffeth at them. He hath said in his heart, I shall not be moved: for I shall never be in adversity. His mouth is full of cursing and deceit and fraud: under his tongue is mischief and vanity. He sitteth in the lurking places of the villages: in the secret places doth he murder the innocent: his eyes are privily set against the poor. He lieth in wait secretly as a lion in his den: he lieth in wait to catch the poor: he doth catch the poor, when he draweth him into his net. He croucheth, and humbleth himself, that the poor may fall by his strong ones. He hath said in his heart, God hath forgotten: he hideth his face; he will never see it (Ps. 10:4–11).

The Psalmist—Solomon's father—then called on God to avenge the victims.

> Arise, O LORD; O God, lift up thine hand: forget not the humble. Wherefore doth the wicked contemn God? he hath said in his heart, Thou wilt not require it. Thou hast seen it; for thou beholdest mischief and spite, to requite it with thy hand: the poor committeth himself unto thee; thou art the helper of the fatherless. Break thou the arm of the wicked and the evil man: seek out his wickedness till thou find none (Ps. 10:12–15).

Conclusion

God sees. He evaluates in terms of His permanent ethical standards. He judges men's weights and measures in terms of His weights and measures. Through the supernatural handwriting on the wall, God told Babylon's final king, "TEKEL; Thou art weighed in the balances, and art found wanting" (Dan. 5:27).

A constant theme in the Mosaic law and Old Testament revelation is the necessity of honest weights and measures. This is a crucial manifestation of a society's commitment to God's covenant.

30

DEFENSIVE WALLS

Riches profit not in the day of wrath: but righteousness delivereth from death.

PROVERBS 11:4

A. The Day When Everything Changes

There is no concept of the final judgment in the Old Testament. The doctrines of the final judgment, hell, heaven, the lake of fire, and the post-resurrection new heaven and new earth are all exclusively New Testament doctrines.[1] So, this proverb refers to history. This is not to say that these dual principles do not apply also to eternity. They do. But that is not its focus here. If we are to understand how it applies to us, we must first understand how it was believed to apply under the Mosaic covenant.

The day of wrath in the Old Testament was a day of judgment that altered a person's life. This might be a military battle. It might be a personal confrontation between rivals. It was a day of judgment for men or institutions. Such an event would permanently change the pattern of history, either personal or national. The prophet Isaiah warned Judah of the day of the Lord.

> The lofty looks of man shall be humbled, and the haughtiness of men shall be bowed down, and the LORD alone shall be exalted in that day. For the day of the LORD of hosts shall be upon every one that is proud and lofty, and upon every one that is lifted up; and he shall be brought low (Isa. 2:11–12).

---

1. The new heavens and the new earth are both taught in Isaiah 65, but they refer to the earth. There are still sinners. There is still death (Isa. 65:17–20). This is a millennial prophecy, not a final judgment prophecy.

When that judgment arrived over a century and a half later, the prophet Jeremiah lamented,

> The young and the old lie on the ground in the streets: my virgins and my young men are fallen by the sword; thou hast slain them in the day of thine anger; thou hast killed, and not pitied. Thou hast called as in a solemn day my terrors round about, so that in the day of the LORD's anger none escaped nor remained: those that I have swaddled and brought up hath mine enemy consumed (Lam. 2:21–22).

B. The Walls of Protection

Men build up walls. In the era of gunpowder, city walls no longer protect against invaders. Cities no longer bother to build walls. But there are walls nonetheless. The favored wall is wealth. "The rich man's wealth is his strong city, and as an high wall in his own conceit" (Prov. 18:11).[2] The rich man's assumption is this: "Every person has a price." He assumes that he can buy his way out of every predicament. But to do this, he needs wealth. The greater the predicament he expects, the greater the wealth he thinks he will require.

This proverb challenges this assumption. There will come a predicament that is too great for a rich man to escape through his wealth. When an invading army penetrates the city's walls, its troops will collect the wealth of all the inhabitants. Why bargain with a rich man? Besides, who can enforce the terms of the agreement? The more ruthless the army, the less reliable the enforcement of contracts.

In contrast is the wall of righteousness. It offers hope that wealth does not. But why? This proverb does not say. But we know this: in an impersonal universe, there could be no such guarantee, no such hope. There would be no sovereign agent to enforce the promise. So, this proverb is a testimony to the cosmic personalism of the created universe.[3] Causation is not impersonal, nor is it ethically neutral.

This being the case, this proverb's message is that *ethics is preferable to riches as a way to avoid the threat of destruction*. The rich man's wall will be breached by the enemy. The righteous man's wall will not.

Conclusion

This proverb deals with faith. It raises this question: What should a wise person trust as his barrier against disaster, money or righteousness?

---

2. Chapter 54.

3. Gary North, *Sovereignty and Dominion: An Economic Commentary on Genesis* (Dallas, Georgia: Point Five Press, [1982] 2012), ch. 1.

This proverb is clear: righteousness. Yet this covenantal fact is difficult for even covenant-keepers to believe in their own lives. It takes
years of self-discipline in terms of God's law to persuade a person that
this proverb is true. A covenant-keeper should know this in principle
from the day he reads this proverb and others like it, but it usually
takes years of evidence to persuade him. People are slow learners.
They are also evidentialists rather than presuppositionalists when it
comes to truths that are difficult to believe.

31

A MULTITUDE OF COUNSELORS

Where no counsel is, the people fall: but in the multitude of counsellors there is safety.

PROVERBS 11:14

A. Corporate Society

Here we have a corporate view of society. The Hebrew word, *'am,* is a collective noun. The context is national. The national covenant forms the basis of this collective.

Societies require counselors. Every society has counselors. At every level of society, decision-makers seek counsel. So, the phrase, "where no counsel is," has to be a metaphor for unwise counsel. It is empty counsel. It counts for nothing. This principle is not limited to civil government.

In Israel, there were court prophets who were on the king's payroll. They were usually false prophets. They spoke what the king wanted to hear, but in the name of God. This counsel is contrasted with a multitude of counsel. So, it must be a form of poor counsel. This proverb's words contrast no counsel with a multitude of counsel. But this is never the situation, for someone is always advising the representatives of society to take a particular course of action on behalf of the society. I conclude that the contrast is between unitary counsel and a cross-section of opinion.

Unitary counsel has multiple defects. First, it must exclude competing views. To do this, there must be a system of information filtering, so that the decision-makers hear only one side regarding any decision. This filtering system must involve conscious deception of

135

those at the top by those in charge of the flow of information. This proverb indicates that this kind of unitary counsel is the equivalent of no counsel at all.

The second problem is that a committee with a unified agenda is after something. Its members have something to gain: fame, influence with key groups outside the counsel, money from a special-interest group, or the approval of the decision-makers, who hear only what they want to hear. When the decision-makers seek confirmation rather than counsel, the Bible speaks of this arrangement as being without counsel.

B. What Is Counsel?

Counsel is an assessment of the unknown future by specialists who know something about the past. The problem for the decision-maker is to assess the degree of correspondence of counsel regarding the past with that which is unknown about the future. First, counselors with expertise regarding the past are always in conflict. The more of them who are consulted, the greater the degree of disagreement over what really happened, what it meant, and what the objective results were.

Second, that which is asserted about the past must be assessed by the decision-makers in terms of three problems: its accuracy, its relevance to the problem at hand, and its enforceability by the hierarchical system of control available to the decision-maker. A decision-maker can issue lots of orders. Will the orders be carried out as he intended, or even at all? Bureaucrats are self-serving. They are also specialists in blocking or deflecting orders from above, as well as requests from below.

This proverb assumes that there is covenantal agreement, established by confession and institutional discipline, in the nation. That is, it assumes that there is a *unitary worldview* regarding God, man, law, causation, and time. This is a society created by covenant. There is a unitary confession: "Hear, O Israel: The LORD our God is one LORD" (Deut. 6:4).

Second, this proverb assumes that within this unitary confession there is disagreement regarding the appropriate course of action. There are experts and non-experts in society who have strong opinions. They are in possession of truth. Information is widely dispersed. In order to gain the advantage of access to the truth that is relevant to the decision at hand and enforceable by the chain of command, the decision-makers must listen to a wide range of opinions.

These opinions are not matched with authority. They are opinions without judicial responsibility. The decision-makers have both authority and responsibility. They cannot evade the problem at hand. So, they seek to deal with it by gaining access to information that a screening committee of court prophets could not possess.

C. The Division of Intellectual Labor

The economist and social theorist F. A. Hayek made this principle, the intellectual division of labor, the cornerstone of his long and distinguished academic career. In what has become a classic essay, "The Use of Knowledge in Society" (1945), Hayek argued against central economic planning because no committee of planners can possess the knowledge that individuals possess across the society. They know the relevant facts of their particular situations. No distant committee can know this.[1]

Unlike a free market, which has a price system to adjust specific supply and demand, which in turn pressures market participants to adjust their plans in terms of prices, the central government possesses no comparable method of bringing this decentralized knowledge to bear on the problem at hand. The decision-makers are not able to collect and assess all the relevant information. So, they listen to representatives of particular groups or viewpoints. There is always screening of information. Decision-makers are not God. They are not omniscient. But by putting information suppliers on notice that many viewpoints will be heard and assessed, the decision-makers call forth far more information than a closed screening committee representing one interest group could possibly produce.

This proverb recommends that decision-makers listen to many points of view before deciding. Their goal should be better information. Solomon understood another principle of decision-making. "He that is first in his own cause seemeth just; but his neighbour cometh and searcheth him" (Prov. 18:17). This also applies to decision-making outside of the courtroom.

D. Every Level of Decision-Making

The principle of multiple counsel applies to every level of decision-making. The individual must make decisions. He should seek multiple counselors.

---

1. F. A. Hayek, "The Use of Knowledge in Society" (1945), in Hayek, *Individualism and Economic Order* (Chicago: University of Chicago Press, 1948), ch. 4.

The free market is the consummate social institution for seeking and gaining counsel. The price system is a constant source of updated information. People buy and sell in terms of a price, which in turn sends more signals and therefore more information.

Everyone is responsible for what he does. Jesus warned: "A good man out of the good treasure of the heart bringeth forth good things: and an evil man out of the evil treasure bringeth forth evil things. But I say unto you, That every idle word that men shall speak, they shall give account thereof in the day of judgment. For by thy words thou shalt be justified, and by thy words thou shalt be condemned" (Matt. 12:35–37). If this applies to words, how much more does it apply to deeds. This should create an incentive for every individual to seek counsel from others who have experience in the area of decision-making that faces him.

Conclusion

A society will fall when the people have no counsel. In this context, this refers to empty counsel: counsel in opposition to God's counsel, as revealed in the Bible. A society of covenant-breakers operates in terms of empty counsel.

Within the covenantal confession of subordination to the trinitarian God of the Bible, there is a wide range of experience, information, and opinion. While decision-makers should be self-governed under biblical law, they also are told to seek a wide range of opinions. The one—the unitary covenant under the trinitarian God—must not exclude the many: a multitude of counsel. Biblically, this principle honors the Trinity. In the Trinity, the one and the many are equally ultimate. This unitary confession requires the consideration of many applications of the confession.

32

TURN LOOSE TO GATHER IN

There is that scattereth, and yet increaseth; and there is that withholdeth more than is meet, but it tendeth to poverty. The liberal soul shall be made fat: and he that watereth shall be watered also himself. He that withholdeth corn, the people shall curse him: but blessing shall be upon the head of him that selleth it.

PROVERBS 11:24–26

This string of proverbs is held together by one theme: *scattering and prospering*. This concept relies on what appear to be contradictions or antinomies. Throw away and gather in; hold on tight and become poor: these seem contradictory. These linked proverbs point to a system of cause and effect that operates outside of men's familiar patterns.

Yet, on closer observation, these patterns are familiar after all. A farmer knows that by scattering seeds, he will reap a great crop. Similarly, if he withholds too much of his seed—more than is "meet," meaning fit—and refuses to scatter them, he will reap almost no crop. He will fall into poverty.

This is a principle of investment. Investment requires future-orientation. A person looks at what he possesses now. He wants greater wealth in the future. In order to attain this goal, he must surrender control over that which he possesses today.

He can plant seed. This seed he cannot grind into flour and bake into bread. To eat seed that is fit—meet—for planting is to "eat your seed corn," the traditional phrase tells us. We eat our future increase. We consume more in the present at the price of consuming less in the future. There is no such thing as a free lunch.

139

A. The Process of Time

Time is on the side of the righteous. All of cause and effect is. Paul wrote: "And we know that all things work together for good to them that love God, to them who are the called according to his purpose" (Rom. 8:28).[1]

When men scatter seed, they expect to prosper over time. When men become grasping, refusing to scatter seed, they become poor over time. The process of compounding—positive and negative—takes time.

Time is relentless. It waits on no man. It has a negative aspect for covenant-breakers and a positive aspect for covenant-keepers. An individual is soon forgotten, but covenant-keepers flourish through the ages. God intervenes to keep the inheritance of covenant-keepers growing.

> As for man, his days are as grass: as a flower of the field, so he flourisheth. For the wind passeth over it, and it is gone; and the place thereof shall know it no more. But the mercy of the LORD is from everlasting to everlasting upon them that fear him, and his righteousness unto children's children; To such as keep his covenant, and to those that remember his commandments to do them (Ps. 103:15–18).

The process of scattering and withholding are aspects of rival views of cause and effect. The covenant-keeper perceives that time is on his side and the side of his covenantal heirs. The covenant-breaker knows, as Satan knows, that his time is short. His legacy compounds at a negative rate. "For the wind passeth over it, and it is gone; and the place thereof shall know it no more." Here today; gone tomorrow.

B. Ownership and Disownership

A farmer owns seed. He will also own any crop produced by this seed. He can increase his wealth in the future by surrendering seed in the present. He invests. What the individual knows to be true within the judicial context of ownership, this proverb implies—but does not explicitly say—also applies to the principle of wealth transfer. This proverb implies that *the same principle of wealth accumulation also applies to the realm of disownership*.

This is contrary to what the world regards as common sense. Cause and effect teach that if you give away wealth, you will possess

---

1. Gary North, *Cooperation and Dominion: An Economic Commentary on Romans*, 2nd ed. (Dallas, Georgia: Point Five Press, [2000] 2012), ch. 6.

less wealth. There is a finite quantity of goods, including time. That which is given away is transferred to someone else. Aristotelian logic says that one object cannot be in two places at once. Is this proverb arguing against Aristotelian logic?

The farmer surrenders control over seeds in the present. He hopes to own more seeds in the future. The process of agricultural production takes time.

This proverb relies on the same concept of time. When men surrender control over their wealth in the present, they can accumulate greater wealth in the future. But in this case, the control is *legal* control. Donors will not own the increase, if any, of whatever they give away. When you turn grain into bread and then give away the bread, you have neither seed nor bread. You do not have grain in the ground, either. Yet this proverb says that in fact you do have the equivalent of seed in the ground. The Preacher—Solomon—wrote elsewhere: "Cast thy bread upon the waters: for thou shalt find it after many days" (Eccl. 11:1).

"The liberal soul shall be made fat: and he that watereth shall be watered also himself" (v. 25). The Hebrew word, *berakah*, is translated "liberal." This is a rare translation. In dozens of passages, it is translated as "blessing" or "blessed." We see this in these related passages:

I have been young, and now am old; yet have I not seen the righteous forsaken, nor his seed begging bread. He is ever merciful, and lendeth; and his seed is blessed (Ps. 37:25–26).[2]

He that hath a bountiful eye shall be blessed; for he giveth of his bread to the poor (Prov. 22:9).

A faithful man shall abound with blessings: but he that maketh haste to be rich shall not be innocent (Prov. 28:20).[3]

He that giveth unto the poor shall not lack: but he that hideth his eyes shall have many a curse (Prov. 28:27).

Give, and it shall be given unto you; good measure, pressed down, and shaken together, and running over, shall men give into your bosom. For with the same measure that ye mete withal it shall be measured to you again (Luke 6:38).[4]

---

2. Gary North, *Confidence and Dominion: An Economic Commentary on Psalms* (Dallas, Georgia: Point Five Press, 2012), ch. 6.

3. Chapter 83.

4. Gary North, *Treasure and Dominion: An Economic Commentary on Luke*, 2nd ed. (Dallas, Georgia: Point Five Press, [2000] 2012), ch. 11.

The blessed soul is the liberal soul. He is also the *blessings* soul—the source of others' blessings. He waters the parched soil. So will he be watered. There is cause and effect. This is a system of expansion—growth—but not for the covenant-breaker.

In contrast is the man who withholds corn in a crisis. "He that withholdeth corn, the people shall curse him: but blessing shall be upon the head of him that selleth it" (v. 26). Note: the blessed man sells grain. He does not give it away. He asks for something in return. But the cursed man keeps grain for himself. Presumably, he is not planning to eat it. Someone with only enough corn to feed his family will not be the target of curses. The accused is a forestaller: a person who controls a sufficient quantity of grain to raise the price by refusing to sell it. What he does is in contrast with the liberal man.

What is unique here is the suggestion that the man who sells grain in a food shortage is like one who scatters his wealth. He will tend toward prosperity. In contrast, the man who holds onto more than is meet—fitting—tends toward poverty. Yet the grain seller receives less money than if he waited until the famine grew worse. The grain hoarder hopes to receive more money per quantity of grain. Yet he tends toward poverty.

This is not the system of cause and effect imagined by the modern economist, who affirms a world of cosmic impersonalism. It is rather the system of cause and effect proclaimed by God, in both the Old and New Testaments. Jesus Christ is the ultimate liberal soul, the example of the system of prospering by letting go.

> And Jesus answered them, saying, The hour is come, that the Son of man should be glorified. Verily, verily, I say unto you, Except a corn of wheat fall into the ground and die, it abideth alone: but if it die, it bringeth forth much fruit. He that loveth his life shall lose it; and he that hateth his life in this world shall keep it unto life eternal (John 12:23–25).

Conclusion

We live in God's world. Men are governed by God in terms of the ethical principles of biblical law. This includes societies. God governs cause and effect in terms of biblical law. This is the Bible's covenantal theory of sanctions.

This proverb describes the principle of turning loose in order to gather in. This principle applies to seeds in farming, where the farmer owns the seeds and also any future crop. It also applies to entire societies. So, a covenant-keeper can turn loose (disown a little) and confidently expect to gather in (own more), even though he surrenders ownership of whatever is turned loose. This covenantal system of cause and effect operates within God's sphere of ownership, not just inside the individual's sphere of ownership. God owns everything: "For every beast of the forest is mine, and the cattle upon a thousand hills" (Ps. 50:10).[5] The individual covenant-keeper, acting as a steward of God's property, can safely give away God's property for covenant-honoring projects. More will follow, as surely as a crop follows planting, because it is God's property.

---

5. North, *Confidence and Dominion*, ch. 10.

33

TWO KINDS OF EXPANSION

He that trusteth in his riches shall fall: but the righteous shall flourish as a branch.

PROVERBS 11:28

This proverb parallels Proverbs 11:4: "Riches profit not in the day of wrath: but righteousness delivereth from death."[1] This proverb is more general. The earlier proverb is true because this proverb is true.

This proverb is an application of an even more general proverb: "No man can serve two masters: for either he will hate the one, and love the other; or else he will hold to the one, and despise the other. Ye cannot serve God and mammon" (Matt. 6:24). What is mammon? It is this principle: "More for me in history."[2]

A. Across Generations

The Old Testament had no explicit concept of a final judgment. So, this proverb refers to this world: history. Yet we know that some people who pursue riches do not fall. They die rich. How can this fact—a fact acknowledged by Asaph in Psalm 73—be reconciled with this proverb? The proverbs are rules illustrating the operation of God's covenant in history. The fifth point of the biblical covenant is inheritance.[3] The following principle governs inheritance: "A good man leaveth an inheritance to his children's children: and the wealth of the sinner is laid up

---

1. Chapter 30.
2. Gary North, *Priorities and Dominion: An Economic Commentary on Matthew*, 2nd ed. (Dallas, Georgia: Point Five Press, [2000] 2012), ch. 14.
3. Ray R. Sutton, *That You May Prosper: Dominion By Covenant*, 2nd ed. (Tyler, Texas: Institute for Christian Economics, [1987] 1992), ch. 5. Gary North, *Unconditional Surrender: God's Program for Victory*, 5th ed. (Powder Springs, Georgia: American Vision, [1988] 2010), ch. 5.

for the just" (Prov. 13:22).[4] Applying this insight to this assertion—he who trusts in his riches shall fall—we conclude that *the mammon-worshipping person falls by way of inheritance*. What a man does in this life will be judged by God finally. This was not an Old Testament insight. But there is a preliminary manifestation of final judgment: *God's judgment of the heirs*. This is a constant theme of the Old Testament: Who will inherit, and what will he inherit? This was Abram's question to God in what he believed (inaccurately) was his old age.[5]

> And Abram said, Lord God, what wilt thou give me, seeing I go childless, and the steward of my house is this Eliezer of Damascus? And Abram said, Behold, to me thou hast given no seed: and, lo, one born in my house is mine heir (Gen. 15:2–3).

Inheritance was on his mind. Inheritance had been the positive sanction God had offered him before he left Ur.

> Now the Lord had said unto Abram, Get thee out of thy country, and from thy kindred, and from thy father's house, unto a land that I will shew thee: And I will make of thee a great nation, and I will bless thee, and make thy name great; and thou shalt be a blessing: And I will bless them that bless thee, and curse him that curseth thee: and in thee shall all families of the earth be blessed (Gen. 12:1–3).

So, the biblical covenant testifies against any concept of personal success that is limited to the lifetime of the achiever. To assess a man's success, we must ask: "Who were his heirs, and what did they do with their inheritance?"

Solomon was a personal failure. His son Rehoboam lost the kingdom because of his policy of high taxation (I Kings 12). He did not possess his father's wisdom—a wisdom that his father had surrendered by marrying hundreds of wives (I Kings 11:3), which violated God's law for Israel's kings (Deut. 17:17),[6] a law that Solomon's father David had also violated (I Sam. 25:42–43; II Sam. 5:13), with terrible consequences for his family (II Sam. 13).

Solomon did not pursue riches, but riches came to him. He did not give these riches away. Thus, he accumulated riches, in violation

---

4. Chapter 41.

5. "And Isaac brought her into his mother Sarah's tent, and took Rebekah, and she became his wife; and he loved her: and Isaac was comforted after his mother's death. Then again Abraham took a wife, and her name was Keturah. And she bare him Zimran, and Jokshan, and Medan, and Midian, and Ishbak, and Shuah" (Gen. 24:67–25:2).

6. Gary North, *Inheritance and Dominion: An Economic Commentary on Deuteronomy*, 2nd ed. (Dallas, Georgia: Point Five Press, [1999] 2012), ch. 42:C.

of God's law for Israel's kings. "Neither shall he multiply wives to himself, that his heart turn not away: neither shall he greatly multiply to himself silver and gold" (Deut. 17:17).[7] He acted contrary to his own principles, as set forth in the Book of Proverbs. These wealth-related proverbs are difficult to believe. They are even more difficult to implement personally.

B. A Flourishing Branch

In most instances, the KJV translators translated this Hebrew word as "leaf." The word relates to foliage. Leaves are temporary things. Branches are more permanent. So, the translators selected "branch." There are multiple Hebrew words translated as "branch."

A leaf reflects the health of a tree. A deciduous tree with no leaves in summer is a dead tree. Leaves in abundance indicate growth. This proverb indicates that righteousness is like a flourishing leaf. To flourish is to possess a benefit. "The righteous shall flourish like the palm tree: he shall grow like a cedar in Lebanon. Those that be planted in the house of the LORD shall flourish in the courts of our God" (Ps. 92:12–13).

To be righteous is to become the recipient of God's tokens of the good life. There is expansion. Yet this is what the man who pursues riches also desires. He wants the expansion of his wealth because riches are a positive sanction. Yet this proverb and others tell us that the pursuit of riches is a snare and a delusion.

> Surely every man walketh in a vain shew: surely they are disquieted in vain: he heapeth up riches, and knoweth not who shall gather them (Ps. 39:6).[8]

> The righteous also shall see, and fear, and shall laugh at him: Lo, this is the man that made not God his strength; but trusted in the abundance of his riches, and strengthened himself in his wickedness (Ps. 52:6–7).

> Wilt thou set thine eyes upon that which is not? for riches certainly make themselves wings; they fly away as an eagle toward heaven (Prov. 23:5).[9]

> As the partridge sitteth on eggs, and hatcheth them not; so he that getteth riches, and not by right, shall leave them in the midst of his days, and at his end shall be a fool (Jer. 17:11).

---

7. Idem.

8. Gary North, *Confidence and Dominion: An Economic Commentary on Psalms* (Dallas, Georgia: Point Five Press, 2012), ch. 7.

9. Chapter 72.

Conclusion

This proverb is clear: he who trusts in riches will fall. He trusts in a visible sanction rather than in the God who awards positive sanctions. This is what Moses warned against. "And thou say in thine heart, My power and the might of mine hand hath gotten me this wealth. But thou shalt remember the LORD thy God: for it is he that giveth thee power to get wealth, that he may establish his covenant which he sware unto thy fathers, as it is this day" (Deut. 8:17–18).[10]

In contrast, the righteous man flourishes. It is not what he owns but *what he is ethically* that marks him as a beneficiary of covenant blessings. Ethical conformity to God's law is of great positive consequence. The piling up of riches is of great negative consequence.

> And he spake a parable unto them, saying, The ground of a certain rich man brought forth plentifully: And he thought within himself, saying, What shall I do, because I have no room where to bestow my fruits? And he said, This will I do: I will pull down my barns, and build greater; and there will I bestow all my fruits and my goods. And I will say to my soul, Soul, thou hast much goods laid up for many years; take thine ease, eat, drink, and be merry. But God said unto him, Thou fool, this night thy soul shall be required of thee: then whose shall those things be, which thou hast provided? So is he that layeth up treasure for himself, and is not rich toward God (Luke 12:16–21).[11]

---

10. North, *Inheritance and Dominion*, chaps. 21, 22.
11. Gary North, *Treasure and Dominion: An Economic Commentary on Luke*, 2nd ed. (Dallas, Georgia: Point Five Press, [2000] 2012), ch. 25.

34

CONFIDENCE IN THE FUTURE

The wicked are overthrown, and are not: but the house of the righteous shall stand.

PROVERBS 12:7

This proverb deals with inheritance. Inheritance is the fifth point of the biblical covenant.[1]

The proverbs refer to temporal affairs. There was no explicit concept of final judgment in the Old Testament. So, the events described here relate to history: in time and on earth.

A. Dreams and Schemes

The general contrast is between the wicked and the righteous. The wicked are overthrown. They do not survive. Yet no person survives. Death takes all men. So, in what does the contrast consist?

This proverb indicates that there is no trace of the wicked after they are gone. This does not mean that the historical record does not provide documentation of their deeds. It means that their dreams and schemes do not survive their overthrow. Their institutions do not persevere. In modern times, this was demonstrated on December 31, 1991, when the Soviet Union committed suicide. The Communist Party ceased to rule the nation. There was a revolution without bloodshed. The leaders simply gave up their attempt to rule as the Party had ruled since 1917. The Soviet Union was the largest empire in recorded history to surrender power without bloodshed.

---

1. Ray R. Sutton, *That You May Prosper: Dominion By Covenant*, 2nd ed. (Tyler, Texas: Institute for Christian Economics, [1987] 1992), ch. 5. Gary North, *Unconditional Surrender: God's Program for Victory*, 5th ed. (Powder Springs, Georgia: American Vision, [1988] 2010), ch. 5.

The context of this proverb becomes clearer with respect to the righteous. This proverb says that "the house of the righteous shall stand." Whereas the wicked are no more, the righteous leave an institutional legacy: a house. It is not overthrown. It sustains the dreams and schemes of the founders.

The issue is covenantal. Covenants are established by confession, mutual promises, and oath-signs. To survive the process of time, these three factors must persevere. The confession may be modified. "Hear, O Israel: The LORD our God is one LORD (Deut. 6:4) does not change, but it is modified. "And without controversy great is the mystery of godliness: God was manifest in the flesh, justified in the Spirit, seen of angels, preached unto the Gentiles, believed on in the world, received up into glory" (I Tim. 3:16). The promises do not change, but the recipients do.

> But ye are a chosen generation, a royal priesthood, an holy nation, a peculiar people; that ye should shew forth the praises of him who hath called you out of darkness into his marvellous light: Which in time past were not a people, but are now the people of God: which had not obtained mercy, but now have obtained mercy (I Peter 2:9–10).

Finally, the requirement of the oath is not abolished, but the oath-signs are replaced with new ones. The Lord's Supper has replaced Passover. Baptism has replaced circumcision.

B. The Perseverance of the Saints' Legacy

There is preservation through time for the institutional legacy of the righteous. This does not apply to the wicked. There is an historical problem here: Islam. It came out of nowhere in 632. Islam conquered North Africa in eight decades, 632–712, and there has been no trace of reconquest by Christianity. In 732, Arab warriors crossed the Pyrenees and moved into what is now France. They were defeated at the Battle of Tours that year. They retreated back into Spain. They were not completely driven out by Spanish military forces until 1492. Today, Muslims are in the process of reconquering Spain through immigration and high birth rates. They are doing the same in Italy and France. Unless their birth rates fall—as seems to be happening—below the non-Muslim population's birth rates—this is not happening—Europe will go Islamic unless Muslims abandon Islam or else Christian revival sweeps through Europe's non-Muslim population.

If this proverb remains true, then it has yet to be proven by all the facts. Christianity and Islam are the two largest religions. They have about the same number of adherents. Each side professes belief in this proverb. Each side awaits the disappearance—the overthrow—of the other.

C. Confidence in the Future

The righteous have a legitimate hope in the future. Their legacy will persevere. The legacy of the wicked will not. The capital and labor that they invest today will produce consequences in the future. *The work of the covenantally faithful is cumulative*. This proverb denies that the righteous will be overthrown in history. It affirms that the wicked will be overthrown, just as their covenant-breaking ancestors were overthrown. The forces of history are not impersonal. They are personal.[2] God in history brings to pass what this proverb insists must happen.

Covenant-keepers can confidently sacrifice present income and leisure for the sake of building up the house of the righteous. This house will not be overthrown in history. In contrast, covenant-breakers have no legitimate hope that their house will not be overthrown in history, for it will be. This proverb is clear.

Conclusion

Covenant-keepers possess legitimate hope in the process of compound growth. Their house will persevere. Investments made today in building up God's kingdom institutions will multiply: compound over time. This is not true of investments made by covenant-breakers. While some of their institutional legacy can persevere, covenant-keepers will inherit it. "A good man leaveth an inheritance to his children's children: and the wealth of the sinner is laid up for the just" (Prov. 13:22).[3]

When covenant-keepers understand and believe this proverb, they receive a remarkable gift: confidence in the long-run pay-off of their efforts. This is a tremendous psychological advantage.

---

2. Gary North, *Sovereignty and Dominion: An Economic Commentary on Genesis* (Dallas, Georgia: Point Five Press, [1982] 2012), ch. 1.
3. Chapter 41.

35

MORE IS BETTER

He that is despised, and hath a servant, is better than he that honoureth himself, and lacketh bread.

Here are a pair of comparisons, each with two aspects. The first person is despised: a negative factor. He possesses sufficient wealth to afford a servant: a positive factor. The second person is a self-inflated person who possesses so little wealth that he lacks bread, which is a low-priced yet vital commodity. He therefore suffers from two negative factors. The first person is said to be better than the second.

In what sense is he better? The Hebrew word translated as "better," *towb*, is as broad as the English word, "good." It conveys the sense of positive. "And God saw the light, that it was good: and God divided the light from the darkness" (Gen. 1:4). It also can mean ethically good, as in the tree of the knowledge of good and evil (Gen. 2:9). It can mean good as in good looking. "And the damsel was very fair to look upon" (Gen. 24:16a).

The first man is despised. Those around him assess his contribution to society negatively. They impute a negative image to him. But no one doubts that he possesses wealth. He has a servant. He has therefore earned or inherited wealth. He is not respected as a person, but what he possesses is desirable.

The second man is a self-promoter. Perhaps he has great self-esteem. If so, he is severely self-deceived. He has achieved nothing of value. He does not sell a service to the community for which anyone is willing to pay him much. His lack of accomplishment is revealed by his economic condition: hunger. There is therefore a great discrepancy between his words and his deeds.

151

A. Wealth as a Positive Factor

This proverb contrasts two negatives: being despised and self-promotion that is not justified by actual performance. Being despised is a negative factor. Self-promotion is also a negative factor. "Let another man praise thee, and not thine own mouth; a stranger, and not thine own lips" (Prov. 27:2). But this proverb insists that the despised man is better than the self-promoter.

The distinguishing factor between them is wealth. This is why this proverb is important in an economic commentary on the Bible. The first man possesses wealth. The second man does not. The disparity is considerable. To have enough wealth to hire a servant is to possess considerable wealth. Human labor is the most versatile factor of production. It can be used to produce value in many ways. It therefore commands a high price, for many employers compete for labor services. A servant has numerous employment opportunities. If he is a slave, he is nonetheless valuable. Other men will bid for his labor services by seeking to purchase him from his owner. His owner has wealth.

In stark contrast to the servant's owner, the self-promoter cannot even afford bread. Bread is a low-cost commodity in most circumstances. It is widely produced. It is at the low-price end of the food supply. It is also vital. A person who cannot afford bread is in desperate shape. He surely cannot afford more expensive food. Yet if he cannot obtain food, he will die of starvation. He is therefore close to becoming either a thief or a charity case. Anyone in Mosaic Israel who was a charity case had no services worth purchasing for the price of bread. Such a person might seek to become a gleaner during the harvest season, which did not last very long. The laws governing this form of charity were seasonal; they did the poor person no economic good outside of the harvest season. Gleaners worked hard in the fields to collect the morally compulsory charity that God specified for the poor (Lev. 19:10;[1] Deut. 24:26[2]). But that law applied only during the harvest season, a short period. This man is so destitute of productive skills that he cannot feed himself.

This proverb does not compare negatives: being despised vs. self-promotion. It compares a positive factor to a negative. The positive factor is wealth. The negative is poverty.

---

1. Gary North, *Boundaries and Dominion: An Economic Commentary on Leviticus*, 2nd ed. (Dallas, Georgia: Point Five Press, [1994] 2012), ch. 11.

2. Gary North, *Inheritance and Dominion: An Economic Commentary on Deuteronomy*, 2nd ed. (Dallas, Georgia: Point Five Press, [1999] 2012), ch. 62.

This would seem to be a straightforward conclusion. Few societies would not recognize its truth. But in modern Christian socialist circles, this conclusion is unacceptable. The socialist endorses some version of egalitarianism. He insists that the primary economic role of civil government is forcibly to redistribute income and capital toward equality. The socialist regards great disparities of wealth as morally objectionable and therefore socially objectionable. So, he must reject the conclusion I have made regarding the presence of a significant disparity of wealth as being the biblically deciding factor in evaluating the preferability of being either a despised man with a servant or a hungry self-promoter.

If my conclusion is correct, then egalitarianism is a false ideal. The Bible not only does not recommend the use of force to redistribute wealth, it presents wealth as a legitimate success indicator. The despised man with a servant is better off than a hungry self-promoter. This concept of "better off" is to be taken here in a broad sense, not merely as an accounting concept.

B. Accurate Self-Assessment

The person who is despised is not despised for having a servant. From Abram to the kings of Israel, men hired servants. There are almost 600 references to the Hebrew word for "servant" or "servants" in the Old Testament.

Having a servant is part of the social division of labor. A servant does work of lower value, or work that is beyond the skill of his employer. More work gets done by two men working together than by one man working alone. The Preacher—Solomon—insisted: "Two are better than one; because they have a good reward for their labour. For if they fall, the one will lift up his fellow: but woe to him that is alone when he falleth; for he hath not another to help him up" (Eccl. 4:9–10).[3] A servant is low in the hierarchy, but he is nonetheless part of the social division of labor.

To hire a servant requires productivity or inherited wealth. This person has enough wealth or productivity to put a servant to work. He provides employment to the servant. Together, they provide output for others. For some reason, the person with the servant is despised. But those who despise him are aware that he is sufficiently successful to hire a servant.

---

3. Gary North, *Autonomy and Stagnation: An Economic Commentary on Ecclesiastes* (Dallas, Georgia: Point Five Press, 2012), ch. 14.

In contrast is a person who announces to others that he is a success. He honors himself. Yet he lacks sufficient wealth or productivity to buy bread, let alone hire a servant. This proverb says that he is a failure—worse than a despised person. He should not be imitated.

The Bible is clear on this issue: the self-promoter is self-deluded. He is skating on thin ice. Jesus warned:

> When thou art bidden of any man to a wedding, sit not down in the highest room; lest a more honourable man than thou be bidden of him; And he that bade thee and him come and say to thee, Give this man place; and thou begin with shame to take the lowest room. But when thou art bidden, go and sit down in the lowest room; that when he that bade thee cometh, he may say unto thee, Friend, go up higher: then shalt thou have worship in the presence of them that sit at meat with thee. For whosoever exalteth himself shall be abased; and he that humbleth himself shall be exalted (Luke 14:8–11).[4]

C. A False Front

This man lacks bread. In an urban setting, where most people do not know each other, he may be able to get away with the deception for a time. If he wears good clothes, using debt to buy these clothes, he may escape detection. A salesman may buy an expensive new car in an attempt to create the illusion of his success. But such subterfuge rarely works. He runs out of money before his false front produces the deals he hopes to make as his way out of poverty. In a rural or small-town community, this deception has no possibility of being successful. People know that he does not have money. They are well aware of the discrepancy between his talk and his performance.

This proverb does not indicate that this man is an urban resident. He is pictured as a more universal personality type. He is a man who seeks to inflate his own ego by claiming a degree of success that he does not possess. He has no success. He is poverty-stricken.

This proverb indicates that such a person is at the bottom of the social pyramid. He is the model of what not to be. He is used for comparison's sake. Better to be despised with only one servant than a self-honoring poor person. He lacks humility. As Jesus pointed out, such a person is ready to sit at the head of the table. But his self-assessment is not the assessment that matters. The host's assessment is what counts. The host is not deceived. He will lead the person to the

---

4. Gary North, *Treasure and Dominion: An Economic Commentary on Luke*, 2nd ed. (Dallas, Georgia: Point Five Press, [2000] 2012), ch. 33.

lowest place—not exactly a place of dishonor, but barely inside the feast. It becomes a place of dishonor because the host leads the man, in full public view, to the fringes of social acceptance.

In some cases, according to Jesus, the stakes are even higher. "Many will say to me in that day, Lord, Lord, have we not prophesied in thy name? and in thy name have cast out devils? and in thy name done many wonderful works? And then will I profess unto them, I never knew you: depart from me, ye that work iniquity" (Matt. 7:22–23).

Conclusion

Wealth is not the only success indicator. This proverb implies that it would be better to be wealthy and loved than wealthy and despised. What society would not acknowledge this? But the contrast here is not between a wealthy despised man and a wealthy beloved man. It is between two negative conditions: being despised and being a self-promoter. The distinguishing characteristic is not found in the primary descriptions of these two men. It is the secondary characteristic: wealth vs. poverty. Wealth is better than poverty.

A self-promoter had better have a degree of success that corresponds to the level of his self-promotion. This is not the case here.

It is best to follow Jesus' recommendation: start at the bottom and let the host lead you to a higher position. Entry is easier at the bottom.

36

THE OBJECT OF OUR LABOR

He that tilleth his land shall be satisfied with bread: but he that followeth vain persons is void of understanding.

PROVERBS 12:11

A. Contentment

A farmer tills his land. He produces the grain that in turn produces bread. His labor input—tilling the soil—is part of the necessary process for producing bread. His labor has a specific goal: the production of bread. This is a universally known product. It is a source of life, but it is common. Common men produce it. There is nothing prestigious about producing bread. There is also nothing prestigious about producing the grain used to bake it.

The core issue here is personal satisfaction: contentment. This is one of God's greatest gifts. This is stressed in the New Testament far more than in the Old Testament.

> Not that I speak in respect of want: for I have learned, in whatsoever state I am, therewith to be content (Phil. 4:11).[1]

> And having food and raiment let us be therewith content (I Tim. 6:8).[2]

> Let your conversation be without covetousness; and be content with such things as ye have: for he hath said, I will never leave thee, nor forsake thee (Heb. 13:5).[3]

---

1. Gary North, *Ethics and Dominion: An Economic Commentary on the Epistles* (Dallas, Georgia: Point Five Press, 2012), ch. 27.
2. Gary North, *Hierarchy and Dominion: An Economic Commentary on First Timothy*, 2nd ed. (Dallas, Georgia: Point Five Press, [2001] 2012), ch. 10.
3. North, *Ethics and Dominion*, ch. 29.

The farmer has found his area of service to God and to the society at large. He is content to plow the fields. It is hard work, but he is content to be doing it. His work and knowledge and tools over time produce his food. He is not looking to do big things. He is looking to do personally important things, beginning with producing a crop.

B. The Pursuit of Vanity

The Hebrew word translated here as "vain" is elsewhere translated as "empty." "And they took him, and cast him into a pit: and the pit was empty, there was no water in it" (Gen. 37:24). The Bible compares this kind of moral emptiness with lack of moral weight. "And they gave him threescore and ten pieces of silver out of the house of Baal-berith, wherewith Abimelech hired **vain** and light persons, which followed him" (Jud. 9:4).

We speak of someone important in his field as a heavyweight. We speak of someone without importance in his field as a lightweight. The word in this context goes beyond importance. These people are leaders. They are able to attract followers. Yet they themselves are empty. They do not perceive that they are empty. If they did, they would depart from their leadership positions. Their followers also do not perceive that they are empty. If they did, they would follow others.

The follower is devoid of understanding. So, there is a match-up. Empty people without sufficiently good judgment to assess their own emptiness attract followers who are devoid of understanding, who do not have the ability to assess the condition of their leaders. Jesus had a metaphor for this situation. "Let them alone: they be blind leaders of the blind. And if the blind lead the blind, both shall fall into the ditch" (Matt. 15:14).

If a vain person and his judgment-lacking followers pursue a goal, it is clear what the goal is: vanity. This is what the Preacher—Solomon—warned against in Ecclesiastes. "I have seen all the works that are done under the sun; and, behold, all is vanity and vexation of spirit" (Eccl. 1:14). Then what is to be done? After surveying the affairs of life, he comes to a recommendation:

> Rejoice, O young man, in thy youth; and let thy heart cheer thee in the days of thy youth, and walk in the ways of thine heart, and in the sight of thine eyes: but know thou, that for all these things God will bring thee into judgment. Therefore remove sorrow from thy heart, and put away evil from thy flesh: for childhood and youth are vanity. Remember now thy Creator

in the days of thy youth, while the evil days come not, nor the years draw nigh, when thou shalt say, I have no pleasure in them (Eccl. 11:9–12:1).

This recommendation is based on a conclusion—a conclusion that in turn was based on a lifetime of contemplation, observation, and personal experience.

> Let us hear the conclusion of the whole matter: Fear God, and keep his commandments: for this is the whole duty of man. For God shall bring every work into judgment, with every secret thing, whether it be good, or whether it be evil (Eccl. 12:13–14).[4]

C. Satisfaction With Conventional Returns

The issue of satisfaction is one of the most difficult to solve. The more opportunities that men possess for both service and consumption, the more complex the problem of satisfaction becomes. The dying words of Cecil Rhodes of Rhodesia come to mind: "So much to do. So little time."

This proverb contrasts two people: a tiller of the soil and a follower of vain people. The farmer has a goal: bread. The goal of the follower is unspecified.

The farmer's goal is limited. Bread is called the staff of life, but it is exceedingly common. It was far more common in Mosaic Israel. Grain was the chief product of most farming in the Middle East. For a low-productivity, pre-capitalist agricultural society, grain is the source of life. It sustains most of the population. A man toils over the ground to grow grain, which is used to make bread, which sustains life. Bread is a no-frills product that is central to society. Jesus' recommended prayer request, "Give us this day our daily bread" (Matt. 6:11),[5] encapsulates the fundamental request: to sustain life.

This is a central goal. It is also a limited goal. The farmer must devote most of his time to the procedures of producing bread. There is neither significant spare time nor spare output in a pre-capitalist agricultural society. Output is low. The farmer is not easily sidetracked. He budgets his time and his capital well in advance. He pursues a narrow goal by means of a specific plan. The plan reflects decades of tradition. Things are to be done in a familiar pattern. There is limited creativity involved.

4. Gary North, *Autonomy and Stagnation: An Economic Commentary on Ecclesiastes* (Dallas, Georgia: Point Five Press, 2012), ch. 45.

5. Gary North, *Priorities and Dominion: An Economic Commentary on Matthew*, 2nd ed. (Dallas, Georgia: Point Five Press, [2000] 2012), ch. 12:A–B.

In contrast is the man who follows vain persons. The word for "follows" is literally "runs after." The meaning of vanity here is emptiness. The person's life is marked by vain pursuits. A later proverb says: "He that tilleth his land shall have plenty of bread: but he that followeth after vain persons shall have poverty enough" (Prov. 28:19).[6] Following empty leaders, he comes up empty-handed.

People do not deliberately follow losers. They prefer to follow winners. They hope to participate in the successful ventures of successful people. They expect success to trickle down to them because of their joint participation.

The person described here is not following winners. He is following empty people. But these empty people radiate the trappings of success. Their followers do not perceive that the leaders' dreams and schemes are futile. It is a case of the blind leading the blind into the ditch.

> Then came his disciples, and said unto him, Knowest thou that the Pharisees were offended, after they heard this saying? But he answered and said, Every plant, which my heavenly Father hath not planted, shall be rooted up. Let them alone: they be blind leaders of the blind. And if the blind lead the blind, both shall fall into the ditch (Matt. 15:12–14).

Folk sayings drive home the warning: "All that glitters is not gold." In Texas, they say: "He is all hat and no cattle." There is a deception as old as paper money: a roll of worthless counterfeit bills wrapped in a high-denomination bill. There is also the hidden phenomenon of consumer debt. A person may wear fine clothes and drive an expensive car, but he is living on the edge of bankruptcy.

Such people attract followers. If they also talk a good line, their appeal is even greater. But they are empty in every sense. They live a lie. Those who are attracted to them will participate, not in their success, but in their failure.

D. Rates of Return

The message of this proverb is this: the day-to-day activities of a farmer who plants seed and cares for his crop will pay off. He and his family will eat. There is no hint that he will get rich. But he will survive. In contrast is the vain pursuit of the man who follows empty people. His plans will come to nothing.

The systematic pursuit of conventional returns on one's conventional labor is the working model of this proverb. There is nothing

---

6. Chapter 82.

spectacular about bread. There is nothing spectacular about farming. Yet the man who diligently sets a conventional goal and follows a conventional plan will find success. The person who has big plans for achieving above-average returns, and who then seeks out smooth talkers who promise above-average returns, will find that he achieves below-average returns.

When a man adopts an innovation in the field in which he has experience, he is seeking an above-average rate of return. He is not satisfied with his previous level of success. He seeks greater output per unit of resource input. This is the motivation for economic progress. It is the underlying impetus for compound growth in every field. Does this proverb suggest that such a motivation is illegitimate?

The proverb's farmer is not being contrasted with a highly innovative farmer. He is being contrasted with a chaser after dreams. The man who runs after vain persons has no experience in the day-to-day activities of specialized production. Or, if he has such experience, he has abandoned it. He is not evaluating the potential success of a new technology in terms of his long experience with older technology. Instead, he is following after empty people. He does not recognize counterfeit claims and strategies when he sees them.

Real estate entrepreneur John Schaub sells a seminar, "Making It Big on Little Deals." The wealth-accumulation strategy works. For over three decades, I watched as he accumulated dozens of homes, now mostly paid off by his renters. He has done this one house at a time. His long-term goal is to leave most of them to charity when he dies, with the funds to be used to build housing for the working poor. Meanwhile, he has provided clean housing for renters at slightly below-market rents. This way, they move out of his houses less often, which saves him time and money in replacing them with new tenants.

In the congested field of get-rich-quick schemes, real estate is a popular one. Late-night television hucksters sell the dream of great wealth through real estate speculation. Schaub does not promote his courses or newsletter in this way. He barely promotes at all, as I have been telling him for three decades. He recommends buying strategies similar to those recommended by the hucksters, but accompanied by careful, self-disciplined, time-intensive preparation. He does not oversell his subscribers and attendees. He has made a fortune in real estate, not through the sale of courses on real estate. He offers only two courses per year, always in the same two cities.

The difference between the two sorts of information sellers is the difference between plowing a field and speculating in grain futures. The farmer will probably bring in a crop and re-plant next season. The commodity speculator will probably lose his money. Most of them do.

Conclusion

The farmer is a steady-as-you-go fellow. The vanity-chaser is ready to buy based on flash, glitter, and promises. The farmer knows his field. The vanity-chaser does not. The farmer is satisfied with the most mundane of products: bread. The vanity-chaser is not satisfied with anything. The farmer wants bread. The vanity-chaser wants more. The pursuit of more is the pursuit of mammon. Jesus warned: "No man can serve two masters: for either he will hate the one, and love the other; or else he will hold to the one, and despise the other. Ye cannot serve God and mammon" (Matt. 6:24).[7]

Bread sustains life. *More* is unbounded: beyond mere sustenance. Bread is produced with a systematic plan with a specific time of completion. *More* is open-ended, which means that no plan is appropriate. Successful plans must have identifiable, measurable goals, i.e., limits. Vanity-chasers resist the concept of limits. Therefore, they reject the idea of systematic plans with limited, measurable goals.

The steady work of a farmer tilling his fields is preferable to a life spent in pursuit of goals announced by empty men. The grand schemes of empty men can absorb a lifetime of effort. But when life is over, all the effort has been wasted. It is like seed planted in rocky soil in a parched place (Matt. 13:5–6). The labor theory of value is incorrect. Labor's value derives from the value of labor's output. In the case of farmers: bread. In the case of vain men: emptiness that matches their spiritual condition.

---

7. North, *Priorities and Dominion*, ch. 14.

37

DILIGENCE AND DOMINION

power — rulership   Taking responsibility

The hand of the diligent shall bear rule: but the slothful shall be under tribute.

PROVERBS 12:24

This proverb deals with hierarchy, point two of the biblical covenant.[1] There will always be rulers who rule over servants. The institutional question is this: What is the basis of hierarchy in any organization? This is an application of a more comprehensive question: What is the foundation of rulership in a godly social order?

What is the meaning here of "hand"? It means power in the sense of rulership. It implies taking responsibility. We see this meaning in God's transfer of civil power to Noah after the Flood. "And surely your blood of your lives will I require; at the hand of every beast will I require it, and at the hand of man; at the hand of every man's brother will I require the life of man" (Gen. 9:5).

What does "tribute" mean? It has to do with subordination. "Yet it came to pass, when the children of Israel were waxen strong, that they put the Canaanites to tribute; but did not utterly drive them out" (Josh. 17:13). This was tribute extracted politically. The Canaanites were forced to serve the Israelites by paying them something of value.

The text of this proverb does not imply political tribute. It implies economic tribute. But what is economic tribute? This proverb does not say.

Deuteronomy 28 outlines a two-fold system of sanctions: positive

---

1. Ray R. Sutton, *That You May Prosper: Dominion By Covenant*, 2nd ed. (Tyler, Texas: Institute for Christian Economics, [1987] 1992), ch. 2. Gary North, *Unconditional Surrender: God's Program for Victory*, 5th ed. (Powder Springs, Georgia: American Vision, [1980] 2010), ch. 2.

and negative. Verses 1–14 present the positive.[2] Among the list is this:

> The LORD shall open unto thee his good treasure, the heaven to give the rain unto thy land in his season, and to bless all the work of thine hand: and thou shalt lend unto many nations, and thou shalt not borrow. And the LORD shall make thee the head, and not the tail; and thou shalt be above only, and thou shalt not be beneath; if that thou hearken unto the commandments of the LORD thy God, which I command thee this day, to observe and to do them (Deut. 28:12–13).[3]

Verses 15–68 present the negative sanctions, among which is this:

> The stranger that is within thee shall get up above thee very high; and thou shalt come down very low. He shall lend to thee, and thou shalt not lend to him: he shall be the head, and thou shalt be the tail (Deut. 28:43–44).

The defining issue here is debt. He who is in debt is subordinate to his creditor. "The rich ruleth over the poor, and the borrower is servant to the lender" (Prov. 22:7).[4] The servant is paying the ruler for the loan that the ruler had extended to him. He is in a form of legal bondage.

This proverb indicates that the slothful person is not in a strong bargaining position in relation to the diligent person. This could mean debt. It could also mean employment options. The slothful person has no economic reserves. When labor becomes plentiful at yesterday's wages, the slothful person may have to lower his asking price for his labor. He has no money or food in reserve. He cannot take time to shop for better employment opportunities. He pays tribute to the employer in the form of low-cost labor services.

This proverb in no way hints that this hierarchical relationship is immoral. Throughout Proverbs, the reader is warned of negative economic sanctions that face slothful workers. These warnings are consistent with the negative sanctions presented in Leviticus 26 and Deuteronomy 28. There is a system of ethical cause and effect in history. Ethical performance has predictable wealth effects. This is an aspect of point four of the biblical covenant.[5]

The diligent person becomes the beneficiary of the tribute paid by the slothful person. The focus here is on production. The slothful person is not highly productive. This is his problem. He would be far

---

2. Gary North, *Inheritance and Dominion: An Economic Commentary on Deuteronomy*, 2nd ed. (Dallas, Georgia: Point Five Press, [1999] 2012), ch. 69.

3. *Ibid.*, ch. 70.

4. Chapter 67.

5. Sutton, *That You May Prosper*, ch. 4. North, *Unconditional Surrender*, ch. 4.

better off financially if he were diligent. So, for that matter, would the diligent person be. It is better to hire the services of a productive person than an unproductive person. This is why the unproductive person must offer to work at low wages. This is all that his productivity warrants.

A diligent person is better off in a society of diligent people than in a society of slothful people. In a land of sloth, he may find more people to pay tribute to him, but their output is below par. This is why they are cheap to hire. He is a ruler in a land of losers. It is better to be a common person in a society of high producers. The economic competition is stiffer, but the wealth per capita is higher.

There is a phrase, "in the land of the blind, the one-eyed man is king." But he is king over people who cannot see. Better to be a two-eyed man in a society of two-eyed men.

Conclusion

Dominion through diligence is the pattern. The slothful person is unlikely to exercise dominion. He is more likely to be in debt to, or on the payroll of, the diligent person. The diligent person leads. He makes decisions as to what must be done. The slothful person is a follower. He is not in a position to make decisions for others. He does what he is told. He does this ineffectively.

38

CHARACTER AND CAPITAL

dreamer | Doer

The soul of the sluggard desireth, and hath nothing: but the soul of the diligent shall be made fat.

life PROVERBS 13:4

A. The Dreamer and the Doer

Here are another pair of contrasts: the sluggard and the diligent. The first is a dreamer. The second is a doer.

The Book of Proverbs is forthrightly opposed to sluggards. Lazy people are contemptuous of work, Solomon informs us in proverb after proverb. They are losers, and they deserve to be losers. A continuing message of Proverbs is that God's system of causation is rigged against sluggards (3:9–10).[1] They cannot win.

We have to deal with the Hebrew word translated here as "soul." It refers to anything that breathes. It means "life."

> And it came to pass, when they had brought them forth abroad, that he said, Escape for thy life; look not behind thee, neither stay thou in all the plain; escape to the mountain, lest thou be consumed (Gen. 19:17).

> Behold now, thy servant hath found grace in thy sight, and thou hast magnified thy mercy, which thou hast shewed unto me in saving my life; and I cannot escape to the mountain, lest some evil take me, and I die (Gen. 19:19).

The soul of the sluggard, like the soul of the diligent, is his life. It defines him. His life is marked by longings. He wants to achieve certain things or obtain certain things. Yet he faces a problem: he has

---

1. Chapter 8.

nothing. He has no capital. Without capital, he cannot finance projects that might enable him to buy the things of his dreams.

In contrast is the soul of the diligent. It will be made fat. What is fatness? Sometimes, it refers to bodily weight. "The light of the eyes rejoiceth the heart: and a good report maketh the bones fat" (Prov. 15:30). In this case, the fatness promised is not the product of calories. The soul of man is not fattened up like an animal being prepared for the butcher. What does fat have to do with life? This passage refers to the fatness of life.

The sluggard has a lean soul. This condition is expressly attributed to the Israelites in the wilderness. "They soon forgat his works; they waited not for his counsel: But lusted exceedingly in the wilderness, and tempted God in the desert. And he gave them their request; but sent leanness into their soul" (Ps. 106:13–15).[2] The word for soul here is *nephesh*—just as it is in this proverb.

B. Dreaming and Doing

This proverb says that the soul of the sluggard desires. The soul of the diligent will be made fat. This contrasts what the sluggard wants with what the sluggard possesses. The sluggard is frustrated by his lack of wealth. He has great dreams and no assets. There is a complete disconnect between dream and reality.

The diligent person is defined by his work. This proverb points to the connection between cause and effect. He works, and the result is fatness. His life is complete. He is not longing after things he cannot have. He has a strong work ethic. This is the source of his fatness. There is a tight connection between labor and reward. "He becometh poor that dealeth with a slack hand: but the hand of the diligent maketh rich" (Prov. 10:4).[3]

One man dreams but does not do. The other man does and reaps a reward. These are two ways of life. The apostle James offered a similar connection: "But be ye doers of the word, and not hearers only, deceiving your own selves" (James 1:22). The sluggard is self-deceived. He has great dreams and no output. He does not have a path to his dreams based on diligent labor.

The diligent person also has dreams. "The thoughts of the diligent tend only to plenteousness; but of every one that is hasty only to want"

---

2. Gary North, *Confidence and Dominion: An Economic Commentary on Psalms* (Dallas, Georgia: Point Five Press, 2012), ch. 23.

3. Chapter 21.

(Prov. 21:5).[4] He has a pathway in mind: from here to there. What is the meaning of plenteousness? The Hebrew word only occurs three times in Scripture. It is translated as "profit" and "preeminence."

> In all labour there is profit: but the talk of the lips tendeth only to penury (Prov. 14:23).[5]

> For that which befalleth the sons of men befalleth beasts; even one thing befalleth them: as the one dieth, so dieth the other; yea, they have all one breath; so that a man hath no preeminence above a beast: for all is vanity (Eccl. 3:19).[6]

Plenteousness means *advantage*. The diligent person seeks personal advantage. He wants to distinguish his work, and therefore himself, from the run-of-the-mill performer. He has great things in mind. What distinguishes him from the sluggard is not the presence of dreams. What distinguishes him is his diligence. He does high quality work. God rewards him for both his dreams and his effort.

C. Fat Souls

The Hebrew word translated "soul" is *nephesh*. It can mean breath. It means life.

Fatness in the Old Covenant era was a thing to pursue. It was a sign of God's blessing. "The sword of the LORD is filled with blood, it is made fat with fatness, and with the blood of lambs and goats, with the fat of the kidneys of rams: for the LORD hath a sacrifice in Bozrah, and a great slaughter in the land of Idumea" (Isa. 34:6). In a low-productivity agricultural world, meat was a special meal. Meat was for special occasions. Fat is what gives flavor to meat. Fat was reserved for God in the sacrificial system: the whole burnt offering (Lev. 1).[7]

The meaning of this proverb is that the diligent person's life is marked by special blessing. There is therefore a predictable relationship between diligence and success. This success is not merely the accumulation of possessions. It is successful living generally.

---

4. Chapter 62.
5. Chapter 46.
6. Gary North, *Autonomy and Stagnation: An Economic Commentary on Ecclesiastes* (Dallas, Georgia: Point Five Press, 2012), ch. 7:C.
7. Gary North, *Boundaries and Dominion: An Economic Commentary on Leviticus*, 2nd ed. (Dallas, Georgia: Point Five Press, [1994] 2012), ch. 1.

D. Unfulfilled Dreams

In contrast to the full life of the diligent person is the life of the sluggard. This person is not committed to his work. He prefers leisure to work. This attitude is reflected in his performance.

The sluggard desires success. He dreams of success. He possesses nothing. Here, the focus is on goods. The contrast between dream and reality is sharp.

Why does he possess nothing? This proverb does not say, but it implies that his performance is substandard. He is a sluggard. He is not marked by a commitment to labor. He is not diligent about his work.

The message here is clear: there is a relationship between laziness and poverty. The sluggard has great dreams, but these dreams are not translated into performance.

There is a book written by a mind-over-matter promoter, Napoleon Hill: *Think and Grow Rich*. It has sold millions of copies. His most famous statement is this: "What the mind of man can conceive and believe, it can achieve." This is humanism's creed. It is also a form of mysticism: an affirmation of temporal causation that is directed by autonomous thought without physical mediation. Those who adopt his techniques of mental visualization are generally unaware that these are techniques of eastern mysticism, which kept Asia poverty-stricken while the West grew rich, 1500–2000. The basic outlook of this philosophy of causation is this: "You can become anything you believe you can become. This is because you make your own reality through imagination." There is a pseudo-Christian variant of this philosophy, made famous in the 1950s by Rev. Norman Vincent Peale, especially in his best-selling book, *The Power of Positive Thinking* (1953). Peale became a national figure in the United States. He was a pastor in the Reformed Church of America, whose official theology has nothing to do with Peale's philosophy.

This proverb challenges any philosophy of think and grow rich. The sluggard can think all he wants; he is still a sluggard. He can think of himself as overcoming the limits around him. He is still a sluggard. The biblical concept of causation has to do with a positive confession—not of faith in man but faith in God. It is tied to goal-setting and careful planning, not visualization and repetition of self-affirming formulas. The most famous of these formulas in the early twentieth century was French pharmacist Emile Coué's dictum, to be repeated at the beginning and end of each day: "Every day in every way, I am getting better and better." He called his system "autosuggestion."

Conclusion

The sluggard is not dreaming of achieving psychological satisfaction. He is dreaming of measurable wealth. He possesses nothing.

His condition is contrasted with the condition of the diligent person. This contrast leads to a conclusion. *The diligent person has a legitimate expectation of measurable wealth*. This success is not limited to psychological satisfaction, which is perceptible only to the individual. The fatness described here is not limited to the internal realm of feeling.

Solomon does not denigrate measurable wealth. On the contrary, he affirms its legitimacy. He disparages the slothful person because that man's dreams of success—dreams not matched by diligence—produce poverty. Poverty is seen as a liability.

Here is another presentation of the basics of success and failure. The sluggard is a moral failure; therefore, he fails visibly. His character marks him as a moral failure. He is lazy. His character manifests itself in his behavior and then in his capital. He has nothing.

The contrast is between laziness and diligence. This is a continuing theme in Proverbs. "How long wilt thou sleep, O sluggard? when wilt thou arise out of thy sleep?" (6:9). He is easily thwarted by discomfort. "The sluggard will not plow by reason of the cold; therefore shall he beg in harvest, and have nothing" (20:4). He is conceited, believing himself to be beyond limits than hamper others. "The sluggard is wiser in his own conceit than seven men that can render a reason" (26:16). In contrast is the diligent man. The diligent man is a moral success; therefore, he succeeds visibly. His character marks him as a moral success. He is not lazy. His character manifests itself in his behavior and then in his capital. He has a fat soul.

Confession of faith in God
+ goal-setting & careful planning

39

WEALTH AND POVERTY

There is that maketh himself rich, yet hath nothing; there is that maketh himself poor, yet hath great riches.

PROVERBS 13:7

A. Success: Real and Illusionary

This proverb presents two views of wealth and poverty. The rival views divide over the correct covenantal definition of success. A man is described as successfully accumulating riches, yet he is really poor. Another man deliberately pursues poverty, yet he is rich.

Riches are an illusion, the proverb says. An individual heaps up possessions, yet none of it counts for anything. Why not? The author does not say. Poverty is also an illusion. A man pursues a life of poverty, yet he attains riches. How? The author does not say.

To make sense of this proverb, we must answer two questions. The first question is this: *Who is deceived by the illusion of wealth?* The person who has pursued wealth is self-deceived. But, given the widespread desire to attain marketable wealth, the illusion of a man's wealth is shared by those who know of the extent of his possessions. The proverb warns us not be taken in by the illusion.

The second question is this: *Who is deceived by the illusion of poverty?* Answer: all those who are deceived by the illusion of wealth. But the person who actually pursues poverty is not taken in. He understands that the road to great riches is poverty.

The author was familiar with the Mosaic law. He understood Deuteronomy 28, which lists sanctions for covenant-keeping and covenant-

170

breaking.[1] He understood Deuteronomy 8, which speaks of wealth as a testimony to the covenant (v. 17).[2] Then why does he teach here that wealth and poverty are illusions?

There are two views of wealth and two views of poverty. The first view can be described as trust in tangible riches. These are assets that can be bought and sold in markets. The second view can be described as trust in non-tangible riches. These assets cannot be bought and sold in markets.

We can say that riches are success indicators. They are not success. Wealth as a success indicator is valid, Moses said, but it is not a substitute for right standing with God. The psalmist said the same thing in Psalm 73. Evil men can attain wealth for a time, but they stand on slippery slopes (v. 18).[3] This proverb describes such a condition. Those who regard themselves as rich are in fact impoverished.

There are poor men who are poor for the sake of the kingdom of God. Jesus is the supreme example. He did not have a place to lay His head (Matt. 8:20).[4] He taught His disciples not to pursue marketable riches, but to seek first the kingdom of God. All these marketable things will be added (Matt. 6:33).[5] It is not that they are wrong to own. It is that they are worth owning only when they are the result of covenant-keeping, not the result of autonomy.

B. The Source of Wealth

The source of wealth matters. It can be attained in two general ways: covenant-keeping and covenant-breaking. The only basis of long-term wealth is covenant-keeping (Deut 28:1–14). The positive sanctions of God are visible and historical. But there are ways to attain wealth that are not the result of covenant-keeping.

The man described here as wealthy yet impoverished has mistaken the success indicator, marketable wealth, for success. Success is what the poor man attains. He has pursued a course of life that produces poverty. Think of the foreign missionary. A good example is J. Hudson Taylor, who started the China Inland Mission in the late nine-

---

1. Gary North, *Inheritance and Dominion: An Economic Commentary on Deuteronomy*, 2nd ed. (Dallas, Georgia: Point Five Press, [1999] 2012), ch. 69.

2. *Ibid.*, ch. 21.

3. Gary North, *Confidence and Dominion: An Economic Commentary on Psalms* (Dallas, Georgia: Point Five Press, 2012), ch. 18.

4. Gary North, *Priorities and Dominion: An Economic Commentary on Matthew*, 2nd ed. (Dallas, Georgia: Point Five Press, [2000] 2012), ch. 19.

5. *Ibid.*, ch. 15.

teenth century. He ate and dressed like the Chinese in his region. He began a regimen of eating simple Chinese food in England, before he went on his first mission. He ate very little, just as most of his future cultural peers did. He pursued poverty for the sake of riches. These riches were non-marketable.

Most religions maintain the distinction between wealth as a snare and poverty as a holy ideal. Biblical religion is no exception. But biblical religion sees marketable wealth as neither exclusively a snare nor a testimony of spiritual success. The criteria for judging the success or failure of wealth are ethical. This also applies to poverty as a failure indicator. Neither wealth nor poverty is an autonomous, self-justifying standard of success.

Jesus amplified the insight of this proverb. He asked a rhetorical question: What does it profit a man to gain the whole world and lose his soul (Matt. 16:36).[6] This contrast is based on the New Testament's doctrine of final judgment and resurrection. Jesus also taught that covenant-keepers are supposed to lay up treasures in heaven by giving away marketable wealth in history (Matt. 6:19–20).[7] This was more explicit than anything taught in the Old Testament, but it was not inconsistent with Old Testament doctrine, as this proverb indicates.

Conclusion

The rich man accumulates marketable wealth, yet he is poor. The poor man accumulates little marketable wealth, yet he is rich. This gives an indication of God's evaluation of wealth and poverty. He imputes nothing of value to wealth accumulated on the basis of autonomy. It does not matter if the rich man obeyed biblical law or not, whether he was a thief or highly productive. What matters is his judicial standing with God: "guilty" or "not guilty." Legal standing is a matter of God's grace. It is not purchased by the recipient. The grace of eternal life is the greatest wealth of all, yet it is non-marketable.

---

6. *Ibid.*, ch. 35.
7. *Ibid.*, ch. 13.

40

WEALTH ACCUMULATION

Wealth gotten by vanity shall be diminished: but he that gathereth by labour shall increase.

PROVERBS 13:11

This proverb acknowledges that it is possible for morally empty people to accumulate wealth. It also asserts that this wealth will eventually be diminished. That which is accumulated in the short run is not retained in the long run.

In contrast, the fruits of labor are positive. In this case, labor means honest labor. It is not that vain people do not labor. It is that their labor is an extension of their worldview. They are spiritually empty. Thus, the visible results of their efforts do not persevere. This view is consistent with the more general proverb: "A good man leaveth an inheritance to his children's children: and the wealth of the sinner is laid up for the just" (13:22).[1]

What is vanity? The word appears again and again in Ecclesiastes. It refers to emptiness. Something looks appealing; in fact, it is empty. It does not deliver what the seeker had expected. Ecclesiastes dismisses as vanity all of the world's preferred benefits.

Then there is outright deception. This also is a form of vanity. "The getting of treasures by a lying tongue is a vanity tossed to and fro of them that seek death" (21:6).[2] This deception is literally suicidal.

---

1. Chapter 41.
2. Chapter 63.

A. Built on Emptiness

Men can accumulate wealth through vanity. Vanity is one basis of accumulation. But in what sense? Is this vanity in the mind of the seller or the buyer? Is the foundation of the accumulated wealth the producer's vanity or the consumer's?

To answer this, we must look at the contrast. The person who accumulates assets through honest labor will see his wealth increase. The focus of this proverb is the dedication of the producer. There is no mention of the buyer.

The vain person also heaps up wealth. This wealth is insecure. It rests on the efforts of a spiritually empty person.

Why should his wealth be threatened? If he is spiritually empty, but his product meets the desires of buyers, the buyers will continue to buy. The flow of funds from the buyers to the producer is not threatened by the spiritual condition of the producer, just so long as he meets the wants of the buyers at prices they are willing to pay.

There are several threats. First, the empty person or his heirs will squander the income, shrinking the net worth of the capital base. Second, the vain person will eventually reduce the value of his output by trying to cut costs by cutting quality. Third, demand will fall because of new competition. Fourth, the buying public's tastes will change, leading to falling demand. The producer's moral flaw will eventually begin to affect the competitiveness of his output.

B. Built on Honest Work

In contrast, the person who works honestly and pays attention to his budget will accumulate capital. He recognizes the positive relationship between good work and high income. He goes about his business in a methodical way. Over time, this attitude toward wealth produces an increase. The laborer does not attempt to take shortcuts that reduce the buyer's benefits. He may try to become more efficient, but the buyer is not short-changed.

This proverb promotes the idea of the value of labor. It does not teach that the value of labor's output is based on the labor's input. In other words, it does not teach the labor theory of value. It does not teach that labor, apart from consumer demand, produces wealth. It does teach that the person who seeks to gather through his own efforts has the correct attitude toward wealth. Wealth can be attained through vanity or through honest labor. The correct approach is honest labor, which secures increasing wealth. Labor is necessary for the preservation of wealth.

God labored to create the world. This gives meaning to the mandated day of rest (Ex. 20:11).[3] This also serves as an example for those who seek wealth. God has built into the social order a system of causation. Labor, when added to land (the environment), produces lasting wealth.

Inherent in creation is the requirement that people work. All warnings that labor-saving machinery or software will produce widespread unemployment are misguided. Labor-saving innovations release men from laboring in one field. This does not reduce the quantity of labor required to maintain the social order. Human labor is the least specific of production inputs. It can be shifted to new fields. *There is always more work to be done*. Manufacturing in the twentieth century declined in economically advanced countries, but service industries replaced manufacturing. Labor became ever-more valuable as capital accumulated. This was because labor became ever-more productive as capital accumulated.

Conclusion

Built into the creation is a program of capital accumulation. At the heart of this process is labor. Men must devote time, thought, and energy in their quest to accumulate wealth. *Labor is desirable as a tool of self-dominion*. It is part of the dominion covenant.[4] When labor is applied to a program of wealth accumulation, the results are positive. Any attempt to get rich apart from labor is a snare and a delusion. It is an empty quest. Such a quest may work for a while, but the program is self-destructive. It undermines long-term capital appreciation.

Capital accumulation

tool of self-dominion — Labor
time
thought
energy

---

3. Gary North, *Authority and Dominion: An Economic Commentary on Exodus* (Dallas, Georgia: Point Five Press, 2012), Part 2, *Decalogue and Dominion* (1986), ch. 24.

4. Gary North, *Sovereignty and Dominion: An Economic Commentary on Genesis* (Dallas, Georgia: Point Five Press, 2012), chaps. 3, 4.

41

ETHICS AND INHERITANCE

A good man leaveth an inheritance to his children's children: and the wealth of the sinner is laid up for the just.

PROVERBS 13:22

This is the most important verse in the Bible that deals with inheritance: point five of the biblical covenant.[1] It establishes a principle of interpretation: *economic sanctions[2] are related to ethical performance.*[3] This brief aphorism summarizes the system of sanctions that is presented in Leviticus 26 and Deuteronomy 28.

A. Generation-Skipping

The proverb establishes the legitimacy of wealth accumulation. A good man accumulates wealth, which he passes on to his grandchildren. In summary, "you can't leave it behind if there isn't any."

Why doesn't the proverb specify children? Why does it refer to grandchildren? The text does not say, but I can offer possible suggestions.

First, the behavior of grandchildren reveals the success of their parents in transferring the ethical precepts of the grandparents. There is visible evidence of the degree of *intergenerational covenantal inheritance.* Depending on how old the grandchildren are, the grandfather can see which grandchildren are likely to extend the kingdom of God

---

1. Ray R. Sutton, *That You May Prosper: Dominion By Covenant*, 2nd ed. (Tyler, Texas: Institute for Christian Economics, [1987] 1992), ch. 5. Gary North, *Unconditional Surrender: God's Program for Victory*, 5th ed. (Powder Springs, Georgia: American Vision, 2010), ch. 5.

2. *Ibid.*, ch. 4.

3. *Ibid.*, ch. 3.

in history. This is a matter of their confession and performance: *word and deed*.

Second, parents should be accumulating capital to transfer to their as yet unborn grandchildren. Wealth from the grandparents can be used to capitalize the grandchildren. This saves the parents money, which can then be used to build up family capital. Part of this accumulated capital will in turn go to their children.

Third, the grandparents should not let the parents inherit all of their wealth. The heirs may squander this legacy. By leaving wealth to grandchildren, a grandfather reduces the risk of the decapitalization of the family's inheritance. This is a strategy of risk diversification.

This raises the question of the administration of capital. The parents may not be effective trustees. If the grandparents place the grandchildren's legacy under the authority of the parents, the grand-children may be disinherited through parental mismanagement. This is why trusts can be effective instruments for transferring wealth. An independent trustee, chosen by the grantor, will act on behalf of the trust's beneficiaries until they come of age, as specified by the trust.

the wealth of the sinner is laid up for the just

B. The Flow of Funds

The second part of this proverb is the heart of the matter: *the wealth of the sinner is laid up for the just*.

There is a common saying: "The rich get richer, and the poor get poorer." This saying is refuted by the effects of compound growth in the West after 1780. The rich have indeed grown richer, but so have the poor. The poor person today lives better than most rich people did in 1800 or even 1900. He has access to far better medical care. His children are more likely to survive childhood diseases and accidents. He has more entertainment.

This proverb says that the righteous get richer at the expense of the unrighteous. How? Through inheritance. Wealth accumulated by the covenant-breaker is inherited by the covenant-keeper. How can this be?

There are two ways. First, the heirs abandon covenant-breaking for covenant-keeping. This is inheritance through adoption into the family of God. Second, covenant-keepers become more productive than covenant-breakers. The covenant-breaking heirs of rich cov-enant-breakers spend their inheritances on goods and services pro-duced for sale by covenant-keepers.

This proverb rests on an assumption: *the structure of covenantal inheritance favors covenant-keeping over the long term*. There can be a build-up of wealth. But this is alienable wealth. Covenant-breakers cannot maintain possession of it in the long run. The covenantal structure of society militates against covenant-breaking. *God has not established a level playing field. He has tilted it in favor of His covenant people.*

How is it tilted? In five ways. First, God is sovereign over creation. He who acknowledges this publicly is specially favored by God. "Wherefore the LORD God of Israel saith, I said indeed that thy house, and the house of thy father, should walk before me for ever: but now the LORD saith, Be it far from me; for them that honour me I will honour, and they that despise me shall be lightly esteemed" (I Sam. 2:30).

Second, men must covenant with either God or Satan. God is the source of blessings. Satan is not. "Every good gift and every perfect gift is from above, and cometh down from the Father of lights, with whom is no variableness, neither shadow of turning" (James 1:17).[4]

Third, society is governed by biblical law. This law is inherently ethical. There is a difference between right and wrong. This is the difference between covenant-keeping and covenant-breaking.

Fourth, there are predictable sanctions in history, positive and negative. Covenant-keeping brings positive sanctions (Deut. 28:1–14).[5] Covenant-breaking brings negative sanctions (Deut. 28:15–68).

Fifth, the process of positive sanctions compounds wealth over time as a testimony to God's covenantal faithfulness. "But thou shalt remember the LORD thy God: for it is he that giveth thee power to get wealth, that he may establish his covenant which he sware unto thy fathers, as it is this day" (Deut. 8:18).[6] This process transfers the inheritance of history to God's people. "For evildoers shall be cut off: but those that wait upon the LORD, they shall inherit the earth" (Ps. 37:9).

C. Per Capita Economic Growth

This proverb directs our attention to the future. It reminds us that our efforts in history extend down through history through our grandchildren. But they also come under the covenantal structure of

---

4. Gary North, *Ethics and Dominion: An Economic Commentary on the Epistles* (Dallas, Georgia: Point Five Press, 2012), ch. 33.

5. Gary North, *Inheritance and Dominion: An Economic Commentary on Deuteronomy*, 2nd ed. (Dallas, Georgia: Point Five Press, [1999] 2012), ch. 69.

6. *Ibid.*, ch. 22.

inheritance. They will someday be reminded of the intergenerational nature of inheritance in history.

The compounding process through time is a way to extend God's dominion in history. Population multiplies. Heirship extends to numbers like the sand of the sea. God promised Abraham: "That in blessing I will bless thee, and in multiplying I will multiply thy seed as the stars of the heaven, and as the sand which is upon the sea shore; and thy seed shall possess the gate of his enemies; And in thy seed shall all the nations of the earth be blessed; because thou hast obeyed my voice" (Gen. 22:17–18). But the heirs do not get poorer as a result: same size pie, but with more pieces to share. On the contrary, they get richer. The promise of God's covenant is per capita economic growth. There will be leisure for all of God's people. "But they shall sit every man under his vine and under his fig tree; and none shall make them afraid: for the mouth of the LORD of hosts hath spoken it" (Micah 4:4).[7]

Not only does the Bible teach *linear history*—creation, Fall, redemption, final judgment—it teaches *historical progress*: ethically, intellectually, economically. Nowhere in the Bible is this made clearer than in Isaiah 65.

And ye shall leave your name for a curse unto my chosen: for the Lord GOD shall slay thee, and call his servants by another name: That he who blesseth himself in the earth shall bless himself in the God of truth; and he that sweareth in the earth shall swear by the God of truth; because the former troubles are forgotten, and because they are hid from mine eyes. For, behold, I create new heavens and a new earth: and the former shall not be remembered, nor come into mind. But be ye glad and rejoice for ever in that which I create: for, behold, I create Jerusalem a rejoicing, and her people a joy. And I will rejoice in Jerusalem, and joy in my people: and the voice of weeping shall be no more heard in her, nor the voice of crying. There shall be no more thence an infant of days, nor an old man that hath not filled his days: for the child shall die an hundred years old; but the sinner being an hundred years old shall be accursed. And they shall build houses, and inhabit them; and they shall plant vineyards, and eat the fruit of them (Isa. 65:15–21).[8]

7. Gary North, *Restoration and Dominion: An Economic Commentary on the Prophets* (Dallas, Georgia: Point Five Press, 2012), ch. 26.
8. *Ibid.*, ch. 15.

Conclusion

If the wealth of the sinner is laid up for the just, then God's people should be optimistic regarding the future. A high level of future-orientation should mark their thinking. Future-orientation is the premier feature of an upper-class individual.[9]

To maintain this outlook, men must act consistently with it. This means that they should strive to build up an inheritance, not merely for their children but also for their grandchildren. They must transfer wealth and vision to grandchildren, who are too young to have secured their place in the world, but whose confessions and outward behavior mark them as covenant-keepers. Such a transfer of wealth takes faith that God will keep the terms of His covenant and not dissipate the inheritance.

---

9. Edward C. Banfield, *The Unheavenly City: The Nature and Future of Our Urban Crisis* (Boston: Little, Brown, 1970), pp. 48–50.

42

DESTRUCTIVE INJUSTICE

Much food is in the fallow ground of the poor, but it is swept away by injustice.

This is the translation of the New American Standard Bible. The King James translation is not clear: "Much food is in the tillage of the poor: but there is that is destroyed for want of judgment."

A. Fallow Ground

The Hebrew word translated by the King James as "tillage" is translated as "fallow ground" elsewhere in the Old Testament.

> For thus saith the LORD to the men of Judah and Jerusalem, Break up your fallow ground, and sow not among thorns (Jer. 4:3).

> Sow to yourselves in righteousness, reap in mercy; break up your fallow ground: for it is time to seek the LORD, till he come and rain righteousness upon you (Hosea 10:12).

Fallow ground is ground that has not been plowed or seeded. It may be fallow for a season, as was to have been the case in the seventh, sabbatical year (Lev. 25:1–7).[1] It may be fallow only until plowing time.

The contrast of Proverbs 13:23 with Hosea 10:12 indicates that fallow land in this case was temporarily fallow. The prophet called on the Israelites to ethical behavior: "Sow to yourselves in righteousness, reap in mercy." *Seeding the land* is described here as *practicing righteousness*. Repentance is the equivalent of plowing fallow soil, which

---

1. Gary North, *Boundaries and Dominion: An Economic Commentary on Leviticus*, 2nd ed. (Dallas, Georgia: Point Five Press, [1994] 2012), ch. 24.

precedes planting: "Break up your fallow ground." When Israelites repent and work in terms of their new ethical vision, there will be a positive sanction from God: "rain righteousness upon you." Then will come the harvest. Hosea spoke of repentance and restoration in terms of plowing, seeding, and harvesting what had been fallow land.

This prophetic context points to the exegetical content of this proverb. The fallow ethical land of Israel contains the fruits of righteous labor. But to produce these fruits, there must be conformity to the Mosaic law. This was the continuing message of the prophets: a call to restore the nation by conforming the Mosaic law.

B. Injustice

Injustice under the Mosaic covenant was any law enforcement that was in conflict with the terms of the Mosaic law, including its civil sanctions. The prophets did not come before the nation to call the people back to ethics in general or to natural law as revealed to autonomous human wisdom. King David set the example for every future king of Israel.

> Now the days of David drew nigh that he should die; and he charged Solomon his son, saying, I go the way of all the earth: be thou strong therefore, and shew thyself a man; And keep the charge of the LORD thy God, to walk in his ways, to keep his statutes, and his commandments, and his judgments, and his testimonies, as it is written in the law of Moses, that thou mayest prosper in all that thou doest, and whithersoever thou turnest thyself (I Kings 2:1–3).

After the Babylonian captivity, the people who returned to the land of Israel made this public confession to God.

> Howbeit thou art just in all that is brought upon us; for thou hast done right, but we have done wickedly: Neither have our kings, our princes, our priests, nor our fathers, kept thy law, nor hearkened unto thy commandments and thy testimonies, wherewith thou didst testify against them (Neh. 9:33–34).

With this in mind, consider the message of this proverb. In fallow land there is a means of growing food. To fallow ground must be added labor: plowing it, seeding it, irrigating it, and keeping it free of crop-consuming insects. Labor must be paid for. So must seeds. All this takes time. Time has a price: interest.

Fallow ground does not normally produce a crop that will sustain an owner economically. So, for fallow ground to bear fruit, the owner or renter must add something of value. He makes an investment: time. A poor man makes a large investment proportional to his capital. He has no reserves if he makes a mistake. Converting a fallow field to food is a high-risk proposition for him.

What is the effect of the threat of injustice on the motivation of a poor man? Highly negative. He is just barely scraping by. Now he faces a new uncertainty: the misuse of the legal system to reduce his income. People with power become his enemies. He can do little to thwart their plans, once his seeds are sown. His land cannot be concealed. The fruits of his labor will be visible to everyone. He is vulnerable. He has no money to hire a lawyer or bribe an official. He operates at the mercy of the legal system. But he cannot trust the legal system.

Injustice is like a harvesting tool. It sweeps away the crop. But this proverb does not say that a crop is ready for harvesting. It says that food is in a fallow field. It speaks metaphorically. Injustice is like a pre-planting harvesting tool. It sweeps away the crop that will not be planted. How is an unplanted crop swept away? By sweeping away the planter's willingness to plant.

C. Marginal Loss = Total Loss

Men make investments of land, labor, time, and capital for the sake of a hoped-for return on their investments. They expect to harvest a return that is higher than what they invested. They work in hope.

Hope is undermined by the threat of injustice. If the land's owner or renter does not expect to gain more than he invests, he will look for other places to make his investment. He will not willingly sacrifice money, time, and energy for the sake of a negative rate of return. He will not work for free in order to benefit unjust people.

Injustice is destructive. This proverb says that it is as destructive as a harvesting tool that sweeps away an entire crop. The threat of injustice at the margin produces the complete destruction of the crop. There will be no crop.

The disincentive produced by injustice is very great, this proverb says. It does not explain why this is true. Solomon expected the reader to understand how men plan for the future. But even if the reader does not understand the logic of the example, he perceives the basic message: injustice is destructive. It could be compared with a plague of locusts that strips away a crop.

Conclusion

Injustice is destructive. The poor man who does not plant a field is harmed. The would-be buyers of his crop are harmed. Even the purveyors of injustice are harmed. They will have less wealth to confiscate through their misuse of the legal system.

Injustice reduces production, but it does so in a way that cannot be perceived directly. A fallow field that remains fallow can be blamed on many factors. But the supreme factor, according to this proverb, is injustice. Someone had planned to gain part of someone else's crop at a below-market price. Now he will do without. So will everyone else.

43

COSTS OF
PRODUCTION

Where no oxen are, the crib is clean: but much increase is by the strength of the ox.

PROVERBS 14:4

The opening clause points to one seemingly beneficial aspect of low productivity: it takes less work. A man owns a stall, suitable for an ox. He does not own or lease an ox. The stall is economically useless unless it is inside a building, which could be used for storage. A holding pen for an animal is a highly specific form of capital. If there is no animal to be penned in, what good is it?

When used, an ox's stall is a mess. It is filled with droppings. Nobody wants the job of cleaning out an ox's stall. But the two available alternatives are even more unpleasant: an uncleaned stall or an empty stall. The former may kill the ox through disease. The latter indicates the lack of a tool of production.

A. Increasing Returns to
Capital Investment

The second clause gets to the economic point: "much increase is by the strength of the ox." The Hebrew word translated here as "increase" is elsewhere translated as "fruit" or "fruits." The meaning is the same: the net output of the land.

> Then I will command my blessing upon you in the sixth year, and it shall bring forth fruit for three years (Lev. 25:21).[1]

---

1. Gary North, *Boundaries and Dominion: An Economic Commentary on Leviticus*, 2nd ed. (Dallas, Georgia: Point Five Press, [1994] 2012), ch. 27.

185

Thou shalt truly tithe all the increase of thy seed, that the field bringeth forth year by year (Deut. 14:22).[2]

The man who owns an ox and land can combine these capital assets to produce a crop. Without an ox, the landowner is limited to whatever he and hired workers can plant by hand. The work is arduous and time-consuming. A man's physical strength is minimal compared to an ox's strength. So, the output of land plus human labor is low when compared to the output of land plus a trained ox's labor. It is a matter of strength, as this proverb says.

Farmland without an ox is not productive. This is because of the low output of human labor in agriculture, compared to an ox's labor. Land becomes far more productive agriculturally by the addition of an ox. Put in economic terminology, there is an increasing rate of return to both land and labor when the labor moves from human labor to ox labor. The ox makes the land more productive for the owner of the land. The land makes the ox more productive for the owner of the ox.

An owner was required to care for both the land and the ox. The land was not to be planted in year six (Lev. 25:1–6).[3] Fallow land had time to be restored. The ox was to share a portion of this increased output with the ox. "Thou shalt not muzzle the ox when he treadeth out the corn" (Deut. 25:4).[4] Paul invoked this law to make the same point with respect to men. "For the scripture saith, Thou shalt not muzzle the ox that treadeth out the corn. And, The labourer is worthy of his reward" (I Tim. 5:18;[5] cf. I Cor. 9:8–9[6]).

Separated, ox and land are not highly productive for their owner. Together, as part of an integrated system of production, they are quite productive. This is another example of the division of labor in action. By combining two different forms of capital, a person can greatly increase his wealth.

B. Good News and Bad News

The good news is that by adding an ox to the production mix, the owner can increase his wealth. The word "increase" is the equivalent

2. Gary North, *Inheritance and Dominion: An Economic Commentary on Deuteronomy*, 2nd ed. (Dallas, Georgia: Point Five Press, [1999] 2012), ch. 34.

3. North, *Boundaries and Dominion*, ch. 25.

4. North, *Inheritance and Dominion*, ch. 62.

5. Gary North, *Hierarchy and Dominion: An Economic Commentary on First Timothy*, 2nd ed. (Dallas, Georgia: [2001] 2012), ch. 8.

6. Gary North, *Judgment and Dominion: An Economic Commentary on First Corinthians*, 2nd ed. (Dallas, Georgia: Point Five Press, [2001] 2012), ch. 11.

of wealth. The bad news is that the ox requires additional capital: a stall. This tool of production must be maintained. Someone must clean the stall. Either the owner does this, or else he hires someone to do this. This is a cost of production.

The owner can defer this maintenance expense for a time. He can let the stall get worse and worse. But the end result will be the loss of his capital asset. The ox will get sick or die.

Of course, this same principle of maintenance applies to every capital good. Capital wears out. In a cursed world, though not in the pre-Fall uncursed world, this is the result of entropy: the tendency of everything to become random.[7] Sharp blades get dull. Sharp minds get dull. Things wear out.

Land wears out, too. Agricultural land is depleted of minerals and vegetation. This is why farmers adopt counter-depletion measures: crop rotation, fertilizer, and fallow land for a season. In this sense, land is a capital good. There is pure land: bedrock support that does not wear out. Then there are topsoil, earthworms, and other living matter, which are consumed by agricultural production.

One of the nice things about the interrelationship between oxen and land is that the contents of stalls can then be spread over land to increase its productivity. This is more work to do, but the result of this work is increase.

All of this points to extra work for men. This is all part of the curse (Gen. 3:17–19).[8]

Conclusion

The lesson of scarcity is this: there are no free lunches. Output requires inputs. In the case of agricultural land, output requires input: land and work animals. Both land and work animals are capital assets. Capital requires additional investment in order to maintain it. This cost of production is required to maximize output.

When an asset's output is significantly increased by the addition of a complementary factor of production, the owner of the initial asset finds that it pays to buy or lease the complementary factor. But in making this decision, he should count the cost of maintaining the complementary factor. Only when the *expected* value of the *expected*

---

7. Gary North, *Is the World Running Down? Crisis in the Christian Worldview* (Tyler, Texas: Institute for Christian Economics, 1988), ch. 2.

8. Gary North, *Sovereignty and Dominion: An Economic Commentary on Genesis* (Dallas, Georgia: Point Five Press, [1982] 2012), ch. 12.

increased output is greater than the *expected* value of the increased inputs should he hire or purchase the second factor of production.

44

BUYING FRIENDSHIP

The poor is hated even of his own neighbour: but the rich hath many friends.

The translators underplayed the power of riches. The Hebrew word translated as "friends" is more accurately translated as "lovers." This word is stronger than the other Hebrew word for "friend" and "friendly." "A man that hath friends must shew himself friendly: and there is a **friend** that sticketh closer than a brother" (Prov. 18:24). The loving friend is more faithful than a brother. This is the meaning of friendship available to the rich person.

We teach our children that money cannot buy friendship. This proverb says the opposite. If we tell children that a friend loves us for ourselves, we must face the dual truth of this proverb. First, poverty produces hatred by neighbors who know a person. Second, wealth produces love. This hatred or love is specifically said to be the result of one's economic condition.

A. The Use of Irony

Why should we imagine that parents in Solomon's day taught their children any differently from the way parents teach their children today? Parents want to protect their children from false friends. From an early age, parents warn their children against trusting in friends who exhibit friendship for the sake of whatever the child possesses. Such friends are false friends. They are committed only to sharing the wealth of the possessor.

He who possesses great wealth usually has an entourage close by. Those who are poor do not have anyone close by. A popular song in

189

the United States during the economic depression of the 1930s was *Nobody Knows You When You're Down and Out* (1922). The song closely paralleled Proverbs 14:20.

> Nobody knows you when you're down and out.
> In your pocket, not one penny,
> And your friends, you haven't any.
> And as soon as you get on your feet again,
> Everybody is your long-lost friend.
> It's mighty strange, without a doubt, but
> Nobody wants you when you're down and out.

In his empty pockets phase, the person had no friends. This proverb goes even further: "The poor is hated even of his own neighbour." This is actual animosity. I think this is literary irony, just as "lovers" is. He is hated in the same sense that a rich man is loved. The poor person feels rejected. His neighbors abandon him. They are not part of his entourage. He has no entourage. The person with a lot of money has an entourage.

Solomon was not unaware of this love-and-hate phenomenon. He described life as it has been down through the ages. Some people's commitment to others is based on what they expect to receive from this commitment. The rich man is expected to spend money on his friends. The poor man is expected to ask his friends for a loan. So, people are generally favorable to the rich people they associate with. This is a great ethical error, Jesus warned the Pharisees. He said to consider the poor when making out the invitation list for your feast.

> When thou makest a dinner or a supper, call not thy friends, nor thy brethren, neither thy kinsmen, nor thy rich neighbours; lest they also bid thee again, and a recompence be made thee. But when thou makest a feast, call the poor, the maimed, the lame, the blind: And thou shalt be blessed; for they cannot recompense thee: for thou shalt be recompensed at the resurrection of the just (Luke 14:12–14).[1]

So, the neighbor described by this proverb is not neighborly. The lover is unlovely. Both are motivated by what they expect to receive from the other person. They are motivated by economic self-interest.

---

1. Gary North, *Treasure and Dominion: An Economic Commentary on Luke*, 2nd ed. (Dallas, Georgia: Point Five Press, [2000] 2012), ch. 34.

B. Winners and Losers

This proverb describes something familiar. People are motivated by economic self-interest. To the extent that this motivation is at the foundation of personal relationships, friendship becomes a matter of wealth. To gain such a friend requires that you gain wealth first. To keep such a friend requires that you retain your wealth and share it. Such friendship is fleeting.

Those who are committed to a personal relationship because of wealth are generally poorer than the recipient of their commitment. The likelihood that they will be named in the person's will is remote. So is his death. The likelihood that he will hand over a large portion of his wealth to friends is also remote. So, the hanger-on is seeking only spare change. He may receive trickle-down wealth, but nothing substantial. He is not productive. He sees his time as most profitably spent with a rich man for the trickle-down wealth and the token benefits it may provide. He establishes a relationship of dependance. He sees this as the highest return on his time.

A seller of goods or services is not equally dependent. He establishes a relationship based on mutually beneficial exchange. He sells something he produces. In all likelihood, he does not seek to establish a relationship of friendship with a wealthy buyer. He keeps the relationship professional, for his competitive advantage in the marketplace is based heavily on the reputation of excellence that his output possesses. Excellence rests on *objective merit*, irrespective of favoritism based on personal friendship. He seeks repeat business. He also seeks referrals if he is a good marketer. If the rich man recognizes that the seller supplies an inferior product, which is offset only by friendship, he may not be ready to recommend the seller to his associates, for they will think him deceived. No one wants to appear to be hampered by poor judgment, least of all a highly successful person.

This means that the rich man's lovers are losers. They probably know this. They correctly perceive themselves to be dependent on creating an illusion of unself-interested friendship. If they do not recognize this, then they are self-deceived as well as self-interested.

Furthermore, their goals are minimal. They do not seek a professional relationship with the rich man based on their objective productivity. They do not seek a stream of predictable income based on supplying something desired by the rich person because of the advantage it gives him. Instead, they seek handouts disguised as participation in joint celebrations. Basically, they are party people. Their personal horizons are limited to whatever wealth can be obtained at a party. This is legitimate as a career, but only if you are a professional party planner or performer. The difference here is the difference between a fee for services rendered and a handout for old times' sake.

Conclusion

Solomon was a very rich man. He was also powerful. He possessed the power of life and death, even to the point of executing his conniving half-brother (I Kings 2). Such men attract hangers-on. If they are wise, they do not let such people into their inner circles. They do not become dependent on them. They treat them, at best, as party people: fun people to have around at unimportant functions. Being invited to unimportant functions is important to unimportant people. A wise man recognizes this. An unscrupulous rich man will take advantage of this moral defect of hangers-on. They become his prey.

45

DEALING WITH THE POOR

He that despiseth his neighbour sinneth: but he that hath mercy on the poor, happy is he.

PROVERBS 14:21

This proverb follows a related one: "The poor is hated even of his own neighbour: but the rich hath many friends."[1] Here, Solomon focuses on the neighbor, who is contrasted with the merciful person.

In the previous proverb, the neighbor's hatred is related to his victim's poverty. The contrast is between the poor man's hating neighbor and the rich man's hanger-on. The difference is not based on comparative moral fiber. Both are morally weak and short-sighted. But the hanger-on is not sinning. The hating neighbor is.

A. Pressured to Give

The hating neighbor has no judicially objective claim against his neighbor. He has not been harmed in any way. The poor man's plight did not come at the expense of his neighbor. Thus, there is no legitimate reason for the hatred. Then on what is it based? The previous proverb tells us: the person's poverty. This proverb is related to the previous proverb. We can legitimately conclude that this is based on the proverb's contrast: the merciful person who gives to the poor.

The poor man is in need of charity. This may be in the form of a charitable zero-interest loan (Deut. 15:1–6).[2] It may be in the form of an outright gift. The point is, his presence places his neighbor in a

---

1. Chapter 44.
2. Gary North, *Inheritance and Dominion: An Economic Commentary on Deuteronomy*, 2nd ed. (Dallas, Georgia: Point Five Press, [1999] 2012), ch. 36.

painful moral situation. Will the neighbor turn his back on the suffer-
ing man, just as the priest and Levite did to the robbed man lying in
the road (Luke 10:31–32)?[3] Or will he lend, asking nothing in return?
Jesus commanded:

> Give to every man that asketh of thee; and of him that taketh away thy
> goods ask them not again. And as ye would that men should do to you, do
> ye also to them likewise. For if ye love them which love you, what thank
> have ye? for sinners also love those that love them. And if ye do good to
> them which do good to you, what thank have ye? for sinners also do even
> the same. And if ye lend to them of whom ye hope to receive, what thank
> have ye? for sinners also lend to sinners, to receive as much again. But love
> ye your enemies, and do good, and lend, hoping for nothing again; and
> your reward shall be great, and ye shall be the children of the Highest: for
> he is kind unto the unthankful and to the evil. Be ye therefore merciful, as
> your Father also is merciful (Luke 6:30–36).[4]

The sinner reacts by blaming the victim. He despises the victim
because of his own dilemma: to give or not to give? He sees the poor
man as the source of guilt. It is easier to blame the poor person for
his condition than to open one's wallet. It is easier to find an explanation of his poverty that is related to some moral weakness on his
part. He is seen as deserving his poverty. He is therefore deserving of
condemnation. Condemnation then becomes hatred. Such hatred is
sinful, this proverb says.

B. Happy to Give

In contrast to the hate-filled person is the merciful person who gives
to the poor. This proverb says that this person is happy. This is consistent with what Jesus taught. Indeed, it is the foundation of what Jesus
taught: "It is more blessed to give than to receive" (Acts 20:35b).[5]

Why should this be true? People are self-centered. Modern economics ever since Adam Smith has rested, above all, on this assertion:
"After the assumption of scarcity, individual self-interest is the most
fruitful assumption undergirding economic theory and practice."
Why should we conclude that giving makes people happy?

We can begin with grandparents' attitude toward their grandchildren. This is the most obvious example, in every culture, at all times.

---

3. Gary North, *Treasure and Dominion: An Economic Commentary on Luke*, 2nd ed.
(Dallas, Georgia: Point Five Press, [2000] 2012), ch. 21.
    4. *Ibid.*, ch. 10.
    5. Gary North, *Sacrifice and Dominion: An Economic Commentary on Acts*, 2nd ed. (Dal-
las, Georgia: Point Five Press, [2000], 2012), ch. 9:A:2.

Then there is gift-giving between spouses. This is not done in the spirit of mutual exchange. So, within the context of the family, giving is more common than mutual exchange. It is when we move beyond the family that most people's motivation moves to self-interest.

This proverb says that giving to the poor makes the giver happy. This is the testimony down through the ages of those who have been exceptional givers. But their number has been limited. Their attitude is generally respected, but their example is not widely imitated.

Why should this positive psychological connection between giving to the poor and happiness exist? To answer this, consider God, in whose image man is made. God is the source of all good gifts. "Every good gift and every perfect gift is from above, and cometh down from the Father of lights, with whom is no variableness, neither shadow of turning" (James 1:17).[6] Peter concluded:

> And above all things have fervent charity among yourselves: for charity shall cover the multitude of sins. Use hospitality one to another without grudging. As every man hath received the gift, even so minister the same one to another, as good stewards of the manifold grace of God (I Peter 4:8–10).

Grace is best defined as an unmerited gift—unmerited by the recipient. God is the source of original grace. God has this advantage: *He is not affected by scarcity*. He did not have to pay for whatever He owns. He is the original owner. "For every beast of the forest is mine, and the cattle upon a thousand hills" (Ps. 50:10).[7] So, when He gives something, He loses nothing. Jesus taught that this is also true of covenant-keepers. What they give up in history for the sake of Christ and His kingdom, they amass in eternity. Jesus said:

> Fear not, little flock; for it is your Father's good pleasure to give you the kingdom. Sell that ye have, and give alms; provide yourselves bags which wax not old, a treasure in the heavens that faileth not, where no thief approacheth, neither moth corrupteth. For where your treasure is, there will your heart be also (Luke 12:32–34).[8]

Conclusion

The attitude we have toward the poor is important. If we despise them and blame them for their poverty in order to reduce the sense

---

6. Gary North, *Ethics and Dominion: An Economic Commentary on the Epistles* (Dallas, Georgia: Point Five press, 2012), ch. 33.
7. Gary North, *Confidence and Dominion: An Economic Commentary on Psalms* (Dallas, Georgia: Point Five Press, 2012), ch. 10.
8. North, *Treasure and Dominion*, ch. 26.

of obligation that we should have for them, then we sin. If we open our wallets to them when they are in trouble through no fault of their own, we gain happiness. This is not a matter of giving in order to receive back from the poor. But it surely is a matter of giving in order to gain great gifts from God: happiness in history and treasure in eternity.

46

EXPENSIVE TALK

In all labour there is profit: but the talk of the lips tendeth only to penury.

PROVERBS 14:23

Here is another proverb of comparisons. One result is beneficial. The other is not. We should choose which action to take in terms of the respective result.

The opening clause is a universal statement: "In all labour there is profit." Did Solomon include theft, arson, and other crimes? No. Then why did he make such a sweeping statement? To emphasize this fact: *the superiority of labor over talk*.

There are people who talk for a living: teachers, preachers, television news anchors, and other members of the chattering class. Some of them make a lot of money. Was Solomon really convinced that talk always leads to poverty? No. Then why did he make such a sweeping statement? To emphasize the superiority of labor over talk.

There are times when a biblical author makes an outrageous statement for effect. This communications technique is called *rhetoric*. For example, a lazy man really does not defend his laziness by referring to a lion in the streets. Yet Solomon used this example twice (Prov. 22:13;[1] 26:13). This is a comparable example of rhetoric.

A. "Action Speaks Louder Than Words"

This is a familiar slogan in American history. Americans like to think of themselves as doers more than talkers. They contrast action, which produces objective results, with talk, which wastes time by not producing any results. This attitude is grounded in the message of Prov-

---

1. Chapter 68.

erbs 14:23. A related passage is James 1:22. "But be ye doers of the word, and not hearers only, deceiving your own selves." The main idea in both passages is not to dismiss talk as worthless, for that would dismiss hearing as worthless. *What is worthless is talk without action consistent with the talk.* Americans have another saying: "You must walk the talk." To act inconsistently with whatever you say you believe is hypocritical and self-destructive. To do nothing is equally hypocritical.

In this passage, "talk with the lips" means talk without action. A person talks in order to impress the listener with his own wisdom. But then the speaker does not take action. His words subsequently condemn him. In order for the talk to become meaningful, the speaker must take action—action that is consistent with what he said.

If a speaker is limited to talk, those around him are unwise to follow his advice. He is not "putting his money where his mouth is." He does not really believe what he is saying, or if he does, then he suffers from mental paralysis. In either case, the listener should not follow his advice without verifying what he has heard. He should also not subordinate himself to this person.

This proverb says that *talk without action produces poverty*. Why should talk lead to poverty? Because action is what makes a profit. Doing nothing produces a loss. Why? Because of the curse of the ground. The land produces weeds and thorns (Gen. 3:17–19).[2] If left to itself, it reverts to wilderness. Wilderness is fit for beasts, not for men. Men are required by God to take dominion (Gen. 1:27–28).[3] Put differently, taking no action leads to the triumph of entropy: nature's constant movement toward disorder.

To work on projects that customers do not want to pay for produces a loss. Talk, when it leads to consumer-satisfying action, produces an increase. The deciding factor is ultimately a sanction. Someone with the power to provide a reward—a paying consumer—decides retroactively that the laborer's effort was praiseworthy.

B. Wasted Time

Talk is cheap, an American proverb says. This proverb says that talk is expensive. It produces poverty. In contrast is labor, which takes effort but produces an increase. Effort is a cost, but this cost produces a profit: a net increase.

---

2. Gary North, *Sovereignty and Dominion: An Economic Commentary on Genesis* (Dallas, Georgia: Point Five Press, [1982] 2012), ch. 12.

3. *Ibid.*, ch. 4.

Solomon indicates here that talk without action appears to be cost-free, but it produces poverty. It is therefore expensive. Why? Because the talker has wasted precious time, which is an irreplaceable resource. He is making a point: he who seeks something for nothing will fall into poverty. In contrast, labor is costly, but it produces an increase. Time spent on labor is profitable. The worker seeks something of greater value from the time he invests in labor. *The distinguishing feature is time*.

This conclusion is not stated in this proverb. But it is implied by this proverb. What do talk and labor have in common? Time. Neither the talker nor the laborer can escape the expenditure of time. Both must surrender time back to its owner: God. God gives it, then reclaims it, moment by moment. So, God expects us not to waste our time. We possess it only as stewards.

Conclusion

Solomon uses overstatement to make a point: the investment of time and effort in labor produces superior results to the investment of time and talk without labor. He who says nothing and then works will gain a better reward than he who talks and then does not work.

Jesus used this structure of cause and effect in a parable.

> But what think ye? A certain man had two sons; and he came to the first, and said, Son, go work to day in my vineyard. He answered and said, I will not: but afterward he repented, and went. And he came to the second, and said likewise. And he answered and said, I go, sir: and went not. Whether of them twain did the will of his father? They say unto him, The first. Jesus saith unto them, Verily I say unto you, That the publicans and the harlots go into the kingdom of God before you. For John came unto you in the way of righteousness, and ye believed him not: but the publicans and the harlots believed him: and ye, when ye had seen it, repented not afterward, that ye might believe him (Matt. 21:28–32).

Action speaks louder than words.

47

OPPRESSION AND MERCY

He that oppresseth the poor reproacheth his Maker: but he that honoureth him hath mercy on the poor.

A. Oppression Is Theocentric

This proverb highlights the ethical aspect of several Mosaic laws dealing with the economic oppression of the poor. Ultimately, the Mosaic laws prohibiting oppression are theocentric. *How you treat the poor reveals what you think of God.* The oppressor is said to reproach God. The Hebrew word can also mean "defy." But the contrast here is with honoring in the sense of upholding. So, the translators chose an English word that is an antonym of "honoring." To reproach God is to act as though God is not the kind of God He says He is. The person rebukes God in the sense of dishonoring him.

The merciful person has an open hand. Legally, he does not have to show favor to the poor man. This is a matter of voluntary action. *Mercy is optional, judicially speaking.* The Hebrew word is often translated as "gracious." "And he said, I will make all my goodness pass before thee, and I will proclaim the name of the LORD before thee; and will be **gracious** to whom I will be gracious, and will shew mercy on whom I will shew mercy" (Ex. 33:19). Grace is an unearned or undeserved blessing from God. *God is not obligated to show His grace.* David called on God to lift him up. "Have mercy upon me, O LORD; consider my trouble which I suffer of them that hate me, thou that liftest me up from the gates of death" (Ps. 9:13). The imagery here is that of God's bending down and lifting up. He stoops to give aid.

200

This is the sense of the Hebrew word in this proverb. Someone lifts up another person, who has fallen. He puts the person back on his feet. This decision is at the discretion of the one who shows mercy or grace.

In my commentary on Leviticus 25:17, "Ye shall not therefore oppress one another; but thou shalt fear thy God: for I am the LORD your God," I made the point that this oppression involved the misuse of civil government. A political insider gains power over others through the monopoly of violence possessed by the civil government.[1] This same misuse of civil government applied in a law of Exodus, "Thou shalt neither vex a stranger, nor oppress him: for ye were strangers in the land of Egypt" (Ex. 22:21).[2] The element of *legalized coercion* was involved.

This connection with the state is not self-evident in this proverb. The reader is assumed by Solomon to be aware of Mosaic laws relating to oppression. Whatever the source of the advantage possessed by the oppressor, he reproaches God by taking advantage of the person subordinate to him. This same element of subordination is implied by the Hebrew word translated as "mercy" in this proverb. The hierarchical relationship is not to be used to take advantage of the weaker party. To do this is to make a statement about God.

God is the supreme party in every relationship. He possesses complete power. If He wishes to impose negative sanctions on anyone, for any reason, He is legally able to do so. This was the main lesson that God taught Job (Job 38–41).[3] Judicially, man cannot claim innocence before God. He deserves whatever God hands out to him. But God is said to be merciful in history. So, in imitating God, covenant-keepers are not to take unfair advantage of the poor. On the contrary, they are to show mercy in the sense of grace: an unearned gift. This is what God does for mankind. Thus, when those calling themselves by His name show mercy and refrain from oppression, they testify accurately to the nature of God in history. They honor God.

---

1. Gary North, *Boundaries and Dominion: An Economic Commentary on Leviticus*, 2nd ed. (Dallas, Georgia: Point Five Press, [1994] 2012), ch. 26.

2. Gary North, *Authority and Dominion: An Economic Commentary on Exodus* (Dallas, Georgia: Point Five Press, 2012), Part 3, *Tools of Dominion* (1990), ch. 48.

3. Gary North, *Predictability and Dominion: An Economic Commentary on Job* (Dallas, Georgia: Point Five Press, 2012), ch. 6.

B. The Welfare State

Verses such as this one can be misused in the name of God. Promoters of coercion by the state in the name of social justice invoke Old Covenant passages that commend mercy. But their appeal to such passages is a cover for oppression. *The heart of mercy is its voluntarism.* The fact that a person is not compelled by civil law to lift up another person is what constitutes an act of compassion as merciful. If the person in need of assistance has a legal claim on compassion, then the issue is obedience to the civil law rather than grace.

Coercion goes beyond the undermining of mercy. The state takes money from one group and transfers it to another group. This transforms politics into special-interest competition. Gaining a majority in a civil government allows wealth redistribution by force. *This is the essence of judicial oppression.* It is common for defenders of the welfare state to justify this because the official targets of state power possess greater wealth than the official recipients. But the issue of economic oppression has to do with the use of the state's monopoly of violence to extract wealth from a targeted group of voters who did not win elections.

Consider the example of Nazi Germany. State laws restricting Jews and businesses operated by Jews were passed in the late 1930s. The fact that Jews as a voting bloc possessed greater per capita wealth than the Nazis who ran the government did not justify the use of state power to place them in a subordinate position. This should be obvious to every defender of the welfare state. So should the real name of the Nazi Party: the National Socialist Democratic Workers Party. But the universal response of welfare state advocates is to criticize these oppressive laws because of their racist and religious official justification, not because a socialist government took money from a group whose members possessed greater per capita wealth than the average German voter. They ignore the fact that had the German government not been socialistic, such legislation would not have been legal. It is the old issue of whose ox gets gored. It is not the fact of Nazi Germany's economic oppression that bothers welfare state proponents. Rather, it is the religious targets of this economic oppression that gains the criticism. Had the Jews been Presbyterians, welfare statists would be quite content with the state-enforced redistribution of wealth.

Conclusion

Oppression is evil. This includes economic oppression by the state. Mercy is righteous. Both statements constitute an affirmation of voluntarism. The state is to be put on a tight leash, neither oppressing the poor nor oppressing the less poor. In order to allow men to act mercifully, the state is not supposed to extract wealth by force from members of one group and then transfer it to members of other groups, all in the name of mercy. State-enforced mercy is state-enforced compulsion. The state is to be an agency of justice, not an agency of plunder.

48

THE FEAR OF THE LORD

Better is little with the fear of the LORD than great treasure and trouble therewith.

PROVERBS 15:16

Proverbs is filled with comparisons: better this than that. The *this* is usually reduced economic means. Consider the next proverb. "Better is a dinner of herbs where love is, than a stalled ox and hatred therewith" (v. 17).[1] Or these:

> Happy is the man that findeth wisdom, and the man that getteth understanding. For the merchandise of it is better than the merchandise of silver, and the gain thereof than fine gold (3:14).[2]

> Better is a little with righteousness than great revenues without right (16:8).[3]

> How much better is it to get wisdom than gold! and to get understanding rather to be chosen than silver! (16:16).[4]

Solomon understood the universality of men's quest for wealth. This quest was as all-encompassing then as it is today, whenever your today happens to be. Jesus referred to this desire to lay up treasure on earth. "But lay up for yourselves treasures in heaven, where neither moth nor rust doth corrupt, and where thieves do not break through nor steal: For where your treasure is, there will your heart be also" (Matt. 6:20–21).[5]

---

1. Chapter 49.
2. Chapter 9.
3. Chapter 51.
4. Chapter 53.
5. Gary North, *Priorities and Dominion: An Economic Commentary on Matthew*, 2nd ed. (Dallas, Georgia: Point Five Press, [2000] 2012), ch. 15.

The contrast here is between two conditions: (1) little with the fear of God and (2) great treasure with vexation or turmoil. The economist never wants to deal with rival conditions with more than one criterion in each. He wants to compare more with less. He wants especially to compare prices, which are conveniently numerical. He wants condition A with condition B, "other things being equal." But this is not the procedure of Solomon. He made his point by comparing mixtures.

He is really comparing the fear of the Lord vs. great treasure, but he adds qualifiers to catch our attention: a lack of wealth vs. vexation. Given the universality of the quest for great treasure, readers down through the ages and across borders have lived in societies that fully understood the benefits of wealth. Wealth is widely regarded as bringing happiness rather than vexation. Wealth is higher on most people's operational scale of values than the fear of the Lord. They spend more time worrying about their lack of wealth than worrying about their lack of any fear of the Lord.

To catch the reader's attention, Solomon compartmentalizes great treasure and vexation. This is what the great religious leaders have taught down through the ages, but it is still not widely believed by their followers. "I'm different," they think. "I would be content with great wealth." The great religious leaders have not been great in terms of the number of people, including their disciples, who personally adopted the leaders' teachings on wealth. There have always been more official believers than begging monks, which is why monks can make a living by begging. It there were more monks than followers, the competition for alms would be very great indeed.

Great treasure brings vexation to most people. This is because wealth has a social function. It requires owners to allocate it. There are many requests for wealth, many alternative and mutually exclusive uses for wealth. *With great wealth comes great responsibility.* Close behind wealth comes a stream of people, each with a suggestion about what the owner should do with his money. Jesus said, "For unto whomsoever much is given, of him shall be much required: and to whom men have committed much, of him they will ask the more" (Luke 12:48b).[6]

So, a wise person would rather possess little rather than accumulate trouble. But most people are not wise. Most people possess little

6. Gary North, *Treasure and Dominion: An Economic Commentary on Luke*, 2nd ed. (Dallas, Georgia: Point Five Press, [2000] 2012), ch. 28.

and accumulate trouble. They think, "Better to have a lot plus trouble than little plus trouble." This is the economist's preferred decision. But Solomon does not offer this choice. He offers the fear of God accompanied by little vs. great treasure accompanied by vexation.

The assumption underlying this proverb is that the fear of the Lord will provide ways of dealing with poverty, whereas great treasure is impotent in the face of vexation. In other words, there is greater legitimate hope in overcoming poverty by fearing God than in overcoming vexation by accumulating wealth. This proverb does not teach that poverty is a likely outcome of the fear of the Lord. It does teach that vexation is a likely outcome of great treasure.

This proverb is about two rival quests: the fear of the Lord vs. treasure. We are told that the fear of the Lord plus poverty is better than treasure plus vexation. This comparison would elicit a universal "So what?" if this proverb's presupposition were not that treasure leads to vexation.

This proverb does not assume that the fear of the Lord generally leads to poverty. The Mosaic law affirms the opposite (Deut. 28:1–14).[7] It makes a comparison: the fear of the Lord plus poverty (possible) is better than great treasure plus vexation (probable). If this were not the case, this proverb would not persuade treasure-seeking men to mend their mammon-governed ways.

Conclusion

The central issue here is the fear of the Lord. This is the central theme of the Bible's wisdom literature.

> And unto man he said, Behold, the fear of the Lord, that is wisdom; and to depart from evil is understanding (Job 28:28).

> The fear of the LORD is the beginning of wisdom: a good understanding have all they that do his commandments: his praise endureth for ever (Ps. 111:10).

> The fear of the LORD is the beginning of wisdom: and the knowledge of the holy is understanding (Prov. 9:10).

The comparison here is between great wealth and the fear of the Lord, which was also Jesus' primary comparison fear or love of God vs. fear or love of mammon. "No man can serve two masters: for ei-

---

7. Gary North, *Inheritance and Dominion: An Economic Commentary on Deuteronomy*, 2nd ed. (Dallas, Georgia: Point Five Press, [1999] 2012), ch. 69.

ther he will hate the one, and love the other; or else he will hold to the one, and despise the other. Ye cannot serve God and mammon" (Matt. 6:24).[8] Here is the proverb's argument. If the fear of the Lord accompanied by poverty is preferable to great wealth accompanied by vexation, how much more is the fear of the Lord with wealth preferable to wealth with vexation? It is not arguing that the fear of the Lord produces poverty. It is arguing that even if it did, poverty would be preferable to great wealth, for with great wealth comes vexation.

[handwritten note: how much more is the fear of the Lord with wealth preferable to weath with vexatin?]

---

8. North, *Priorities and Dominion*, ch. 14.

49

LOVE IS NOT FOR SALE

Better is a dinner of herbs where love is, than a stalled ox and hatred therewith.

PROVERBS 15:17

A. Love Before Wealth

Here we have another contrast where wealth is on the losing side: love vs. hatred. A dinner of herbs indicates poverty. There is no meat. There is no bread. There is basic nutrition, but calories are lacking. In contrast, there is an ox in a stall. There is capital. Presumably, there is productivity. The ox is working; his owner is benefitting. But his life is cursed by hatred.

Love, which is the superior possession, is accompanied by poverty. Love no more causes poverty than the fear of the Lord does, which is the superior possession in the previous proverb. This proverb rests on the possibility that love and poverty do go together on occasion.

The specific manifestation of poverty is worth considering. The dinner is sparse. Herbs are what people plant in a garden or collect in the woods. They provide flavor and some nutrition, but they cannot sustain life by themselves. If this diet lasts too long, the person dies of starvation. Eating only herbs is therefore a temporary condition. It reflects extreme poverty. This person is close to the bottom of the economic strata. Will he starve? No. David wrote: "I have been young, and now am old; yet have I not seen the righteous forsaken, nor his seed begging bread" (Ps. 37:25).[1] Times will get better very soon, but the transition will be to reduced poverty, not wealth.

---

1. Gary North, *Confidence and Dominion: An Economic Commentary on Psalms* (Dallas, Georgia: Point Five Press, 2012), ch. 6.

208

In contrast is a person with an ox and a stall. He is not facing disaster. He is nowhere near the bottom of the economic strata. But in his house is hatred. The very poor man will soon escape his life-and-death situation. This man has no comparable assurance of deliverance from hatred. He may get richer. He may get poorer. In either case, his situation would remain less preferable than the poor man's, for the poor man has love.

B. Love and Hatred

In neither case is the person's economic condition said to be either the cause or the effect of his emotional condition. Love and poverty can and do accompany each other. So do wealth and hatred. So desirable is love in comparison with hatred that this proverb insists that poverty with love is superior to wealth with hatred. This is not to say that poverty and hatred would not be worse. They would be worse, as surely as love and wealth would be better than love and poverty.

The focus of concern is not the economic condition of each of the two people, but rather their respective emotional conditions. This proverb implies that love and hatred are of greater concern than wealth and poverty. It implicitly recommends that we deal with first things first. The nearly universal concern of the poor man is to escape poverty. The almost equally universal concern of the rich man is to avoid poverty. Rich people and poor people focus their concern on their economic situation. This proverb indicates that this is a mistake. Of much greater concern are matters of the heart.

It is possible to work your way out of poverty. More important, it is possible to sleep your way into poverty. Several of Solomon's proverbs say this. If you can sleep your way into poverty, the presumption is that you can work your way out. Love and hatred are not so easily dealt with. Someone who works three extra hours a day and saves his wages will begin to climb out of poverty. There is no comparably predictable procedure for working your way out of hatred.

This proverb does not say whether the hatred is directed outward or inward. Hatred being what it is, it is usually a joint effort. Someone who responds with love to one who hates steadily undermines the hater's ability to maintain the hatred. Love disarms hatred. Jesus said: "Ye have heard that it hath been said, Thou shalt love thy neighbour, and hate thine enemy. But I say unto you, Love your enemies, bless them that curse you, do good to them that hate you, and pray for them which despitefully use you, and persecute you" (Matt.

5:43–44).[2] It takes a supremely self-conscious hatred to survive the weapon of love.

People are more ready to pay for a program on how to get rich than they are for a program on how to achieve love. This may be because they are more interested in wealth than love. It could also be that they think they are less likely to achieve love than wealth. They go for what they believe is likely to have greater success.

People who do not have riches are so besieged with problems related to poverty, which are highly specific, that they cannot imagine that being delivered from these problems will not make them happy. But with greater wealth inescapably comes greater responsibility. "For unto whomsoever much is given, of him shall be much required: and to whom men have committed much, of him they will ask the more" (Luke 12:48b).[3] These responsibilities involve greater care and wisdom to deal with than the decision to buy food at the market or to pay to get a car repaired.

There is a familiar aphorism: "Money can't buy happiness." Most adults are aware of this, yet they find it difficult to internalize it and make it a principle of their own decision-making process. The suggestion that money can buy love is not taken seriously even by children. In 1964, the Beatles had a #1 song, "Can't Buy Me Love." Supposedly, it expressed a fundamental principle of the revolutionary generation of 1965–70—"the 'sixties."

> Can't buy me love, love
> Can't buy me love.
>
> I'll buy you a diamond ring, my friend, if it makes you feel all right.
> I'll get you anything, my friend, if it makes you feel all right.
> 'Cause I don't care too much for money; money can't buy me love.

The irony here is that the person singing it had been able to accumulate so much money that buying the listener a diamond ring was nothing special. The Beatles went on to make more money—hundreds of millions of dollars, yen, pounds, deutschmarks—than any singing group in history.

> Can't buy me love, everybody tells me so.
> Can't buy me love, no, no, no, no.

2. Gary North, *Priorities and Dominion: An Economic Commentary on Matthew*, 2nd ed. (Dallas, Georgia: Point Five Press, [2000] 2012), ch. 10.
3. Gary North, *Treasure and Dominion: An Economic Commentary on Luke*, 2nd ed. (Dallas, Georgia: Point Five Press, [2000] 2012), ch. 28.

The group broke up in 1970, abandoning a gigantic stream of income. They could no longer stand to work with each other. Each of the members had at least one divorce. Ringo Starr, the drummer, became an alcoholic. (Alcoholics Anonymous helped restore him to sobriety.) In 1980, John Lennon was shot in front of his New York City apartment by someone who a few hours before had him autograph a record album cover. He died a few hours later. Money did not buy them love—not for long, anyway.

As for their American fans, the 1970s became the "me decade," marked by self-centeredness and the pursuit of wealth. The message of the 1964 lyrics did not stick.

Conclusion

The lure of wealth is great. So is the lure of love. Wealth is not evenly distributed. The ability to create it or receive it is limited to an elite. Love appears to be more randomly distributed, although proving this would be impossible. Wealth is expressed numerically. Love is not.

This proverb indicates that love is available to those who seek it. Otherwise, there would be no reason to put this in a long list of calls to ethical action. Men can pursue wealth. They can pursue love. But the ways to wealth are clearer than the ways to love.

50

MOVING FORWARD

The way of the slothful man is as an hedge of thorns: but the way of the righteous is made plain. ⤳ to cast up or raise

PROVERBS 15:19

A. Why Sloth Is an Ethical Issue

The contrast here is ethical: slothful vs. righteous. Initially, the passage seems to compare different patterns of behavior: sloth vs. righteousness. Sloth is a preference for doing as little as possible. Righteousness is a commitment to do that which is bounded by ethical standards. Why the contrast? It makes sense only if sloth is an ethical matter. A preference for doing as little as possible in any situation is identified here as a violation of God's ethical standards.

The Book of Proverbs is hostile to sloth. This proverb offers a unique assessment of sloth. It compares the slothful person's way of life with a hedge of thorns.

The way of the righteous person is different. The question is: In what way? The Hebrew word translated here as "plain" is misleading. It means to cast up or raise. "Sing unto God, sing praises to his name: **extol** him that rideth upon the heavens by his name JAH, and rejoice before him" (Ps. 68:4). "**Exalt** her, and she shall promote thee: she shall bring thee to honour, when thou dost embrace her" (Prov. 4:8). "Go through, go through the gates; prepare ye the way of the people; **cast** up, **cast** up the highways; gather out the stones; lift up a standard for the people" (Isa. 62:10). It is like a highway. It is raised higher than the drainage ditch at the side of the road. The righteous person's path in life is above the worst of the mud.

212

The indication here us that a slothful person's path is hedged by thorns. But why should this be? Does God direct the slothful person onto a pathway specially designed to thwart his efforts? Is life for a slothful person difficult because of an objective difference in his pathway? Or is his pathway filled with thorns subjectively? Is it resistant because he finds all effort distasteful?

B. Subjective Effort

The slothful man prefers ease to effort. He does not like to work. This proverb indicates that his pathway in life is a burden compared to that which the righteous person experiences.

A burden must be either carried or set down. The slothful person wants to lay his burden down. The righteous person wants to carry his own load. He does not want to be a burden to others.

The slothful person faces a life of thorns. It is not just that his path resists him. It is that it inflicts pain on him. It scratches him and scars him as he moves forward. It is easier not to move. It is easier to wait for someone else to clear the path.

The righteous person moves along a different pathway. It does not resist him. He can move faster than the slothful person can. He can move with less pain. He can move for a longer period before resting. The slothful person sees the world as being against him. The righteous person does not. The slothful person sees the world around him as a threat. The righteous person does not. The slothful person's assessment of the challenge he faces persuades him that it is safer to stand pat. The righteous person's assessment of the challenge he faces persuades him to keep moving forward because he is better off on the highway than in the ditch. Besides, if he sits down on the highway, he may get run over.

This passage identifies the covenant-keeper's path as objectively easier than the covenant-breaker's. Jesus taught the same thing.

> Come unto me, all ye that labour and are heavy laden, and I will give you rest. Take my yoke upon you, and learn of me; for I am meek and lowly in heart: and ye shall find rest unto your souls. For my yoke is easy, and my burden is light (Matt. 11:28–30).

Yet He also taught this: "Enter ye in at the strait gate: for wide is the gate, and broad is the way, that leadeth to destruction, and many there be which go in thereat: Because strait is the gate, and narrow is the way, which leadeth unto life, and few there be that find it" (Matt.

7:13–14).[1] The implication is that the more burdensome path is the wider path. Most people choose it. Therefore, either they hate righteousness so much that they prefer the extra burden of the wider path or else they do not perceive that the righteous life is less burdensome.

So, the contrast in this proverb is between the slothful person's perception of the challenge vs. the righteous person's perception of the challenge. By "perception," I do not mean a preliminary assessment of what lies ahead. I mean the actual experience.

This indicates that the righteous person will not only achieve more in life than the slothful person, his psychological experience will be superior. His tasks will seem easier to him than the slothful person's tasks will seem to him.

We are unable scientifically to measure difficulty, as perceived by one person. This is a subjective category. There are no measurements of subjective perception. We are unable to say just how much more difficult life seems to the slothful person in comparison to the righteous person. Yet this proverb speaks authoritatively to this issue. It tells us that life for the slothful person seems more of a burden to him than it seems to a righteous person.

Conclusion

The slothful person is hampered by his own ethical defect. Life seems too painful for him to commit the kind of resources and effort that are necessary to overcome life's challenges. In contrast, the righteous person perceives his challenges as those appropriate to highway existence. His environment does not seem as a threat to him.

Both perceptions are self-reinforcing. The slothful person does not like to work. He pays for this ethical defect by experiencing more trouble and no permanent triumph. In contrast, the righteous person is rewarded by experiencing a sense of liberation. His environment does not overcome his inner strength, which reinforces his perception that moving forward does not require superhuman effort.

---

1. Gary North, *Priorities and Dominion: An Economic Commentary on Matthew*, 2nd ed. (Dallas, Georgia: Point Five Press, [2000] 2012), ch. 17.

51

LAWFUL OWNERSHIP

Better is a little with righteousness than great revenues without right.

PROVERBS 16:8

A. Righteousness vs. Corruption

This is another comparison: righteousness and corruption. This contrast is heightened by a secondary contrast: more vs. less. This proverb does not call on the righteous person to pursue poverty rather than wealth. It calls on him to pursue righteousness rather than corruption.

The word translated "right" is the word *mishpat*. It usually relates to a judicial proceeding. "Thou shalt not wrest the **judgment** of thy poor in his cause" (Ex. 23:6). This law is aimed at members of a court. The sin of rendering false judgment can be the sin of judicial corruption. It can also be injustice, meaning the misuse of the civil law even though the case does not go to court.

This proverb makes its point by comparing a pair of combinations: poverty and righteousness vs. wealth and corruption. It does not imply that righteousness generally produces poverty. It does imply that one of corruption's goals is wealth. It says that when righteousness is accompanied by poverty, it is preferable to corruption accompanied by wealth. The negative condition of poverty is preferable when the price of wealth is corruption.

This proverb does not say that the price of righteousness is poverty. One cannot purchase righteousness with poverty. This proverb is not an affirmation of a vow of poverty or a monastic life. On the other hand, one can sometimes purchase wealth with corruption.

This proverb advises against this. It does so by comparing economic outcomes: wealth vs. poverty. Poverty is preferable.

This proverb makes ethical sense because the comparison is illustrated by rival economic conditions. Solomon knew that men rarely pursue poverty deliberately. Poverty is widely recognized as an undesirable condition. Later, we read: "Remove far from me vanity and lies: give me neither poverty nor riches; feed me with food convenient for me: Lest I be full, and deny thee, and say, Who is the LORD? or lest I be poor, and steal, and take the name of my God in vain" (30:8–9).[1] Yet Solomon says that poverty is superior to riches when riches have been achieved through corruption.

B. A Question of Sanctions

Poverty is not a sanction for righteousness, for it is a negative sanction. Wealth is a sanction for corruption. It is a positive sanction, for it is the goal of corruption. Men do not normally pursue negative sanctions when they break the law. We do not think of corrupt judges placing themselves at risk for the sake of poverty.

This proverb raises a question. Why is a negative sanction preferable to a positive sanction? The deciding factor is corruption. This raises a second question. What is it about corruption that weighs the case against wealth? Wealth is so universally perceived as something worth sacrificing for, and poverty is so universally avoided, that the deciding factor associated with corruption must be weighty indeed.

This proverb does not say what this factor is. There are several possible answers. First, corruption is its own curse, in the same sense that righteousness is its own reward. Corruption, like righteousness, stands alone as a negative value. There are ethical systems built in terms of this presupposition regarding righteousness for its own sake, most notably Immanuel Kant's.[2] Second, corruption brings inescapable eternal negative sanctions that are more fearful than the positive sanction of great wealth. This is the New Testament's teaching. Jesus said: "For what is a man profited, if he shall gain the whole world, and lose his own soul? or what shall a man give in exchange for his soul?" (Matt. 16:26).[3] Third, corruption may bring negative sanctions in his-

---

1. Chapter 85.

2. Immanual Kant, *Lectures on Ethics* (New York: Harper Torchbooks, [1780–81?] 1963).

3. Gary North, *Priorities and Dominion: An Economic Commentary on Matthew*, 2nd ed. (Dallas, Georgia: Point Five Press, [2000] 2012), ch. 35.

tory when it is discovered. This risk is not worth the benefits of great wealth. Fourth, corruption brings guilt, and guilt must be confessed publicly (Lev. 5:17; 6:4; Num. 5:6–7).

This proverb says that great wealth is not worth the price of being corrupt. It is not just that it is better not to gain the wealth that corruption can bring. It is actually better to be poor. Why, then, would a just and wise man become corrupt for the sake of wealth?

Conclusion

Injustice is to be avoided. No matter how much wealth a person can gain from injustice, it produces loss. The loss is so great that poverty is preferable.

52

WEIGHTS AND MEASURES

A just weight and balance are the LORD's: all the weights of the bag are his work.

PROVERBS 16:11

This proverb presents the theological foundation of a related pair of Mosaic laws.

> Ye shall do no unrighteousness in judgment, in meteyard, in weight, or in measure. Just balances, just weights, a just ephah, and a just hin, shall ye have: I am the LORD your God, which brought you out of the land of Egypt (Lev. 19:35–36).[1]

> Thou shalt not have in thy bag divers weights, a great and a small. Thou shalt not have in thine house divers measures, a great and a small. But thou shalt have a perfect and just weight, a perfect and just measure shalt thou have: that thy days may be lengthened in the land which the LORD thy God giveth thee. For all that do such things, and all that do unrighteously, are an abomination unto the LORD thy God (Deut. 25:13–16).[2]

The law in Leviticus refers back to the exodus as the law's justification. This points to God's office as cosmic Judge. He executes judgment in history. He delivered the Israelites out of the injustice of slavery in Egypt. The law in Deuteronomy presents a positive sanction for obedience: long life in Canaan. This is the same promise that is attached to the commandment to honor parents (Ex. 20:12),[3] which Paul identified as the first commandment with a promise (Eph. 6:2).

---

1. Gary North, *Boundaries and Dominion: An Economic Commentary on Leviticus*, 2nd ed. (Dallas, Georgia: Point Five Press, [1994] 2012), ch. 19.

2. Gary North, *Inheritance and Dominion: An Economic Commentary on Deuteronomy*, 2nd ed. (Dallas, Georgia: Point Five Press, [1999] 2012), ch. 65.

3. Gary North, *Authority and Dominion: An Economic Commentary on Exodus* (Dallas, Georgia: Point Five Press, 2012), Part 2, *Decalogue and Dominion* (1986), ch. 25.

Clearly, this was a fundamental law in Mosaic Israel.

This proverb speaks of just (*mishpat*) weights as belonging to God. This is peculiar language. Everything belongs to God (Ps. 50:10).[4] In what way are just weights uniquely His—sufficiently unique to be designated here as His?

Weights and measures are representative of God's law, meaning His ethical standards.[5] To use a false weight is to substitute a deceptive standard for the true one. This is analogous to calling God a deceiver. He establishes standards, and men are to honor these standards. The false weight deviates from a representative standard. It is used to benefit the person who uses the false weight, who is generally the seller of a good. It means treating different people differently judicially. This is a violation of God's rule of law.

> Ye shall not respect persons in judgment; but ye shall hear the small as well as the great; ye shall not be afraid of the face of man; for the judgment is God's: and the cause that is too hard for you, bring it unto me, and I will hear it (Deut. 1:17).[6]

> Thou shalt not wrest judgment; thou shalt not respect persons, neither take a gift: for a gift doth blind the eyes of the wise, and pervert the words of the righteous (Deut. 16:19).[7]

The seller of goods is a specialist in these goods. He possesses specialized information, including information on how to cheat a buyer. Yet he is trusted by the buyer. So, when he uses false weights to deceive the buyer, he has adopted different weights. He buys from his professional suppliers with one set of weights, but he then sells to retail buyers with a different set. This is a violation of the rule of law.

Standard weights are mandatory for every society. These standards must be legally enforceable in a civil court. Of course, there can also be private courts that enforce specialized standards. But final jurisdiction in history requires an agency of law enforcement that possesses the lawful authority to impose negative sanctions on convicted violators. The civil government possesses this authority with respect to weights and measures. There is no other common government in society. Weights and measures are supposed to apply equally to everyone inside the geographical borders of a civil government.

---

4. Gary North, *Confidence and Dominion: An Economic Commentary on Psalms* (Dallas, Georgia: Point Five Press, 2012), ch. 10.

5. North, *Boundaries and Dominion, op, cit.*

6. North, *Inheritance and Dominion*, ch. 4.

7. *Ibid.*, ch. 40.

So important are predictable and legally enforceable weights and measures that this proverb identifies these as belonging to God. Therefore, any alteration of these standards by self-interested individuals constitutes theft. This is more than theft. This is theft of God's property.

God, as the creator and sovereign sustainer of the universe, possesses lawful ownership of the creation. He delegates to individuals, voluntary organizations, and lawfully covenanted associations the authority to impose negative sanctions for violating God's laws. The law of weights and measures is highly important in the overall civil legal order. This law decentralizes law enforcement to individuals whose profession requires weights and measures. In this sense, weights are a matter of civil law and therefore possess covenantal importance. Everyone is required to honor the law, but because the actual weights are owned by profit-seeking sellers, *sellers become agents of the court*. Any attempt on their part to tamper with these weights constitutes a flagrant violation of God's law. This is why a related proverb says, "Divers weights, and divers measures, both of them are alike abomination to the LORD" (20:10),[8] which is a recapitulation of Deuteronomy 25:16. An abomination in the Mosaic law was a flagrant sin. It was often associated with idolatry (Deut. 13:13–15; 17:1–4; 18:10–12).

Conclusion

This proverb identifies weights and measures as belonging to God. Tampering with them is a serious offense: the theft of God's property. A false weight is an abomination in God's sight.

The law of weights and measures decentralizes law enforcement. It begins with self-government. Civil law serves as a back-up to this law. But God warns men that He is the ultimate enforcer of this law. He weighs all men in His balances, which are reliable.

---

8. Chapter 57.

53

VALUE AND PRICE

How much better is it to get wisdom than gold! and to get understanding rather to be chosen than silver!

A. Wisdom Over Gold

This is a famous proverb. It compares the value of wisdom to the value of gold. Understanding is similarly more valuable than silver.

In what way did Solomon contrast wisdom with silver? Gold is always worth more per ounce than silver. Does this proverb imply that wisdom is more valuable than understanding because gold is more valuable than silver? No. The Hebrew words for wisdom and understanding are found together at least 50 times in the same verses. The phrase, "wisdom and understanding," is used as a kind of poetic device. We rarely find the phrase, "understanding and wisdom," and the two most prominent cases where we do are in Daniel, in the mouths of Babylonians.

Solomon selects gold and silver as reference points in order to make a point: *the supreme value of wisdom.* Elsewhere, he selects rubies. "For wisdom is better than rubies; and all the things that may be desired are not to be compared to it" (8:11). Men throughout history have searched for gold and silver. They have sacrificed time and health to accumulate gold and silver. The metals' desirability, coupled with their scarcity, gives them great value. The implication is that wisdom and understanding are even more scarce, but they are not equally desired. Solomon insists that they are even more desirable.

Why are they not highly desired? Because they are in short supply.

221

It takes wisdom and understanding to perceive the high value of wisdom and understanding.

What is the essence of wisdom? Understanding the word of God and God's interpretation of it. Solomon insists, "There is no wisdom nor understanding nor counsel against the LORD" (21:30). Wisdom means being like-minded with God. It means thinking God's thoughts after Him. Paul wrote: "Casting down imaginations, and every high thing that exalteth itself against the knowledge of God, and bringing into captivity every thought to the obedience of Christ" (II Cor. 10:5). In short, *wisdom is the ability to think theocentrically*. God, not man, is the center of the universe. Men should think accordingly.

B. Unreliable Riches

Once accumulated, riches can be lost. Solomon says, "Labour not to be rich: cease from thine own wisdom. Wilt thou set thine eyes upon that which is not? for riches certainly make themselves wings; they fly away as an eagle toward heaven" (23:4–5).[1] Jesus said: "Lay not up for yourselves treasures upon earth, where moth and rust doth corrupt, and where thieves break through and steal" (Matt. 6:19).[2]

Wisdom can also flee, as Solomon discovered. In his old age, he worshipped the false gods of his wives (I Kings 11:4). But the implication of the Proverbs is that wisdom is more stable than wealth.

The Book of Proverbs from beginning to end is about the benefits of possessing wisdom. Everything else is second best, or even less. Yet the market for wisdom is limited. This is why Solomon compiled these proverbs. These proverbs are designed to impart wisdom. Part of that wisdom is the understanding that wisdom is so valuable. Most men do not recognize this, and fewer still follow what wisdom reveals, including Solomon. Solomon multiplied wives, which was prohibited to kings by the Mosaic law. "But he shall not multiply horses to himself, nor cause the people to return to Egypt, to the end that he should multiply horses: forasmuch as the LORD hath said unto you, Ye shall henceforth return no more that way. Neither shall he multiply wives to himself, that his heart turn not away: neither shall he greatly multiply to himself silver and gold" (Deut. 17:17).[3] Solomon multi-

---

1. Chapter 72.
2. Gary North, *Priorities and Dominion: An Economic Commentary on Matthew*, 2nd ed. (Dallas, Georgia: Point Five Press, [2000] 2012), ch. 13.
3. Gary North, *Inheritance and Dominion: An Economic Commentary on Deuteronomy*, 2nd ed. (Dallas, Georgia: Point Five Press, [1999] 2012), ch. 42:E.

Wisdom is Knowing and obeying God's law

plied all of the above (I Kings 10:28). He kept his horses, wives, and gold. He lost his wisdom, which had brought him renown.

C. Marketability

There is a ready market for gold and silver. Where such markets are prohibited by law, there are black markets for them. They are universally desired.

There is no comparable market for wisdom. There are markets for knowledge, since knowledge brings money, power, fame, and influence. Knowledge is not the same as wisdom. *Wisdom is knowing and obeying God's law.* Knowledge is information, and accurate information about the world's affairs can be marketed.

The wide market for gold and silver provides value. Value is imputed by acting individuals. They say, "this is valuable," and if they put their money where their mouths are, the price of the asset increases. In contrast, wisdom has no comparable market. Rulers through history have gone out of their way to exclude counselors who have possessed wisdom.

So, the market price of gold exceeds the price of wisdom. This fact is what gives this proverb its punch. Men can monitor the price of gold; they cannot monitor the price of wisdom.

There is a discrepancy between value and price. This discrepancy lies at the heart of economic theory. If value is subjective, as modern economists say that it is, then it cannot be measured. There is no objective measure of subjective value. There is more or less value, but not *exactly this much* more or less.[4] In contrast, prices are objective. The price of harlotry is higher to the buyer than the price of the gospel is to the recipient. This does not mean that harlotry is more valuable than the gospel. The opposite is true.

Conclusion

There is a saying attributed to a skeptic, Oscar Wilde, that a cynic knows the price of everything and the value of nothing. This saying is an application of this proverb's insight. The value of wisdom is higher than the value of gold. There is an objective price of gold at this moment. There is no objective price of wisdom at this moment. Wisdom can purchased, which is what the Book of Proverbs is all

---

4. Murray N. Rothbard, *Man, Economy, and State: A Treatise on Economic Principles,* 2nd ed. (Auburn, Alabama: Mises Institute, [1962] 2009), ch. 1:5:A.

about. *The price of wisdom is obeying God's word*. It is too high a price for imperfect men to pay. But Christ paid it, and He makes wisdom available through grace to His people. "But he that is spiritual judgeth all things, yet he himself is judged of no man. For who hath known the mind of the Lord, that he may instruct him? But we have the mind of Christ" (I Cor. 2:15–16).[5]

The price of wisdom is obeying God's word.

"But we have the mind of Christ."

5. Gary North, *Judgment and Dominion: An Economic Commentary on First Corinthians*, 2nd ed. (Dallas, Georgia: Point Five Press, [2001] 2012), ch. 2.

54

THE HIGH WALL OF WEALTH

The rich man's wealth is his strong city, and as an high wall in his own conceit.

PROVERBS 18:11

This proverb asserts that wealth is a rich man's strong city. A strong city in the ancient world was a walled city. A wall slowed down invaders. Wealth serves as the equivalent of an ancient high wall for the rich person. It resists invaders. The stated advantage here is the ability to insulate yourself from the calamities that poor people faced until the twentieth century in industrial societies, and which billions of poor people face in India and China in the early twenty-first.

The rich man's family is the next-to-the last to face starvation in a famine, after senior government officials. His family does not freeze in the winter. In summers, he and his family members can journey to a cooler location if he lives without air conditioning, which became universal in the middle-class West after 1960.

The rich man has a lot of money. Money is the most marketable commodity. At some price, everyone wants more of it. So, the rich man can buy protection from specialists who are in a position to provide it. This purchase of safety can take many forms. One is outright bribery of government officials. Another is "protection money" paid to a local criminal gang. Another is commercial insurance. A crisis that a rich man cannot escape through surrendering a portion of his wealth is usually either a society-wide crisis, such as a plague or a lost war, or else a disease that medical science has not yet eliminated.

Money offers protection because it is the most marketable commodity. People under almost all situations are willing to exchange goods and services for money. This means that whatever the circumstances, a

225

rich man can find someone to sell him whatever he wants or needs. So, he need not plan carefully for the future. No matter what time brings, he will be able to buy whatever he wants. This puts him in a situation that few people in history have enjoyed. He is part of an elite.

If events around a rich man cannot penetrate his shield of money, then he is tempted to imagine that he needs no outside agency to protect him. He forgets where he got his wealth. Moses warned against this attitude of confidence, "And thou say in thine heart, My power and the might of mine hand hath gotten me this wealth. But thou shalt remember the LORD thy God: for it is he that giveth thee power to get wealth, that he may establish his covenant which he sware unto thy fathers, as it is this day" (Deut. 8:17–18).[1] Wealth has a covenantal purpose. It is not to make a man impervious to disaster, but rather to make him more aware of God's covenant and its positive sanctions. He should also not forget its negative sanctions. "And it shall be, if thou do at all forget the LORD thy God, and walk after other gods, and serve them, and worship them, I testify against you this day that ye shall surely perish" (Deut. 8:19).[2]

Men are to trust the God of the covenant. Men's trust should be in the Giver, not the gift. "Every good gift and every perfect gift is from above, and cometh down from the Father of lights, with whom is no variableness, neither shadow of turning" (James 1:17). Yet men who accumulate great wealth tend to attribute their success to their own abilities. This is their downfall. "And again I say unto you, It is easier for a camel to go through the eye of a needle, than for a rich man to enter into the kingdom of God" (Matt. 19:24).[3]

This proverb adds, "as an high wall in his own **conceit**." This is an odd translation. The Hebrew word is usually translated as "image" (Lev. 26:1; Num. 33:52) or "picture" (Prov. 25:11). It is translated as "imagery" once (Ezek. 8:11). Closer to the meaning here is this: "Their eyes stand out with fatness: they have more than heart could **wish**" (Ps. 73:7). The English word "wish" is misleading. The word "imaginations" is much closer. The New American Standard Version translates the clause, "and like a high wall in his imagination."

A high wall is his image of the meaning of his wealth. It surrounds him. It keeps troubles away.

1. Gary North, *Inheritance and Dominion: An Economic Commentary on Deuteronomy*, 2nd ed. (Dallas, Georgia: Point Five Press, [1999] 2012), ch. 22.

2. *Ibid.*, ch. 23.

3. Gary North, *Priorities and Dominion: An Economic Commentary on Matthew*, 2nd ed. (Dallas, Georgia: Point Five Press, [2000] 2012), ch. 38.

This proverb makes this comparison of wealth and an image of safety. It does not say that the wealthy person is self-deluded. It does not have to. Moses taught this in Deuteronomy 8. High walls offer no protection against negative covenant sanctions. This was the message of the fall of Jericho, the first city inside Canaan to fall to the invading Israelites.

Conclusion

We are not to trust in anything but the God of the covenant. "Some trust in chariots, and some in horses: but we will remember the name of the LORD our God" (Ps. 20:7). Wealth is a weak reed to rest on in history. It is utterly useless to trust in wealth for eternity. "For we brought nothing into this world, and it is certain we can carry nothing out" (I Tim. 6:7).[4]

Wealth seems to offer protection. Under most circumstances, it does. But this protection for a time in history is an illusion in eternity. To trust in wealth testifies to spiritual error. Yet it is an almost universal error among adults. In this sense, children are much wiser. They trust in their parents, not in their wealth. They trust in a highly personal world of people and commitments. It is adults who trust more in pieces of metal, or worse, plastic.

---

4. Gary North, *Hierarchy and Dominion: An Economic Commentary on First Timothy* (Dallas, Georgia: Point Five Press, 2012), ch. 10.

55

RIVAL INHERITANCE PROGRAMS

House and riches are the inheritance of fathers and a prudent wife is from the LORD.

PROVERBS 19:14

This proverb identifies the proximate source of earthly blessings. A house and wealth come from one's father. God supplies a wise wife. The recipient gains all of these assets from others. Those men who are the heirs of great wealth should not attribute their success to themselves. Neither should a husband of a wise wife attribute this benefit to himself.

In some cases, a man may have accumulated houses and wealth through his own efforts. But a wise wife is uniquely a gift from God. He can take no credit for her. He may be tempted to attribute his economic success to his own efforts, but this is forthrightly a mistake when speaking of a wise wife.

Proverbs identifies a wise wife as an asset of greater value than jewels. "Who can find a virtuous woman? for her price is far above rubies" (31:10).[1] So, Solomon offers a contrast: objects that can be inherited can be attributed to men's efforts, either the original wealth builder or the heir, but a wise wife is a gift from God. This is the greater gift. An inheritance is desirable, but a wise wife is a greater blessing. This greater blessing is not the work of any man's hands or efforts. It is the work of God.

This proverb points to the legitimacy of inherited wealth. The recipient is not warned to beware of his inheritance. This implies that the builder of a fortune can legitimately pass the wealth to his sons.

---

1. Chapter 85.

Intergenerational wealth is a good thing. "A good man leaveth an inheritance to his children's children: and the wealth of the sinner is laid up for the just" (13:22).[2] Wealth gained through righteous behavior is not stigmatized in the Bible. "The LORD shall command the blessing upon thee in thy storehouses, and in all that thou settest thine hand unto; and he shall bless thee in the land which the LORD thy God giveth thee" (Deut. 28:8). "And the LORD shall make thee plenteous in goods, in the fruit of thy body, and in the fruit of thy cattle, and in the fruit of thy ground, in the land which the LORD sware unto thy fathers to give thee" (Deut. 28:11).[3]

So important was inheritance in the Mosaic law that a father was not permitted to disinherit a son without judicial cause. The eldest son of a despised first wife received a double portion, based on his legal status as firstborn, irrespective of a man's greater favor shown to a later wife (Deut. 21:15–17).[4]

The biblical law of inheritance was rejected by European societies. They substituted primogeniture, where the eldest son inherited the landed estate. Then they added entail: a prohibition on the sale of the landed estate. Inheriting eldest sons got around this by indebting the estate. They spent the money, and the creditors inherited the land.

In the twentieth century, this system came under attack. Heavy inheritance taxes stripped European families of large landed estates. Taxes also stripped them of large amounts of money, even if they had no land. A growing hostility of intra-family inheritance became visible, decade by decade. The most famous early advocate of heavy inheritance taxes was Andrew Carnegie, the atheistic, Darwinian American industrialist, in his 1889 essay, "The Gospel of Wealth."

The state has substituted itself for the family. It provides old age pensions and old age medical services, just as sons have done for millennia. It also pays for the education of children, and it has made school attendance compulsory. To pay for all this, the state has drastically increased taxes. So, sons now pay the state rather than their own parents. The inheritance-disinheritance system has become impersonal and statist. This way, politicians get credit for helping people supposedly in need, bureaucrats receive high salaries for administering the programs, and ethical considerations relating to fam-

---

2. Chapter 41.

3. Gary North, *Inheritance and Dominion: An Economic Commentary on Deuteronomy*, 2nd ed. (Dallas, Georgia: Point Five Press, [1999] 2012), ch. 69.

4. *Ibid.*, ch. 50.

ily inheritance are abandoned. Numerical criteria, such as age and income level, are substituted for ethics.

Rich families have evaded taxes in the United States by setting up public trusts and foundations. They have transferred control of the family inheritance to boards of trustees, where the donors and their heirs sit. They can exercise indirect control over the use of what had been family assets. These funds legally must be used for government-approved purposes. The families have maintained influence over the specifics of how the now tax-exempt assets would be used down through the generations. Often, the foundations have borne the donating family's names. A major goal of great families—fame—has thereby been preserved.

Conclusion

We inherit things of real value. The family supplies houses and other physical assets. God the Father supplies a prudent wife. Both inheritances are governed by God's family covenant, which has laws. These laws are the basis of a good inheritance (Deut. 28:1–14).

There is a war against God's laws of inheritance. Unwise men choose imprudent wives. Then they squander their inheritances. The modern state also undermines the family inheritance by substituting tax-funded welfare programs. These programs undermine the ethical standards of the covenant. They substitute the political covenant for the family covenant.

56

LENDING TO GOD

He that hath pity upon the poor lendeth unto the LORD; and that which he hath given will he pay him again.

PROVERBS 19:17

A. An Open Hand for the Poor

The Hebrew word here translated as "pity" elsewhere is translated as "mercy." "He that despiseth his neighbour sinneth: but he that hath mercy on the poor, happy is he" (14:21).[1] "He that oppresseth the poor reproacheth his Maker: but he that honoureth him hath mercy on the poor" (14:31).[2] The idea is not that a person has silent emotional empathy—pity—for the poor but rather that he does something good for the poor.

He who gives something of value to the poor man, which would include his time, is said to lend to God. The meaning of the Hebrew word is the same as it is in the Mosaic law: "He shall lend to thee, and thou shalt not lend to him: he shall be the head, and thou shalt be the tail" (Deut. 28:44). But does this language apply to someone who lends to God? Does God become his tail, to be wagged at will?

The relationship of God to man is always that of lender and borrower. Jesus told His disciples to pray: "And forgive us our debts, as we forgive our debtors" (Matt. 6:12).[3] This reflects a fundamental biblical principle: *grace precedes law*. Man is always beholden to God.

---

1. Chapter 45.
2. Chapter 47.
3. Gary North, *Priorities and Dominion: An Economic Commentary on Matthew*, 2nd ed. (Dallas, Georgia: Point Five Press, [2000] 2012), ch. 12:C.

So, in what way can it be said that by showing mercy to a poor person, a man lends to God?

The second part of this proverb supplies the answer: "and that which he hath given will he pay him again." The English text suffers from what English teachers call "indefinite pronoun reference." Who is "he" who will pay "him" again? It is obvious conceptually, though not grammatically, that God is the person who will repay. Can the giver count on God? Yes. God is reliable. But this willingness on God's part to repay does not place the merciful person in a net creditor position in relation to God. Rather, it marginally reduces the magnitude of the debt owed to God, which is enormous.

Every good gift comes from God. "Every good gift and every perfect gift is from above, and cometh down from the Father of lights, with whom is no variableness, neither shadow of turning" (James 1:17).[4] Moses said the same thing: "But thou shalt remember the LORD thy God: for it is he that giveth thee power to get wealth, that he may establish his covenant which he sware unto thy fathers, as it is this day" (Deut. 8:18).[5] The motivation to show mercy to the poor is no less a gift from God than any other mark of grace in someone's life. The person who shows mercy to the poor is still in debt to God. But in terms of success in history, the message of this proverb is clear: that which is given up for mercy's sake will return. "Cast thy bread upon the waters: for thou shalt find it after many days" (Eccl. 11:1).

B. Representation

Why is a gift to the poor a loan to God? The answer is in the biblical doctrine of representation. Jesus taught this regarding the final judgment.

> Then shall the King say unto them on his right hand, Come, ye blessed of my Father, inherit the kingdom prepared for you from the foundation of the world: For I was an hungred, and ye gave me meat: I was thirsty, and ye gave me drink: I was a stranger, and ye took me in: Naked, and ye clothed me: I was sick, and ye visited me: I was in prison, and ye came unto me. Then shall the righteous answer him, saying, Lord, when saw we thee an hungred, and fed thee? or thirsty, and gave thee drink? When saw we thee a stranger, and took thee in? or naked, and clothed thee? Or when saw we thee sick, or in prison, and came unto thee? And the King shall answer and

4. Gary North, *Ethics and Dominion: An Economic Commentary on the Epistles* (Dallas, Georgia: Point Five Press, 2012), ch. 33.
5. Gary North, *Inheritance and Dominion: An Economic Commentary on Deuteronomy*, 2nd ed. (Dallas, Georgia: Point Five Press, [1999] 2012), ch. 22.

say unto them, Verily I say unto you, Inasmuch as ye have done it unto one of the least of these my brethren, ye have done it unto me (Matt. 25:34–40).

The act of mercy to the poor is an act of repayment to God. The act of mercy to the poor man is not legally mandated. The repayment to God is legally mandated, but by God's court, not man's. Man does not possess sufficient wealth to repay God. God is not in need of repayment economically, but man is in need of a means of repayment judicially. God's honor must be upheld. Adam violated it. Justice, mercy, and humility are the coin of God's realm.

> Will the LORD be pleased with thousands of rams, or with ten thousands of rivers of oil? shall I give my firstborn for my transgression, the fruit of my body for the sin of my soul? He hath shewed thee, O man, what is good; and what doth the LORD require of thee, but to do justly, and to love mercy, and to walk humbly with thy God (Micah 6:7–8)?

So, there is a great need for suitable representatives. The poor serve as God's representatives. What men do for the least of these, they do unto God.

C. Repayment in History

Jesus taught that whatever of marketable value is surrendered in history will be repaid in eternity.

> Lay not up for yourselves treasures upon earth, where moth and rust doth corrupt, and where thieves break through and steal: But lay up for yourselves treasures in heaven, where neither moth nor rust doth corrupt, and where thieves do not break through nor steal: For where your treasure is, there will your heart be also (Matt. 6:19–21).[6]

The Old Covenant had no concept of eternity as a warehouse of treasure to be stockpiled in history. The Old Testament's concept of causation was historical. The kingdom of God is a temporal kingdom, the Old Testament taught. The New Testament teaches that God's kingdom is both temporal and eternal.

> Fear not, little flock; for it is your Father's good pleasure to give you the kingdom. Sell that ye have, and give alms; provide yourselves bags which wax not old, a treasure in the heavens that faileth not, where no thief approacheth, neither moth corrupteth. For where your treasure is, there will your heart be also (Luke 12:32–34).[7]

---

6. North, *Priorities and Dominion*, ch. 13.

7. Gary North, *Treasure and Dominion: An Economic Commentary on Luke,* 2nd ed. (Dallas, Georgia: Point Five Press, [2000] 2012), ch. 26.

Being a temporal kingdom, there is repayment in history.

And Jesus said unto them, Verily I say unto you, That ye which have followed me, in the regeneration when the Son of man shall sit in the throne of his glory, ye also shall sit upon twelve thrones, judging the twelve tribes of Israel. And every one that hath forsaken houses, or brethren, or sisters, or father, or mother, or wife, or children, or lands, for my name's sake, shall receive an hundredfold, and shall inherit everlasting life (Matt. 19:28–29).[8]

So, covenantal causation is not limited to eternity. It operates in history, as a foretaste of eternity—a down payment or earnest payment. This inheritance is mediated by the Holy Spirit, Paul wrote. "In whom ye also trusted, after that ye heard the word of truth, the gospel of your salvation: in whom also after that ye believed, ye were sealed with that holy Spirit of promise, Which is the earnest of our inheritance until the redemption of the purchased possession, unto the praise of his glory" (Eph. 1:13–14).

Conclusion

Showing mercy to the poor is both sacrificial and self-interested. It is an act of sacrifice on behalf of others—immediate loss—but also a self-interested act: future returns. The giver must have faith in God as a creditor who forgives. Otherwise, the act of mercy is perceived by the donor a one-way event. To imagine that it is a one-way event is to lack faith in God's system of covenantal causation. This reduces the amount of mercy shown, since it removes a positive sanction that is a great motivation.

We must not regard God as a debtor who faithfully repays. Such an outlook places man in control over God. After all, the borrower is servant to the lender (22:7).[9] God's covenant is seen as a way to manipulate God. Yet the purpose of the sanctions is to reinforce men's faith in the reliability of God's covenant (Deut. 8:18).[10] The incorrect view is analogous to a cartoon I saw in the early 1960s. Two rats are in a psychologist's rat-training cage, called a Skinner box in honor of experimental psychologist B. F. Skinner. In front of one rat is a horizontal lever and a vertical slot. The rat says to his associate, "I've got this psychologist completely trained. Every time I press this lever, he drops food through the slot."

The giver represents God to the recipient: the true source of un-

---

8. North, *Priorities and Dominion*, ch. 39.
9. Chapter 67.
10. North, *Inheritance and Dominion*, ch. 22.

deserved benefits, i.e., the source of grace. The giver is to give thanks to God. Simultaneously, the recipient represents God to the giver. Man lends to God by way of the recipient. He also is to give thanks to God: for the wealth to give, for the opportunity to give, and for the motivation to give.

57

DIVERSE WEIGHTS

Divers weights, and divers measures, both of them are alike abomination to the LORD.

PROVERBS 20:10

This is a reconfirmation of Proverbs 11:1: "A false balance is abomination to the LORD: but a just weight is his delight."[1] It also recapitulates Proverbs 16:11: "A just weight and balance are the LORD's: all the weights of the bag are his work."[2] These are all brief summaries of the law: "Ye shall do no unrighteousness in judgment, in meteyard, in weight, or in measure. Just balances, just weights, a just ephah, and a just hin, shall ye have: I am the LORD your God, which brought you out of the land of Egypt" (Lev. 19:35–36).[3] The link between the honest weights and justice is made explicit in this text.

The nature of the prohibition is clarified here: *deception*. There are more than one standard being used in exchanges. Presumably, this applies to the sellers of goods. They possess the technical tools of weighing and measuring. When they buy, they use one set. When they sell, they use another set. They play upon the ignorance of buyers and sellers. But it is more likely that buyers are the primary victims. In a division-of-labor society, there is a chain of sellers, from manufacturer to the final retailer. Sellers are likely to possess the weighing and measuring devices of their trade. A wholesaler is less likely to use diverse weights, because he knows that the buyer is a specialist in his particular market niche in the chain of distribution. He will have

---

1. Chapter 29.
2. Chapter 52.
3. Gary North, *Boundaries and Dominion: An Economic Commentary on Leviticus*, 2nd ed. (Dallas, Georgia: Point Five Press, [1994] 2012), ch. 19.

the same measuring devices. The likelihood of a successful deception is low. The more transactions take place, the more likely there is an opportunity for the deception to be revealed.

The retail seller is therefore the most likely culprit. The consumer relies on the seller to use honest scales. He is more likely to be the first victim than a wholesaler further down in the chain of transactions.

The term is used for truly heinous infractions of the Mosaic law. Some were sexual. They threatened the land. "Ye shall therefore keep my statutes and my judgments, and shall not commit any of these abominations; neither any of your own nation, nor any stranger that sojourneth among you" (Lev. 18:26). Others were related to witchcraft. These were crimes for which God drove the Canaanites out of the land. "For all that do these things are an abomination unto the LORD: and because of these abominations the LORD thy God doth drive them out from before thee" (Deut. 18:12). Others were theological. "The graven images of their gods shall ye burn with fire: thou shalt not desire the silver or gold that is on them, nor take it unto thee, lest thou be snared therein: for it is an abomination to the LORD thy God" (Deut. 7:25). "Cursed be the man that maketh any graven or molten image, an abomination unto the LORD, the work of the hands of the craftsman, and putteth it in a secret place. And all the people shall answer and say, Amen" (Deut. 27:15). In short, these were the most serious crimes in Mosaic Israel.

This proverb identifies diverse weights as an abomination. This was also true of Proverbs 11:1. What is the nature of the infraction that justified such a condemnation? There is no other business practice that is so identified.

Conclusion

The use of deceptive scales is a form of theft. It is a continuing form of theft. The false weights are not used only one time. This crime reveals a mentality hostile to justice. God abhors it.

The judicial responsibility associated with every sin is in part related to the representation of God made by the sin in question. False measures seem disproportionately condemned. We should attempt to understand the reason for this condemnation. The use of diverse measures representatively attributes to God the character of an unjust ruler. Such a ruler refuses to honor the rule of law. "One law shall be to him that is homeborn, and unto the stranger that sojourneth among you" (Ex. 12:49).[4] God is pictured as pretending to honor the principle, just as the businessman pretends to have one set of weights as both buyer and seller. God is therefore represented as a deceiver in His capacity as a judge. This is a false witness. We are reminded that God's justice is at the heart of the covenant.

---

4. Gary North, *Authority and Dominion: An Economic Commentary on Exodus* (Dallas, Georgia: Point Five Press, 2012), Part 1, *Representation and Dominion* (1985), ch. 14.

58

THE HIGH PRICE OF SLUMBER

Love not sleep, lest thou come to poverty; open thine eyes, and thou shalt be satisfied with bread.

PROVERBS 20:13

This is another proverb that identifies an unwillingness to work with poverty. A person who prefers sleep to work had better prefer poverty to wealth. In two other proverbs—actually one, which is then repeated—laziness is described as folded hands. "Yet a little sleep, a little slumber, a little folding of the hands to sleep" (Prov. 6:10; cf. 24:33[1]). From excessive slumber to poverty: this is causation. A demonstrated preference for sleep is sufficient to produce poverty.

This cause-and-effect relationship is the result of God's curse of the earth (Gen. 3:17–19).[2] People must labor in order to get the earth to produce the goods they want in the quantities they want. People must become productive. This means that their output should be valued more highly than their inputs. The crucial input, for humanity and for most individuals, is labor. Without labor, the land's output is insufficient to provide people with the environment they want.

We say that a person sees an opportunity. Rarely does anyone see an opportunity, other than a coin in a gutter. He *imagines* an opportunity. He *perceives* an opportunity. But we say that he sees an opportunity. This is poetic language. This proverb uses poetic language.

The second clause says, "open thine eyes, and thou shalt be satisfied with bread." Opened eyes are contrasted with closed eyes. Solo-

---

1. Chapter 75.
2. Gary North, *Sovereignty and Dominion: An Economic Commentary on Genesis* (Dallas, Georgia: Point Five Press, [1982] 2012), ch. 12.

mon is using sleep as a poetic identification of laziness. So, open eyes are the poetic identification of work. Literally, a person with open eyes who is watching a television screen is not productive. He might as well be sleeping.

Causation in history is not from mere open eyes to bread, which is the poetic symbol of abundance. It is from work to bread. So, the terminology is poetic, not literal. A person could have his eyes closed and be imagining the details of some new invention. That could be very productive. Sleep is different. It is a mental escape from coherent causation. Dreams are not limited by the normal processes of nature.

Benjamin Franklin in a letter made the comment, "time is money." He meant this: with time, you can make money. Waste time, and you will not make money.

He who is lazy is not merely a time-waster. He is a wealth-waster. He throws away a crucial source of wealth: time. The result of not gaining wealth is poverty. This proverb is clear about economic cause and effect.

"Open thine eyes, and thou shalt be satisfied with bread." To open one's eyes is to wake up. Of course, waking up is not sufficient. Getting up is also important. So is getting busy.

To be satisfied with bread means to be filled with food, and the text can be translated this way. The person who is an active worker is unlikely to go hungry. The person who is lazy, unless he inherited wealth, is likely to be hungry.

Conclusion

This passage reaffirms a continuing theme in Proverbs. To gain poverty, all it takes is to do nothing. The manifestation of doing nothing is sleep. The sleeping person is not in touch with reality and its limitations. He does not change the world around him. The curse of the ground (Gen. 3:17–19) is not overcome by his active labor.

There is economic cause and effect in history. There is a predictable relationship between work and prosperity, and also between laziness and poverty. This proverb does not affirm the labor theory of value. It affirms the *labor theory of opportunity*. He who slumbers will miss out. He will not be able to make good use of the opportunities that are out there, ready to be implemented.

59

DECEPTIVE BARGAINING

It is naught, it is naught, saith the buyer: but when he is gone his way, then he boasteth.

PROVERBS 20:14

The buyer is described as saying two different things about the same transaction. It is clear from this proverb that what he tells the seller is one thing. What he tells his associates is another.

In the first case, he is in a competitive situation. He is trying to avoid paying what the seller has asked for his good. The buyer wants to pay less. Free market economics ever since Adam Smith has rested on the axiom that people prefer to pay less than more, unless charity is involved. What the buyer says to the seller here is consistent with what free market economics teaches about pricing.

In the second case, he is the proud owner of the item he was seeking to purchase. Part of his pride stems from the low price he paid to purchase it. He wants to impress others with his skill as a bargainer. So, the item he told the seller was worth nothing, he now tells others was a tremendous bargain.

This proverb does not recommend this kind of sharp bargaining. It merely describes what was common in Solomon's day, and what is still common in my day.

A. Negotiating the Price

Buyers (sellers of money) want to buy low. They do not want to pay a seller more than the seller is willing to accept. The description here indicates that the market was open to bargaining. Sellers asked more than they expected to receive. Buyers offered less than they expected to pay.

241

"It is naught." The prospective seller knows that the prospective buyer does not really believe this. The phrase is merely rhetoric—a code phrase for "offer me a lower price." No one pays good money for something he believes is worth nothing. The fact that he is willing to spend time negotiating indicates that he thinks the item is worth something.

Why should the prospective buyer believe that the prospective seller is willing to lower the price? Because the marketplace is commonly marked by sellers who trade on the ignorance of buyers. Buyers do not know for sure what the seller is willing to accept. Sellers do not know what a particular buyer will pay. So, the two compete because of the existence of a zone of ignorance.

When someone walks into a large retail store that has priced all items with bar codes connected to a computer system, he does not bother to negotiate with a clerk. The clerk has no authority or ability to change the price. The price has been set by a third party who does not meet with buyers. The buyer pays and leaves. Pricing is established in terms of volume. The store makes a low profit margin per sale. Its profit comes from large volume: high turnover per unit of time. Large volume requires rapid individual sales. If the buyer wants a lower price, he must go to another store.

The zone of ignorance between buyer and seller is nonexistent in a store that sells with computerized bar codes. The buyer knows exactly what the seller is willing to take for the item. The seller is not concerned with what the individual buyer is willing to pay. Profit comes from high-volume sales, not from successful negotiation with each seller. The seller saves time by refusing to negotiate on price. So does the buyer.

If a buyer wants a lower price, he must spend time shopping. The seller competes against other sellers. The buyer competes against other buyers. In a market in which knowledge is widely distributed and cheap to buy, sellers do not compete against buyers. Such negotiation takes place only where there are zones of ignorance about alternatives. The broader the information base about a specific product, the less relevant is information about what a particular buyer or seller will accept as a transaction price.

The residential real estate market has zones of ignorance because each home is different. Sellers announce prices higher than they are willing to accept. Buyers offer lower prices than they are willing to pay. Negotiation is not face to face. It is done through intermediaries: real estate agents. But any home buyer who says "It is naught" in front of a seller is making a big mistake. The seller's wife will resent such an assessment. The wise approach is to say, "This is lovely. It is too bad we just can't afford it." But in most cases, the agent who shows the home asks the seller to be absent at the time of the walk-through. Bargaining is much more impersonal. It is done with a signed contract and earnest money.[1]

B. More Truth, More Sales

If a seller has a reputation for hard bargaining, well-informed buyers will either bargain sharply or go elsewhere to buy, because they do not think their bargaining skills are superior to the seller's skills.

Sellers who do not stick to their initial prices invite sharp-bargaining buyers. They also lose time negotiating. The time cost per sale increases.

Modern capitalism is generally price competitive. It seeks to broaden the market by lowering prices. A seller seeks to increase his product's market share by lowering prices and attracting buyers who had been priced out of the market.

There are niche markets that are not price competitive. These are usually markets for the rich or the poor. The seller who sells a unique service to rich people, like the junk dealer who sells one-of-a-kind used goods to poor people, does not price their goods to sell in large numbers. So, both men trade on buyers' ignorance of alternatives. The vast majority of buyers do not shop regularly at junk stores or boutiques for custom-made goods.

Mass production encourages more truth. Buyers announce their best price and stick to it unless they are losing a lot of money. If they lose money, they change their pricing structure in one shot by entering new prices in the bar code computer.

Mass production encourages high-volume sales. By lowering prices, highly competitive sellers meet the market. They target a specific kind of buyer and price their goods accordingly. They try to figure out what a representative though hypothetical buyer will pay. This hypothetical buyer represents many buyers who will make a purchase. The seller is highly concerned about what this hypothetical buyer will pay. Once he decides, individual buyers matter only as members of a statistically relevant group.

---

1. Earnest money is money paid by the potential buyer in advance. It is forfeited if the seller agrees to the buyer's contract, and the buyer then refuses to complete the transaction. It is also called "good faith" money.

Conclusion

This proverb applies to a pre-capitalistic society or to niche markets with one-of-a-kind products for sale. There is negotiation between buyer and seller because of zones of ignorance. Neither party knows what price the other party is willing to accept. Because of ignorance, buyer competes against seller. The less the ignorance, the more that buyers compete against buyers, and sellers compete against sellers.

60

DEMAND COLLATERAL FROM FOOLS

Take his garment that is surety for a stranger: and take a pledge of him for a strange woman.

This proverb appears again in Proverbs 27:13. This indicates that Solomon took its message seriously.

A. Avoid Co-Signing

The old English word "surety" means "co-signer." A co-signer pledges that if a debtor defaults on a loan, he will pay off the debt. He places his own assets on the line. Otherwise, the lender will not lend to the debtor. The lender wants someone who has a high credit rating to act as guarantor for the loan. The co-signer owns something worth accepting if the loan goes bad.

The Proverbs are clear: it is unwise to become a co-signer.

> My son, if thou be surety for thy friend, if thou hast stricken thy hand with a stranger, Thou art snared with the words of thy mouth, thou art taken with the words of thy mouth. Do this now, my son, deliver thyself, when thou art come into the hand of thy friend; go, humble thyself, and make sure thy friend. Give not sleep to thine eyes, nor slumber to thine eyelids. Deliver thyself as a roe from the hand of the hunter, and as a bird from the hand of the fowler (6:1–5).[1]

> He that is surety for a stranger [*zoor*] shall smart for it: and he that hateth suretiship is sure (11:15).

> A man void of understanding striketh hands, and becometh surety in the presence of his friend (17:18).

---

1. Chapter 11.

> Be not thou one of them that strike hands, or of them that are sureties for debts (22:26).

This proverb refers to taking a garment. This refers back to the Mosaic law.

> If thou at all take thy neighbour's raiment to pledge, thou shalt deliver it unto him by that the sun goeth down: For that is his covering only, it is his raiment for his skin: wherein shall he sleep? and it shall come to pass, when he crieth unto me, that I will hear; for I am gracious (Ex. 22:26–27).

The garment had to be returned in the evening. Thus, it was not useful to the lender directly. But it was very useful indirectly. It kept the borrower from indebting himself beyond the value of his assets: one garment, one loan. The lender made sure by collecting it during the day that the borrower was not using it to collateralize multiple loans.[2]

B. Foolish Debtors

This proverb rests on this assumption: a person who co-signs for a person outside the covenant is unwise. The word translated here as "stranger" is *zoor*. This word connotes perversion and rebellion. It is neither *geyr* nor *nokree*, which referred to foreigners residing inside Israel. It is something sinister.

> And Nadab and Abihu died, when they offered strange fire before the LORD (Num. 26:61).

> They provoked him to jealousy with strange gods, with abominations provoked they him to anger (Deut. 32:16).

It is always unwise to become a co-signer. It is doubly unwise when the debtor is *zoor*. So, this proverb instructs the listener to collect the garment from the co-signer. It assumes that the stranger will default. Thus, be sure that the co-signer possesses something of value.

The same applies to the strange woman. Here, the Hebrew word is *nokree*. It does not imply perversity, but it does imply foreign legal status. This is a foreign resident inside the land who has not covenanted with God, unlike a *geyr*. Proverbs warns against associating closely with such a woman. "To keep thee from the evil woman, from the flattery of the tongue of a strange woman" (6:24). The co-signer not only associates with such a woman, he goes into debt on her be-

---

2. Gary North, *Authority and Dominion: An Economic Commentary on Exodus* (Dallas, Georgia: Point Five Press, 2012), Part 3, *Tools of Dominion* (1990), ch. 49:J.

half. This is a person devoid of good judgment. Take a pledge from such a person. You may need to foreclose.

Conclusion

It is not mandatory that a creditor demand collateral from a brother in the faith. Moses warned, "If thou at all take thy neighbour's raiment to pledge...." The key word is *if.* In contrast, this proverb says that a wise lender *must* take collateral from someone who co-signs for a covenant-breaker. This person is devoid of good judgment. If it is unwise to become a co-signer for a friend (6:1–5), how much more unwise is it to become a co-signer for a rebel?

61

EASY COME,
EASY GO

An inheritance may be gotten hastily at the beginning; but the end thereof shall not be blessed.

PROVERBS 20:21

A. Covenantal Inheritance

The concept of inheritance was central to Hebrew culture. Inheritance was part of the national covenant. The Book of Deuteronomy is structured in terms of this concept.[1] Inheritance was viewed as part of an intergenerational program of dominion. Each generation was required by God to build up capital to pass on. "A good man leaveth an inheritance to his children's children: and the wealth of the sinner is laid up for the just" (13:22).[2]

The inheritance was more covenantal-ethical than economic.

And these words, which I command thee this day, shall be in thine heart: And thou shalt teach them diligently unto thy children, and shalt talk of them when thou sittest in thine house, and when thou walkest by the way, and when thou liest down, and when thou risest up (Deut. 6:6–7).[3]

The foundation of a sustained inheritance was moral-judicial.

And it shall be, if thou do at all forget the LORD thy God, and walk after other gods, and serve them, and worship them, I testify against you this day that ye shall surely perish. As the nations which the LORD destroyeth

---

1. Gary North, *Inheritance and Dominion: An Economic Commentary on Deuteronomy*, 2nd ed. (Dallas, Georgia: Point Five Press, [1999] 2012).
2. Chapter 41.
3. *Ibid.*, ch. 15.

before your face, so shall ye perish; because ye would not be obedient unto the voice of the LORD your God (Deut. 8:19–20).[4]

B. Early Inheritance

Jesus' parable of the prodigal son rests on this proverb. The son asks for his inheritance early. His father gives it to him. He then goes to a far country, becoming a stranger in a strange land. He squanders his inheritance in riotous living. He is left with nothing (Luke 15:11–16).[5]

The message of this proverb is that an economic inheritance is not autonomous. It must be sustained by personal adherence to the covenantal legal order by which it was created. The heir must govern his life by the same moral order that governed his father's life. The inheritance is more comprehensive than mere wealth. Wealth is not autonomous. This was Moses' warning.

> And thou say in thine heart, My power and the might of mine hand hath gotten me this wealth. But thou shalt remember the LORD thy God: for it is he that giveth thee power to get wealth, that he may establish his covenant which he sware unto thy fathers, as it is this day (Deut. 8:17–18).[6]

The heir is unwise to seek an early inheritance. It comes in a lump sum. The heir does not understand the process of the slow, steady accumulation of wealth. He does not understand that the economic surplus over time, which made possible his inheritance, was an outcome of covenant-keeping entrepreneurship. The heir does not understand how rapidly an inheritance can be consumed. The hasty inheritance can be squandered hastily.

C. Covenantal Sanctions

The sanctions were an integral part of the Mosaic covenant. The blessings of the covenant are listed in Deuteronomy 28:1–14.[7] The cursings are listed in verses 15–68. These are corporate sanctions.

In this proverb, the absence of positive sanctions is a mark of God's negative response to an inheritance hastily received. These are personal sanctions. They apply to individual heirs. The person who inherits hastily, meaning without personal experience in administering wealth, should not expect to retain this wealth.

---

4. *Ibid.*, ch. 23.

5. Gary North, *Treasure and Dominion: An Economic Commentary on Luke*, 2nd ed. (Dallas, Georgia: Point Five Press, [2000] 2012), ch. 37.

6. North, *Inheritance and Dominion*, chaps. 21, 22.

7. *Ibid.*, ch. 69.

This proverb is a warning to heirs. It is also a warning to parents. Parents have an obligation to train their prospective heirs in the basics of the covenantal administration of capital. *For a child to inherit great wealth without prior training in capital management is a curse.* It does not appear to be a curse at the time of the inheritance, but this will become obvious over time. The prodigal son learned this lesson first-hand. "And when he came to himself, he said, How many hired servants of my father's have bread enough and to spare, and I perish with hunger!" (Luke 15:17). By then, his inheritance had been transferred to the covenant-breakers who sold him all those good times.

The sanctions serve as a warning. God's blessings are not random. They are part of a covenantal legal order. We are to assess events as either blessings or cursings in terms of the content of God's Bible-revealed law. This is what the prodigal son did as he slept with the pigs. He had time to repent and then to return to his father's house. The external reality of his condition could not be denied. He had wound up exactly as this proverb says.

Conclusion

Inheritance is covenantal. It is part of the covenantal order established by God. Those who understand the covenant are more likely to recognize the threat of an early inheritance than someone who has not understood it. This proverb is a pithy summary of Deuteronomy 8:17–20.

62

PAY ATTENTION TO DETAILS

The thoughts of the diligent tend only to plenteousness; but of every one that is hasty only to want.

PROVERBS 21:5

A. Diligence as the Model

The diligent person serves as a morally correct model for others. The Book of Proverbs returns repeatedly to this theme.

This proverb can also be translated, "The thoughts of the diligent tend surely to plenteousness." This is closer to the meaning of the text than any suggestion that a diligent person's thoughts are focused solely on plenteousness or profitability. This proverb is saying that there is a correlation between a diligent person's care in thinking through a plan of action and the outcome of this action, which is plenteousness.

Is this correlation 100%? The Hebrew text indicates that it is. The translators added "tend." But did Solomon believe that diligent people's plans produce plenteousness all the time? Elsewhere, he seems to. "The hand of the diligent shall bear rule: but the slothful shall be under tribute" (12:24).[1] Yet in the Bible, evil-doers are said to rule over the righteous. Psalm 73 is a good example.

> But as for me, my feet were almost gone; my steps had well nigh slipped. For I was envious at the foolish, when I saw the prosperity of the wicked. For there are no bands in their death: but their strength is firm. They are not in trouble as other men; neither are they plagued like other men. Therefore pride compasseth them about as a chain; violence covereth them as a garment. (Ps. 73:2–6).[2]

---

1. Chapter 37.
2. Gary North, *Confidence and Dominion: An Economic Commentary on Psalms* (Dallas,

This is not a permanent condition, the Psalmist said. "Surely thou didst set them in slippery places: thou castedst them down into destruction. How are they brought into desolation, as in a moment! they are utterly consumed with terrors" (Ps. 73:18–19). But, for a time, the unrighteous do prosper. So, the translators added "tend" to the verse, which reflects the overall message of the Bible. Still, Solomon wrote more emphatically than this. He sought to persuade his readers that diligent attention to one's plans produces personal success in history.

This is a case where an author's rhetoric conveys what both he and readers know is not true. Diligent plans do not *surely* produce success in history for diligent individuals. The prophets were diligent, yet they suffered at the hands of covenant-breakers. Jesus told the disciples, "Blessed are ye, when men shall revile you, and persecute you, and shall say all manner of evil against you falsely, for my sake. Rejoice, and be exceeding glad: for great is your reward in heaven: for so persecuted they the prophets which were before you" (Matt. 5:11–12). Diligence produces positive sanctions, but not always in history.

B. Haste Makes Waste

In contrast to the diligent planner is the hasty individual. "Every one that is hasty only to want." Again, we find that hasty people sometimes do prosper. But the connection between hasty decisions and poverty does exist. Lot was hasty in his decision to choose Sodom as his dwelling place (Gen. 13:10–11). This eventually cost him his capital and his family (Gen. 19).

Diligence requires attention to detail. Haste involves great confidence that things will work out well despite a lack of attention to details. "Come ye, say they, I will fetch wine, and we will fill ourselves with strong drink; and to morrow shall be as this day, and much more abundant" (Isa. 56:12).

The hasty person believes that the world is based on luck. He does not delay taking action until he can verify the truth of what has been placed before him. He assumes that he has been blessed by impersonal fate or personal luck. This is thought to negate the risks of decision- making based on insufficient facts.

The Bible teaches that there is no such thing as luck. There is also no such thing as impersonal fate. The Bible teaches that God providentially sustains the universe and works out His decree for history.

Georgia: Point Five Press, 2012), ch. 17.

Drop down, ye heavens, from above, and let the skies pour down righteousness: let the earth open, and let them bring forth salvation, and let righteousness spring up together; I the LORD have created it. Woe unto him that striveth with his Maker! Let the potsherd strive with the potsherds of the earth. Shall the clay say to him that fashioneth it, What makest thou? or thy work, He hath no hands?" (Isa. 45:8–9)

Proverbs speaks of wisdom as personified. "When he gave to the sea his decree, that the waters should not pass his commandment: when he appointed the foundations of the earth: Then I was by him, as one brought up with him: and I was daily his delight, rejoicing always before him" (8:29–30).

Careful planning, including diligent prayer, is basic to success in life. The hasty person does not believe this. He does not see the requirement to prepare oneself for years by studying God's law (Ps. 119). He does not think that years of attention to one's occupation are necessary for mastery. He thinks that enthusiastic commitment on short notice will overcome all resistance.

The hasty person thinks, "This is the opportunity of a lifetime. I must not allow it to get away." Yet a person's lifetime is in God's hand. God can bring other major opportunities. The question is: "Is this opportunity consistent with my calling—the most important thing I can do in which I would be most difficult to replace?" God called Moses to become His spokesman before Pharaoh and to lead Israel out of Egypt. This was surely more important than working as a sheepherder for another 40 years. It was the opportunity of a lifetime. But it came after 40 years of herding sheep. With Aaron at his side, Moses became an overnight sensation as far as Pharaoh and Israel were concerned. But he had served time faithfully at a small task in preparation for this new calling.

Conclusion

Diligence is superior to haste as a way of life. Careful attention to detail is a reliable course of action. Haste is not.

The requirement of diligence points to the availability of sufficient time to complete our life's tasks before God. God is not in a hurry. His people should therefore not be in a hurry.

63

NOTHING FOR SOMETHING

The getting of treasures by a lying tongue is a vanity tossed to and fro of them that seek death.

PROVERBS 21:6

A. The Misuse of Deception

This proverb says that it is possible to gain treasure through deliberate deception. It is a form of vanity—chasing after emptiness. Solomon already has warned: "Wealth gotten by vanity shall be diminished: but he that gathereth by labour shall increase" (13:11).[1] In this passage, Solomon escalates the warning. Those who pursue wealth in this way are seeking death. To seek death is suicidal. We have already been informed, regarding wisdom, "But he that sinneth against me wrongeth his own soul: all they that hate me love death" (8:36). Pursuing treasure through deception requires that the pursuer hate wisdom.

The temptation of great wealth is one of the most powerful temptations in life. The question arises: Why? What is it about great wealth that lures people into death? In a very poor society, such wealth might mean the difference between life and death in a crisis, but in modern society, people rarely die from poverty. Great wealth does not add years compared to middle-class wealth. It allows people to live in special ways, yet even here, most people cannot say exactly what these ways are.

In terms of eating, sleeping, learning, and being entertained, the middle-class person has most of the advantages that a wealthy man

---

1. Chapter 40.

254

has. There are middle-class men who would not want great wealth if it meant that their wives would drag them to the opera and ballet, then write large checks to support these narrowly appreciated arts. These men would prefer to write checks in order to escape attending.

The major differences between middle-class living and wealthy living in my era are the ability to afford three things: full-time servants, very large homes, and homes located at a great distance from a street. A wealthy person hires numerous full-time servants to run his household. Given the value of his time, this is an economically rational decision. Second, the very rich live in large homes that cannot be seen from a highway. They can afford expensive land that offers seclusion to large homes. Their properties have long, winding driveways. Servants, large homes, and seclusion are social goods, sometimes called *positional goods*.[2] They identify wealth. Rich men usually want this recognition. So do rich men's wives, especially the second or third wife.

Positional goods are not life-and-death goods. To sacrifice one's integrity in order to obtain positional goods—or, more likely, merely an opportunity to obtain enough wealth to buy positional goods—is to become self-deceived. The price of the positional goods is too high. Jesus asked: "For what is a man profited, if he shall gain the whole world, and lose his own soul? or what shall a man give in exchange for his soul? (Matt. 16:26).[3] This rhetorical question is an extension of Proverbs 21:6 to eternity.

B. Vanity

The biblical meaning of vanity is a combination of success and emptiness. A person pursues something that he considers valuable or worth having, but when he obtains or attains it, he finds that it does not fulfil his expectations. The Book of Ecclesiastes dismisses all things pursued for their own sake as vanity.

Vanity of vanities, saith the Preacher, vanity of vanities; all is vanity (Eccl. 1:2).[4]

I have seen all the works that are done under the sun; and, behold, all is vanity and vexation of spirit (Eccl. 1:14).[5]

---

2. Fred Hirsch, *The Social Limits to Growth* (London: Routledge and Kegan Paul, 1976).

3. Gary North, *Priorities and Dominion: An Economic Commentary on Matthew*, 2nd ed. (Dallas, Georgia: Point Five Press, [2000] 2012), ch. 35.

4. Gary North, *Autonomy and Stagnation: An Economic Commentary on Ecclesiastes* (Dallas, Georgia: Point Five Press, 2012), ch. 1.

5. *Idem.*

> Then I looked on all the works that my hands had wrought, and on the labour that I had laboured to do: and, behold, all was vanity and vexation of spirit, and there was no profit under the sun (Eccl. 2:11).[6]

The warning here is against _autonomy_. Nothing pursued _for its own sake_ is anything but vanity. Only that which is pursued under the law of God for the glory of God escapes from vanity. Self-judgment must be conformed to God's judgment. Nothing is autonomous.

> Let us hear the conclusion of the whole matter: Fear God, and keep his commandments: for this is the whole duty of man. For God shall bring every work into judgment, with every secret thing, whether it be good, or whether it be evil (Eccl. 12:13–14).[7]

Men pursue wealth because it seems to offer a wide range of options. But all of these options are vanity—empty. They all command a price. If wealth is pursued through deception, it produces death. This is nothing (vanity) for something (life).

Conclusion

Solomon identifies a common misconception: imagining that wealth is worth lying to attain. This is a monumental misconception. Yet the lure of treasure is so great that men sacrifice their integrity in order to attain it. Great wealth is vanity whenever pursued for its own sake: empty. When pursued by means of deception, it is suicidal.

---

6. _Ibid._, ch. 2.
7. _Ibid._, ch. 45.

64

MORAL CAUSATION

The robbery of the wicked shall destroy them; because they refuse to do judgment.

PROVERBS 21:7

This is the common view of moral causation in the Mosaic law. Deuteronomy 28:15–68 presents it. There is moral causation in history. Morality shapes economic results. In this case, the message relates to a violation of morality: robbery. The word can also be translated as "spoil" or "oppression."

A. Robbers Lose in History

Wicked men rob others. They do this to benefit themselves. They use coercion or the threat of coercion, or they use deception, to obtain wealth owned by others. They use ungodly methods to lay up treasure. That which God had delivered into the hands of other people, who had acted lawfully, the robbers obtain apart from moral performance or legal claim. The robbers attempt to thwart God's allocation of resources. They seek ownership on a legal foundation other than God's mandated legal order. They seek to establish a new world order, one which favors them uniquely.

This proverb says that robbers will reap a disaster for their efforts. It offers a reason for this: the refusal of the wicked to do judgment. By "judgment," Solomon meant *righteous* judgment. The Mosaic law says: "Ye shall do no unrighteousness in judgment: thou shalt not respect the person of the poor, nor honour the person of the mighty: but in righteousness shalt thou judge thy neighbour" (Lev. 19:15).[1] These are God's judgments.

---

1. Gary North, *Boundaries and Dominion: An Economic Commentary on Leviticus*, 2nd ed. (Dallas, Georgia: Point Five Press, [1994] 2012), ch. 14.

"Ye shall do my judgments, and keep mine ordinances, to walk therein: I am the LORD your God. Ye shall therefore keep my statutes, and my judgments: which if a man do, he shall live in them: I am the LORD" (Lev. 18:4–5).

B. Winners and Losers

The wicked person robs others. He does this in order to increase his wealth at the expense of his victims. His gain is their loss. The exchange between them is not voluntary. It is not an arrangement based on the expectation of mutual benefit. The victim may be the victim of deception, hoping for gain, but the robber understands in advance that the exchange will not rest on mutually shared benefits.

In a free market exchange, both parties benefit, or expect to benefit, from an exchange. Each understands that the other expects to gain from the transaction. The relationship is not based on the expectation of either party that he will gain at the other person's expense. Adam Smith, in Book I, Chapter 2 of *The Wealth of Nations* (1776), wrote these words, which have survived the test of time.

> But man has almost constant occasion for the help of his brethren, and it is in vain for him to expect it from their benevolence only. He will be more likely to prevail if he can interest their self-love in his favour, and show them that it is for their own advantage to do for him what he requires of them. Whoever offers to another a bargain of any kind, proposes to do this. Give me that which I want, and you shall have this which you want, is the meaning of every such offer; and it is in this manner that we obtain from one another the far greater part of those good offices which we stand in need of. It is not from the benevolence of the butcher, the brewer, or the baker, that we expect our dinner, but from their regard to their own interest. We address ourselves, not to their humanity but to their self-love, and never talk to them of our own necessities but of their advantages.

The exchange relationship is not a zero-sum game, where every gain comes at the cost of another player's loss. Both parties expect to gain.

The robber knows better. He knows that his victim will lose. He initiates the transaction on this basis. This is the essence of robbery. It relies either on coercion or deception. It is based on the assumption that gain results from loss. This is not the basis of the free market economy. It is also not the basis of biblical morality. God's law establishes a system of moral causation in history. *Righteousness produces material benefits.* These are not one-sided benefits. All the participants in society can perceive this, even covenant-breakers.

> But ye that did cleave unto the LORD your God are alive every one of you this day. Behold, I have taught you statutes and judgments, even as the LORD my God commanded me, that ye should do so in the land whither ye go to possess it. Keep therefore and do them; for this is your wisdom and your understanding in the sight of the nations, which shall hear all these statutes, and say, Surely this great nation is a wise and understanding people. For what nation is there so great, who hath God so nigh unto them, as the LORD our God is in all things that we call upon him for? And what nation is there so great, that hath statutes and judgments so righteous as all this law, which I set before you this day? (Deut. 4:4–8)[2]

So powerful is this testimony in the hearts of men that God says that the very unwillingness of an individual to evaluate the results of God's law in this positive fashion—in other words, to suppress this understanding—constitutes wilful rebellion against God, a form of rebellion which is the origin of idolatry: worshipping animals and insects (Rom. 1:18–23).[3] The robber refuses to accept this. He believes that he can safely substitute deception or coercion in place of mutually beneficial voluntary exchange. He believes that he can benefit from a violation of God's covenantal legal order.

This proverb says that the robber's assessment is incorrect. It says that such wicked behavior will result in his destruction. The robber expects to benefit from his coercion, but he will not benefit. He will sustain a massive loss. He will become a far greater loser than his victim.

Conclusion

A just man is in a position to extend judgment in history. So is an unjust man. What men do in history reflects their concept of causation.

The robber denies the cause and effect relationship that God announces in His law governs the world of man. His actions reflect his denial of God's legal order. This proverb warns men not to act on any such assumption. It warns them to adhere to the standards established in God's revelation.

A just man is in a position to extend judgment in history.

---

2. Gary North, *Inheritance and Dominion: An Economic Commentary on Deuteronomy*, 2nd ed. (Dallas, Georgia: Point Five Press, [1999] 2012), ch. 8.

3. Gary North, *Cooperation and Dominion: An Economic Commentary on Romans*, 2nd ed. (Dallas, Georgia: Point Five Press, [2000] 2012), ch. 2.

65

THE CRY OF THE POOR

Whoso stoppeth his ears at the cry of the poor, he also shall cry himself, but shall not be heard.

PROVERBS 21:13

A poor person has a right to cry out to God for deliverance. The Hebrews in Egypt cried out to God for deliverance. God heard them and delivered them under Moses. God raised up Moses, who initially resisted the call (Ex. 4:1–13), to deliver His people.

A poor person may also cry out to men who possess more wealth than he does. He seeks deliverance from his immediate situation. He sees that another person may be in a position to help him. He asks for help.

Is this a loud cry? Sometimes the Hebrew word is correctly translated this way. "My heart shall cry out for Moab; his fugitives shall flee unto Zoar, an heifer of three years old: for by the mounting up of Luhith with weeping shall they go it up; for in the way of Horonaim they shall raise up a cry of destruction" (Isa. 15:5). It can also be understood as crying in the sense of shedding tears. "And Tamar put ashes on her head, and rent her garment of divers colours that was on her, and laid her hand on her head, and went on crying" (II Sam. 13:19). It is more likely a cry in the sense of a corporate appeal in the midst of a crisis. It is not an audible cry. It is a representative cry. "At the noise of the taking of Babylon the earth is moved, and the cry is heard among the nations" (Jer. 50:46).

The Hebrew word translated here as "stoppeth" can mean "closed up." It can also mean "narrow." The meaning here is "an unwillingness to consider." Poor people are in need. A somewhat less poor person is in a position to help, yet he does nothing.

There are cause and effect in God's covenantal social order. What a person sows, so shall he reap. "But this I say, He which soweth sparingly shall reap also sparingly; and he which soweth bountifully shall reap also bountifully" (II Cor. 9:6). "Be not deceived; God is not mocked: for whatsoever a man soweth, that shall he also reap" (Gal. 6:7). The laws of society are ultimately covenantal; hence, there is an ethical component.

A merciless person does not listen to the cry of a person in need. Neither will others listen to him, should he come under distress. Every person is threatened by something. Everyone can come under distress of some kind. There is no immunity from distress in this life. Solomon says that so personal are social cause and effect that the person who refuses to help the poor when he can help is going to be overtaken by external events that threaten him.

Hearing the cry of the poor is an ethical issue. Solomon does not call for the civil government to tax members of one income group in order to fund another group. He is not directing his warning to civil magistrates. He is warning people with assets to assist the poor.

Conclusion

The warning is personal. The threatened sanction is personal. Poor people in society should be able to present their case to the public at large. If their case has merit, yet no one lifts a hand to help, then those who have remained judicially deaf will find that their day of trouble will come. What they have sown, they will reap.

66

BIBLICAL BRIBERY

A gift in secret pacifieth anger: and a reward in the bosom strong wrath.

PROVERBS 21:14

A. God Cannot Be Bribed

Solomon, as the king of Israel, was familiar with the strategic use of gifts. The Hebrew word translated as "gift"—*mattawn*—appears three times in Proverbs. The context of Proverbs 21:14 is not clearly that of civil government. It is in Proverbs 19:6. "Many will intreat the favour of the prince: and every man is a friend to him that giveth gifts." Proverbs 18:16 may refer to civil rulers. "A man's gift maketh room for him, and bringeth him before great men." Great men may be civil rulers. If not, then these men have access to civil rulers.

The general principle governing these proverbs is found in Proverbs 18:8. "A gift is as a precious stone in the eyes of him that hath it: whithersoever it turneth, it prospereth." In this proverb, the Hebrew word is different: *sachad*. It is used repeatedly to describe bribery. In most, the texts are hostile. They are governed by this presupposition. "For the LORD your God is God of gods, and Lord of lords, a great God, a mighty, and a terrible, which regardeth not persons, nor taketh reward" (Deut. 10:17). What applies to God must also apply to those who act as judges in His name.

> And thou shalt take no gift: for the gift blindeth the wise, and perverteth the words of the righteous (Ex. 23:8).

> Thou shalt not wrest judgment; thou shalt not respect persons, neither take a gift: for a gift doth blind the eyes of the wise, and pervert the words

262

of the righteous (Deut. 16:19).

Cursed be he that taketh reward to slay an innocent person. And all the people shall say, Amen (Deut. 27:25).

A wicked man taketh a gift out of the bosom to pervert the ways of judgment (Prov. 17:23).

Thy princes are rebellious, and companions of thieves: every one loveth gifts, and followeth after rewards: they judge not the fatherless, neither doth the cause of the widow come unto them (Isa. 1:23).

Then what of the proverb in question? "A gift in secret pacifieth anger: and a reward in the bosom strong wrath." Why in secret? What anger is it pacifying? Isn't the context the same as the other Hebrew word for gift?

B. What We Owe Corrupt Rulers

There is no question that God prohibits bribery that produces corrupt judgments. But this does not directly deal with the question of becoming a willing victim of a corrupt judgment. Corrupt rulers are marked by a willingness to accept bribes. This puts the covenant-keeper at a disadvantage. In a court of law, his opponent may have paid a bribe. A practical question arises: What should a covenant-keeper do to reduce the likelihood of being the victim of paid-for corrupt judgment?

Solomon does not suggest that anything is wrong with this: "A gift in secret pacifieth anger: and a reward in the bosom strong wrath" (21:14). Nor here: "A gift is as a precious stone in the eyes of him that hath it: whithersoever it turneth, it prospereth" (17:8). Yet in the second case, the Hebrew word is *sachad*. We are faced with what initially appears to be an ethical dilemma. Solomon points to the benefits of bribery without condemning it.

There is a reason for this. The Bible condemns bribery. The question is, how does the Bible define bribery? There are two choices.

1. To pay a civil official to deliver a corrupt judgment, i.e., a judgment at odds with what biblical law mandates.
2. To pay a civil official to deliver a judgment different from what he otherwise would hand down.

The Bible clearly condemns the first practice. If the proverbs under consideration here, which deal with the benefits of giving gifts, do not refer to civil government, then bribery may be defined according to the second option. But nowhere in the Bible is gift-giving con-

demned in this way. Bribery is condemned because it perverts righteous judgment. There would have been a righteous decision handed
down, but bribery has led to a different decision.

C. Rival Approaches to Law

Here, we see a fundamental difference between rival views of civil
law. One view defines righteous judgment as consistent with a code of
ethics. A decision is *substantively* righteous. Why? Because it upholds
the ethical foundation of the specific statute or tradition. The other
view defines righteous judgment as procedurally correct. A decision
is *formally* righteous. Why? Because it is technically predictable. The
modern world has moved systematically toward formal rationalism:
procedure over ethics. It steadily has abandoned substantive rationalism: ethics over procedure.

If we define righteous judgment as procedurally correct law, then
all bribery is condemned. If we define righteous judgment as ethically correct law, then bribery is condemned when it tempts a civil
official to enforce ethically incorrect law.

The critic may respond: "Civil law should be both ethically
grounded and procedurally predictable." Yes, this is what civil law
should be. But what is the biblically correct view of bribery in an
ethically corrupt legal system?

Jesus provided a practical answer to this question.

> Ye have heard that it hath been said, An eye for an eye, and a tooth for a
> tooth: But I say unto you, That ye resist not evil: but whosoever shall smite
> thee on thy right cheek, turn to him the other also. And if any man will sue
> thee at the law, and take away thy coat, let him have thy cloke also. And who-
> soever shall compel thee to go a mile, go with him twain (Matt. 5:38–41).[1]

Did Jesus abandon the Mosaic law as an ideal? Moses declared:
"Eye for eye, tooth for tooth, hand for hand, foot for foot, Burning for burning, wound for wound, stripe for stripe" (Ex. 21:24–25).[2]
The context was two men fighting, where an injured pregnant woman
loses her child. If this law is no longer in effect, then the judicial case
against abortion is surrendered.[3]

---

1. Gary North, *Priorities and Dominion: An Economic Commentary on Matthew*, 2nd ed.
(Dallas, Georgia: Point Five Press, [2000] 2012), ch. 9.

2. Gary North, *Authority and Dominion: An Economic Commentary on Exodus* (Dallas,
Georgia: Point Five Press, 2012), Part 3, *Tools of Dominion* (1990), ch. 37.

3. R. J. Rushdoony, *The Institutes of Biblical Law* (Nutley, New Jersey: Craig Press,
1973), pp. 263–69. Cf. North, *Authority and Dominion*, ch. 37:A.

Jesus was speaking to Jews who lived under Roman oppression. They were not in charge of the legal system. So, He recommended that people make an extra payment to those who used compulsion against them. This payment was not owed. It was not even demanded. In the context of civil compulsion, this is correctly identified as a bribe. It is a payment in advance to buy the favor of a person in authority.

There is another example. It involves a positive sanction in the context of a negative sanction. Jesus said,

> There was in a city a judge, which feared not God, neither regarded man: And there was a widow in that city; and she came unto him, saying, Avenge me of mine adversary. And he would not for a while: but afterward he said within himself, Though I fear not God, nor regard man; Yet because this widow troubleth me, I will avenge her, lest by her continual coming she weary me (Luke 18:2–5).

The widow faces an unjust judge. She wants justice. So, she bangs on his door. She nags him. She makes his life miserable. She offers a bribe: "I will stop pestering you if you render judgment." He accepts the bribe. He decides to get some peace and quiet by rendering righteous judgment.

Jesus was illustrating the correct approach to prayer. Be persistent. Treat God as if He were an unjust judge.[4] But if we are allowed to treat God as if He were an unjust judge, when He is not an unjust judge, then we are allowed to treat unjust judges similarly.

Conclusion

Solomon taught that paying a judge to render a judgment against what biblical law mandates is a corrupt form of bribery. God cannot be bought off to render unrighteous judgment. Therefore, do not try to buy off a judge to render unrighteous judgment.

Solomon also taught that "a gift in secret pacifieth anger: and a reward in the bosom strong wrath." When dealing with a judge who systematically renders ethically corrupt judgments, it is legitimate to persuade him to render an incorrupt judgment by paying him in secret. It may not be wise in a particular instance. It is always risky. But it is not morally corrupt.

There is no universal definition of justice that fits all cases. There is no neutral law. There is no neutral court procedure. There are God's

---

4. Gary North, *Treasure and Dominion: An Economic Commentary on Luke*, 2nd ed. (Dallas, Georgia: Point Five Press, [2000] 2012), ch. 42.

law and man's law. There is covenant-keeping and covenant-breaking. The quest for universal definitions of law and law enforcement that reconcile God's Bible-revealed law and man's law is an assault on the Bible, for it is an assertion of covenant-breaking man's ethical neutrality and judicial autonomy. It is an attempt to bring God's law into sovereign man's law court. So, there is no universal definition of bribery.[5] This definition is biblically incorrect: "To pay a civil official to deliver a judgment different from what he otherwise would hand down." This definition is correct: "To pay a civil official to deliver a corrupt judgment, i.e., a judgment at odds with what biblical law mandates."

---

5. Gary North, "In Defense of Biblical Bribery," in Rushdoony, *Institutes of Biblical Law*, pp. 843–44.

67

ECONOMIC HIERARCHIES

The rich ruleth over the poor, and the borrower is servant to the lender.

PROVERBS 22:7

Hierarchy is not a bad thing. On the contrary, hierarchy is an inescapable concept. It is point two of the biblical covenant structure.[1] The question that everyone faces is the nature of the multiple hierarchies under which he or she lives. The hierarchy described in this proverb is economic.

A. The Rich Rule Over the Poor

The rich man has many opportunities. This is the best definition of riches. The poor man has far fewer opportunities.

The rich man can make mistakes and still not have to change his lifestyle. The poor man must make many changes in his pattern of consumption if he makes mistakes. He will be in a weak bargaining position, for he has no economic reserves. The trade-off between money and time works against him. He has little money, so he soon runs out of time in a crisis. He could buy more time with money. He has no money. So, he must accept an employment or credit offer that he would not accept, had he not run out of money and if he were not running out of time.

When a rich man enters the free market and offers to hire less rich men, he faces competition from other rich men. Similarly, when a

---

1. Ray R. Sutton, *That You May Prosper: Dominion By Covenant,* 2nd ed. (Tyler, Texas: Institute for Christian Economics, [1987] 1992), ch. 2. Gary North, *Unconditional Surrender: God's Program for Victory*, 5th ed. (Powder Springs, Georgia: American Vision, [1980] 2010), ch. 2.

poor man enters the market, he is competing against other poor men. The free market is highly competitive, but it is not the competition of one-on-one competition between a rich man and a poor man, or a creditor and a debtor. Only when the contract is signed does the hierarchy become one-on-one.

Think of the analogous competition of courtship. Males compete against males; females compete against females. Only after marriage does a hierarchy prevail.

B. The Creditor Rules Over the Debtor

This proverb teaches that as surely as a rich man is in a superior position in relation to a poor man, so is a creditor in a superior position to a poor man. Poor men know this.

The hierarchy is based on a credit-debt relationship. For most people, it is better to be under economic authority. Most people are not entrepreneurs. They do not want to live with the extensive uncertainty that offers the entrepreneur the opportunity to make a profit, provided he is willing to risk taking a loss. No one can avoid uncertainty entirely, for only God is omniscient. But most people try to limit uncertainty in their lives. This is why most people prefer a wage to investing as a way to support themselves.

Earning a wage is a mark of subordination. A proverb could accurately announce, "The rich ruleth over the poor, and the wage-earner is servant to the wage-payer." The difference is, the wage-earner probably is bound by a revocable contract. He can lawfully quit, and his employer in a free society can lawfully fire him, unless there is a signed contract to the contrary.

A debt contract is more permanent than most wage contracts. It binds the debtor to a repayment schedule. This is a more rigid form of hierarchy. This proverb reminds a potential debtor that debt is a form of servitude.

Servitude is not morally wrong. The Mosaic law had a provision that allowed a servant to pledge lifetime service to his master or employer (Ex. 21:4–6; Deut. 15:16–17). Paul recommended that a slave remain content with his position (I Cor. 7:20). But if he is offered a legal way to go free, he should take it (I Cor. 7:21).[2]

Paul also recommended debt-free living. "Owe no man any thing, but to love one another: for he that loveth another hath fulfilled the

---

2. Gary North, *Judgment and Dominion: An Economic Commentary on First Corinthians*, 2nd ed. (Dallas, Georgia: Point Five Press, [2001] 2012), ch. 8.

law" (Rom. 13:8). But because almost every economic relationship has a time component, there is always some short-term credit/debt.[3]

The debtor is a servant because he has promised to pay. He is less mobile because of this. This mobility may be geographical. It may be related to career. If the debt was used to purchase a capital asset, the income generated by the asset may be well above whatever is required to service the debt. This increases mobility. The problem is the uncertainty of future income compared to the certainty of the debt's repayment schedule. The inherent servitude of the permanent obligation stands as a threat to the person who has contracted the debt.

A debt secured by inanimate collateral is different from debt secured by personal obligation. If someone borrows money to buy a house, and the house serves as collateral for the mortgage, then the threat of foreclosure is always there, but it is not the equivalent of personal bondage. It is not the same as a loan secured by a person's earning ability. The debtor whose home is foreclosed for non-payment can move—indeed, will be probably be asked to move by the new owner of the home. But this threat does not extend to his person or his savings. He retains mobility.

Conclusion

The rich man rules over the poor man because he has financial reserves that the poor man does not have. He can offer a loan to a poor man in a poor man's time of crisis. The poor man is not in a strong bargaining position.

Similarly, the creditor is in a strong bargaining position in relation to the debtor. The debtor may be only one payment away from a crisis. Few creditors are.

The economic hierarchy in a free market is a hierarchy of competition. Rich men compete against rich men for the services of less rich men. Poor men compete against poor men. Creditors compete against creditors. Debtors compete against debtors. There are limits to the severity of the hierarchy.

---

3. Gary North, *Cooperation and Dominion: An Economic Commentary on Romans*, 2nd ed. (Dallas, Georgia: Point Five Press, [2000] 2012), ch. 12.

68

A LION IN THE STREETS

The slothful man saith, There is a lion without, I shall be slain in the streets.

PROVERBS 22:13

A. Excuses, Excuses

Actually, slothful men do not say this. It is doubtful that they said it in Palestine in Solomon's day. Who would believe it? That is Solomon's point. He is implying that all of the other excuses that slothful men offer for not leaving the house every morning are in the same category as worrying about being killed by a lion in the streets. Solomon's contempt for sloth is seen in a parallel passage later in this book.

> The slothful man saith, There is a lion in the way; a lion is in the streets. As the door turneth upon his hinges, so doth the slothful upon his bed. The slothful hideth his hand in his bosom; it grieveth him to bring it again to his mouth. The sluggard is wiser in his own conceit than seven men that can render a reason (26:13–16).

The slothful man rolls from side to side in his bed. He is too lazy to eat. He is puffed up. He is altogether a contemptible person.

He offers an excuse for his sloth: "A lion is in the street." Solomon's intense ridicule indicates that slothfulness in Israel was widely regarded as a moral defect. The slothful person searches for an acceptable excuse for not going to work. He does not want to come out and say, "Look, I am lazy. Work does not agree with me. It never has. I find it a lot more pleasant to just stay home and relax." The public, then as now, looks on such excuses as evidence of a weak moral character. People also think, "I am forced by external circumstances to go to work. Why should this person escape the negative sanctions of not going to work? Who does he think he is?"

There is a familiar American saying, "An honest day's labor for an honest day's pay." Its opposite was popular in the Soviet Union before it collapsed in 1991. "We pretend to work, and they pretend to pay us." Soviet work habits were terrible, and so was output. So was the currency system.[1] The American outlook on work is that it is more than a necessary evil. A man defines himself by what he does for a living, not what he does in his spare time. This is characteristic of Protestantism in general. There really was a Puritan work ethic in the sixteenth and seventeenth centuries. Work was regarded as a holy calling from God, something not to be taken lightly or escaped, even by rich men. Puritans had contempt for the Cavaliers, meaning Great Britain's upper crust society, which was based on inherited wealth in land, not on labor and especially commercial labor. Traces of this pro-work attitude remain in modern Anglo-American society.

B. Evading Responsibility

Work is a form of personal responsibility. Each person is called by God to exercise dominion on God's behalf in his appropriate boundary of responsibility. This is the biblical worldview from Genesis 1 to Revelation 22.

When a person refuses to exercise responsibility in preference for a life of leisure, he rebels against God. Because service to God in the realm of economics is *service to other men,* who represent God, a refusal to work is an attempt to evade service to others. It is not surprising that people recognize the threat to themselves posed by other people's sloth. It means that fewer goods and services are offered for sale or as charitable gifts. Almost everyone is a little poorer. Only those who sell to the slothful are benefited, and only for as long as the slothful have money to spend.

The most memorable case of a slothful man that I can recall was reported in the central column of the *Wall Street Journal*: the human interest section. It was the story of an heir who lived on cruise ships. He had never married. He would hire a prostitute to spend a week or two with him on a cruise. He would hire a different one for the next cruise. He would eat as much as he wanted; cruises are famous for their policy of unlimited servings. Eventually, he would gain so much

---

1. A humorous book on the irrationality of the Soviet economic system is Leopold Tyrmand, *The Rosa Luxemburg Contraceptives Cooperative* (New York: Macmillan, 1972).

weight that he would have to go to a weight-reduction "fat farm" for a few weeks. Then he would return to the cruises. He had lived on cruise ships for all of his adult life. He was finally running low on money. He was unsure of how he would spend the rest of his life after the money ran out.

A vacation cruise is seen as a special treat for married couples. Because of price competition, it is possible for middle-class couples to take a cruise once or twice. There are expensive cruises, too. It does not take many cruises to become jaded with what they offer. But, as a lifetime special event, they have an appeal. Yet the thought of spending one's life on cruises as a passenger is unthinkable to most people, which is why the *Wall Street Journal* ran the story: the bizarre factor. Productive people know the difference between a life of work interspersed with leisure vs. a life of leisure interspersed with crash dieting. They prefer the former.

C. Dropping Out

In 1963, Timothy Leary, a Harvard University lecturer in psychology, was fired for recommending psychedelic drugs to his students. In the second half of the decade, he cashed in on a five-year international cultural rebellion of college-age students. He adopted flowing robes, as if he were an Indian mystic living a life of poverty. He flew around the United States to deliver well-paid lectures, which ended with this slogan: "Turn on. Tune in. Drop out." He became famous for this slogan. He was still promoting the use of psychedelic drugs: "Turn on." What his listeners were supposed to tune into was vague. To drop out would require continuing subsidies from members of the conventional society. His audiences were filled mostly with parentally funded teenagers and young adults, who had temporarily dropped out of middle-class society.

The counter-culture fad faded in 1970, when the United States went into an economic recession. Jobs became scarce. Leary continued to live a chaotic life thereafter, including two prison terms in the first half of the 1970s. He continued to lecture, though without much media attention. In the late 1980s, he resurfaced as a computer software writer. He died of cancer in 1996.

People with Leary's message are found in every society. Usually, they are on the society's fringes. Occasionally, they receive wide attention for a time, but they fade into the shadows again. Their outlook requires subsidies from productive people. Eventually, the subsidies end.

Scarcity was imposed on covenant-breaking mankind and the world in order to keep men from dropping out, i.e., forcing them to cooperate (Gen. 3:17–19).[2] The need to work is imposed by scarcity. Men understand that men who seek to escape from the scarcity-imposed requirement to work are a threat to the social order. The requirement to work preceded the curse (Gen. 2). Scarcity reinforced this requirement after the Fall.

Conclusion

This proverb uses ridicule to reject a view of life that threatens society and threatens the family headed by a person who adopts subterfuge to justify his sloth. It is not a lion in the streets that threatens him. Rather, his own rejection of work threatens him. If adopted widely, this outlook would threaten the progress of society.

The future will not be captured by men who are slothful. It will be captured by people who are not afraid of non-existent lions in the street, but who are afraid of a life of sloth.

2. Gary North, *Sovereignty and Dominion: An Economic Commentary on Genesis* (Dallas, Georgia: Point Five Press, [1982] 2012), ch. 12.

69

POVERTY PREVENTION

If thou hast nothing to pay, why should he take away thy bed from under thee?

PROVERBS 22:27

To understand this proverb, we must first understand the Mosaic law governing collateral.

> If thou lend money to any of my people that is poor by thee, thou shalt not be to him as an usurer, neither shalt thou lay upon him usury. If thou at all take thy neighbour's raiment to pledge, thou shalt deliver it unto him by that the sun goeth down: For that is his covering only, it is his raiment for his skin: wherein shall he sleep? and it shall come to pass, when he crieth unto me, that I will hear; for I am gracious (Ex. 22:25–27).

A person comes to a potential lender, seeking a loan. The lender can lawfully ask for collateral. But it is a strange form of collateral. It must be returned in the evening. It is a coat or other covering for cold weather. So, the borrower can use it when he really needs it. It seems to be useless to the lender, who must return it when it is needed.

This form of collateral is in fact very useful. The borrower is restricted from using the collateral to secure multiple loans. The lender can lawfully require the person to hand over the coat during the day. When he hands it over, he cannot take it to another lender as security for a loan. This law restricts multiple indebtedness.[1]

This proverb assumes the following scenario. A poor man has gone to a lender. As collateral, he has offered his bed. As with a coat, which must be returned to the borrower at night, the bed is useful during the night. The lender must return it during the night. Also

---

1. Gary North, *Authority and Dominion: An Economic Commentary on Exodus* (Dallas, Georgia: Point Five Press, 2012), Part 3, *Tools of Dominion* (1990), ch. 49:J.

274

like the coat, the bed is not needed during the day. The lender can lawfully demand that the borrower deliver it to him during the day.

This proverb says that someone is trying to take away a man's bed from under him. This would be illegal during the evening. So, if the bed is under the person, this is because the sun has risen. He should be off his bed and off to work. But he is still on his bed.

The lender sees the situation. The borrower is lazy. He does not want to get up in the morning. He has an aversion to work. This explains his poverty. This is why he needed a loan in the first place.

The lender has a problem. How will he be repaid? This debtor is a lazybones. He is not driven by conscience to repay loans. He has no money. There is a reason why he has no money. He is lazy.

He needs to change his ways. He needs motivation to change. One way for the lender to motivate him to change his ways is to demand that he surrender his collateral each morning. The lure of staying in bed in comfort can be removed. If the borrower wishes to sleep, he can sleep on the ground.

Solomon presents a rhetorical question: "If thou hast nothing to pay, why should he take away thy bed from under thee?" The answer is this: "Because you are lazy. You prefer to spend your time in bed rather than at work. Your income will fall. You will have to go into debt. You have been so unwise in the past that the only item that you can offer as collateral is your bed. Now that you cannot pay what you owe, your bed will be removed by the lender every morning." This is a warning to lazy men not to stay in bed before they fall into poverty to such a degree that they must get a loan to stay afloat financially. If they are so unwise as to borrow on this basis, the lender may exercise his authority and demand that you get out of bed every morning.

At the same time, this proverb is a warning to lenders not to violate the law governing collateral. If a lender comes at night to collect this form of collateral, the borrower will not sleep well. If he does not sleep well, he will not be efficient on the job. If he loses his job or if his production on the job declines because of sleep deprivation, the lender is unlikely to be repaid. So, to increase the likelihood of being repaid, the lender should honor the law governing collateral.

Conclusion

This proverb is another in a series of proverbs warning men against the sin of laziness. This one is more subtle that the others. It reminds lazy men of a possible outcome of their refusal to work. They will be in their beds when their creditors come to the door demanding the return of their only collateral: their beds. Here is the message: it is better to get out of bed early in the morning and go to work before poverty strikes.

70

LANDMARKS

Remove not the ancient landmark, which thy fathers have set.

This is a reaffirmation of a Mosaic law: "Thou shalt not remove thy neighbour's landmark, which they of old time have set in thine inheritance, which thou shalt inherit in the land that the LORD thy God giveth thee to possess it" (Deut. 19:14).[1] To this law, a curse was attached: "Cursed be he that removeth his neighbour's landmark. And all the people shall say, Amen" (Deut. 27:17).[2]

This proverb indicates that what Moses had revealed as judicially binding five centuries earlier (I Kings 6:1) was still in force in Israel. The landmarks were still visible and still legally binding. The Assyrian and Babylonian captivities were in the future.

A landmark was a rural land boundary marker. Landmarks marked off the property that had been distributed to Israelite families after the conquest of Canaan. Any land marked by these boundaries could not be transferred permanently to other families (Lev. 25:8–13),[3] except under the unique condition of a broken and then unredeemed pledge to a priest (Lev. 27:15).[4]

This law was intended to produce social cooperation. It established property rights. This means that it increased the likelihood that families in specific tribes would cooperate with each other. If an

---

1. Gary North, *Inheritance and Dominion: An Economic Commentary on Deuteronomy*, 2nd ed. (Dallas, Georgia: Point Five Press, [1999] 2012), ch. 44.

2. *Ibid.*, ch. 68.

3. Gary North, *Boundaries and Dominion: An Economic Commentary on Leviticus*, 2nd ed. (Dallas, Georgia: Point Five Press, [1994] 2012), ch. 25.

4. *Ibid.*, ch. 27.

heir resided on the family's land, he would be familiar with the customs of the neighborhood. Nevertheless, the owner could lawfully lease the land to anyone, including a covenantal stranger.

These markers could be more easily removed and moved than boundary markers in a city. Because of the low cost associated with moving a marker, the law imposed a special curse. So binding was this curse that all those who heard this law read by Levites or priests were required to affirm it by shouting "Amen." This was a public, corporate covenantal act. God presented Himself as the guardian of land markers.

Conclusion

Boundary markers identify ownership. They literally apply in real estate: stakes placed on property. But the principle of marked ownership also applies to other items, such as automobiles. Records must be kept. Boundaries must be enforced by civil courts. To break continuity with boundaries is to break continuity with the past. This breaks continuity with the future.

71

IN THE PRESENCE OF KINGS

Seest thou a man diligent in his business? he shall stand before kings; he shall not stand before mean men.

PROVERBS 22:29

Here we find another example of the theme of diligence. The Hebrew word translated here as "business" is usually translated as "work" or "workmanship."

The word for "stand" is sometimes translated as "present." A person who stands in front of a king possesses some kind of authority. "And the LORD said unto Moses, Rise up early in the morning, and stand before Pharaoh; lo, he cometh forth to the water; and say unto him, Thus saith the LORD, Let my people go, that they may serve me" (Ex. 8:20). This is repeated in Exodus 9:13. A different Hebrew word for "stand," but conveying the same meaning, is found in the description of Joseph's authority before Pharaoh. "And Joseph was thirty years old when he stood before Pharaoh king of Egypt. And Joseph went out from the presence of Pharaoh, and went throughout all the land of Egypt" (Gen. 41:46). The ruler invested him with official authority because he trusted Joseph's judgment.

The diligent man will not stand before "mean" men. The Hebrew word translated here as "mean" is found in only one other verse, where it is translated "drowned." "Pharaoh's chariots and his host hath he cast into the sea: his chosen captains also are drowned in the Red sea" (Ex. 15:4). The root Hebrew word means "dark." In this context, the word means "obscure" (NASB), which is appropriate for such an obscure word.

This proverb conveys the idea that a diligent man will not have to waste his time dealing with obscure people. Taken together—kings and

279

obscure people—this proverb conveys the sense of service. It is not that kings grant the diligent person some kind of award for good work. The parallel would not make sense. Obscure people do not grant awards. They are too obscure. The awards would not mean anything. So, the sense of this proverb is that the diligent person serves in some kind of advisory capacity. Kings listen to him. Obscure people would also listen to him, but he has no time to advise everyone. So, he advises kings.

In the world of finance, we see an analogous procedure. As a money manager gains the reputation for making his clients lots of money, he finds that rich people want to invest their money with him. He can then screen access by raising the amount of money required to invest in his fund. Or he can charge a higher percentage for administering the funds. People without much money to invest cannot afford him. There was a time when he might have taken them on as clients, but no longer. There are only so many hours in the day. If a man must devote time to mastering a field, he might as well serve people with money or influence rather than poor people without influence. His time is scarce. He has to allocate it. Those without influence or wealth are no longer able to purchase his labor.

This proverb describes a positive sanction for diligence: to stand before kings. Why is this a positive sanction? Because most people wish to be in the presence of important people. They wish to be known as people with sufficient importance to gain access to the circles of the blessed. This is why people give favors to people who need no favors. They are not seeking money. They are seeking a kind of rubbed-off fame. The public imputes importance to famous people. Other people seek a kind of reflected fame by being in the circles of the famous. This is why people ask famous people to sign autographs. In a few cases, this may be for money, such as an autographed baseball made in a record-breaking game. But normally, people just want a scrap of paper with a celebrity's signature on it.

Here, King Solomon speaks of obtaining an audience before kings. The king wants top-quality service. This person is in a position to provide it. Kings do not want services rendered by obscure people, any more than people with expertise want to serve obscure people. Kings want the best and can afford the best. This person's performance on the job has won him a reputation for excellence. This is the kind of person kings wish to deal with.

So fundamental is diligence in a person's ability to deliver consistently above-average performance that Solomon says diligence will be rewarded by exceptional acclaim. This indicates that diligence is rare. If everyone were equally diligent, most people would not gain access to kings. So, because diligence is exceptional, the reward is exceptional.

Conclusion

There are winners and losers in life. Kings are usually winners. So, to stand before kings is to bask in the reflected light of winners. Solomon presents this as a positive sanction for diligence. In contrast, obscure people are losers. Diligent people will not have to spend time dealing with losers.

This proverb makes it clear that it is better to win than lose. It calls men to greater diligence, so as not to be acclaimed by losers.

72

UNRELIABLE RICHES

Labour not to be rich: cease from thine own wisdom. Wilt thou set thine eyes upon that which is not? for riches certainly make themselves wings; they fly away as an eagle toward heaven.

PROVERBS 23:4−5

Solomon was rich. He had asked for wisdom and had gained great wealth. He did not lose his wealth. Instead, he lost his wisdom. He married too many women.

His wealth did not fly away. But he had not pursued kingship in order to gain wealth. He had hoped to gain the ability to provide sound judgment for the nation. He had achieved this goal. He lost it with respect to his own household. He worshipped the gods of his foreign wives. This cost his son Rehoboam the kingdom. The prophet told Jeroboam, Solomon's successor in the Northern Kingdom, that God would take action after the death of Solomon.

> Howbeit I will not take the whole kingdom out of his hand: but I will make him prince all the days of his life for David my servant's sake, whom I chose, because he kept my commandments and my statutes: But I will take the kingdom out of his son's hand, and will give it unto thee, even ten tribes (I Kings 11:34−35).

Solomon pursued wisdom, a good thing. He attained wisdom, a good thing. But wisdom then escaped him. That which he had pursued with all his might, he lost. He kept what he had not pursued, his wealth.

A. Pursuing Vanity

Nothing pursued for its own sake is reliable. *Autonomy fails to secure permanent benefits.* Solomon initially pursued wisdom for the sake of

282

the nation. But he lost this vision. He turned against God's law. He broke the laws of kingship.

> When thou art come unto the land which the LORD thy God giveth thee, and shalt possess it, and shalt dwell therein, and shalt say, I will set a king over me, like as all the nations that are about me; Thou shalt in any wise set him king over thee, whom the LORD thy God shall choose: one from among thy brethren shalt thou set king over thee: thou mayest not set a stranger over thee, which is not thy brother. But he shall not multiply horses to himself, nor cause the people to return to Egypt, to the end that he should multiply horses: forasmuch as the LORD hath said unto you, Ye shall henceforth return no more that way. Neither shall he multiply wives to himself, that his heart turn not away: neither shall he greatly multiply to himself silver and gold (Deut. 17:14–17).[1]

His heart turned away, just as Moses had predicted. This is the danger of anything pursued for its own sake or for what it offers to men in history. *To pursue anything for its own sake is to pursue the wind.* This is vanity.

This proverb singles out riches. Why riches? Why not the other parts of the triumvirate: sex and power? Because money is the most commonly available of the three. Almost anyone can pursue money. Power is not available to as many people as money is. The number of women available to any man is limited, other than through prostitution. There has been only one Solomon in this respect, and his unique example stands as a lasting testimony to the utter foolishness of the quest.

Money is the most marketable commodity. It makes available most of the other sins, which are for sale.

The popular T-shirt slogan, "He who dies with the most toys wins," is popular for two reasons. First, people know it is not true, that it is a child's outlook. Second, they also know that what the would-be rich and the already rich do to amass ever-greater wealth indicates that they really do believe it. Their behavior testifies to their belief in it. If they do not believe it, then they are sorely confused.

B. Riches Are Fleeting

The imagery of riches making wings to fly away is graphic. Riches are fleeting. So is life. *The fleeting nature of life should remind men of the fleeting nature of riches.* But, for most people, it is difficult to accept this fact emotionally. Jesus warned his disciples of this error.

---

1. Gary North, *Inheritance and Dominion: An Economic Commentary on Deuteronomy*, 2nd ed. (Dallas, Georgia: Point Five Press, [1999] 2012), ch. 42.

And he spake a parable unto them, saying, The ground of a certain rich man brought forth plentifully: And he thought within himself, saying, What shall I do, because I have no room where to bestow my fruits? And he said, This will I do: I will pull down my barns, and build greater; and there will I bestow all my fruits and my goods. And I will say to my soul, Soul, thou hast much goods laid up for many years; take thine ease, eat, drink, and be merry. But God said unto him, Thou fool, this night thy soul shall be required of thee: then whose shall those things be, which thou hast provided? So is he that layeth up treasure for himself, and is not rich toward God (Luke 12:16–21).[2]

Are riches uniquely fleeting, compared to other attributes of success? Solomon did not say they are. Isaiah indicated that all of life suffers from this condition of easy departure.

The voice said, Cry. And he said, What shall I cry? All flesh is grass, and all the goodliness thereof is as the flower of the field: The grass withereth, the flower fadeth: because the spirit of the LORD bloweth upon it: surely the people is grass (Isa. 40:6–7).

Then why did Solomon single out riches? Because riches are the universal surrogate for all the other fleeting pursuits in life. The prices of the other popular vanities are usually denominated in money. If there is a market for a specific vanity, money is the unit of exchange. A person can change his mind about which vanity to pursue. Money lets him make this transition with the least loss to his accumulated portfolio of vanity. *Money is the lowest common denominator in the pursuit of vanity*, for it is the universal medium of exchange.

Riches are fleeting because wealth can be used to pursue so many false trails. Ecclesiastes described all the vanities that he pursued. Solomon had the money to indulge himself. Men with riches face many opportunities to dissipate their wealth, just as the prodigal son dissipated his (Luke 15:11–32).[3]

For most people, it is easier to spend money than to accumulate it. For a tiny elite, this is not true. Their wealth accumulates faster than they can spend it on themselves. There is not enough time in the day to spend it all in consumption. These people are uniquely dangerous to others when they attempt to put their wealth to use in a larger cause. Customers impose limits on wealth-seekers: objective profit and loss. Customers bid money to be served. But in giving

---

2. Gary North, *Treasure and Dominion: An Economic Commentary on Luke*, 2nd ed. (Dallas, Georgia: Point Five Press, [2000] 2012), ch. 25.

3. *Ibid.*, ch. 37.

money away, the rich man finds that there is no agreement regarding objective measures of success. Everyone encourages him to give away even more. He finds himself surrounded by men with grand plans to redeem the world through money—messianic men who dream of spending rich men's money to achieve their own agendas. For most wealth-pursuers, the world is better off when they pursue their wealth than when they begin to give it away.

Conclusion

The central question here is broad: "Wilt thou set thine eyes upon that which is not?" That which is *not* is vanity.

Riches fly away. So does vanity in general. That which is pursued for its own sake becomes vanity. To accumulate it is to accumulate the wind.

It is difficult to see this with respect to riches, so Solomon singles out riches as the universal deceiver of the easily deceived. It is the common representative of man's autonomous wisdom. He warns us: "cease from thine own wisdom."

73

SUPERNATURAL SANCTIONS

Remove not the old landmark; and enter not into the fields of the fatherless: For their redeemer is mighty; he shall plead their cause with thee.

PROVERBS 23:10–11

This refers back to a previous proverb, "Remove not the ancient landmark, which thy fathers have set" (Prov. 22:28).[1] This in turn refers back to a Mosaic law: "Thou shalt not remove thy neighbour's landmark, which they of old time have set in thine inheritance, which thou shalt inherit in the land that the LORD thy God giveth thee to possess it" (Deut. 19:14).[2] This proverb adds two additional pieces of information: (1) there is special protection accorded to orphans; (2) a mighty redeemer will defend their cause against the proverb's violator.

It is clear that the redeemer in question is God. The Hebrew word for redeemer, *ga'al*, is occasionally used to identify God. The most famous example is Job's declaration: "For I know that my redeemer liveth, and that he shall stand at the latter day upon the earth" (Job 19:25). God redeemed Israel from Egypt. "Wherefore say unto the children of Israel, I am the LORD, and I will bring you out from under the burdens of the Egyptians, and I will rid you out of their bondage, and I will **redeem** you with a stretched out arm, and with great judgments" (Ex. 6:6). The word refers to the next of kin, who is not only the redeemer—one who buys his relative out of bondage (Lev. 25:48–49)[3]—but also the blood avenger. "The revenger of blood

---

1. Chapter 70.
2. Gary North, *Inheritance and Dominion: An Economic Commentary on Deuteronomy*, 2nd ed. (Dallas, Georgia: Point Five Press, [1999] 2012), ch. 44.
3. Gary North, *Boundaries and Dominion: An Economic Commentary on Leviticus*, 2nd ed. (Dallas, Georgia: Point Five Press, [1994] 2012), ch. 32.

himself shall slay the murderer: when he meeteth him, he shall slay him" (Num. 35:19). God holds this dual office with respect to His redeemed people: redeemer and blood avenger.

A. Pleading the Orphan's Cause

To plead a cause is to act as a defense attorney for the victim. But, unlike a modern attorney who merely argues a case, the person described here also executes judgment. God sees the evils done to the defenseless. He intervenes on their behalf.

> Ye shall not afflict any widow, or fatherless child. If thou afflict them in any wise, and they cry at all unto me, I will surely hear their cry; And my wrath shall wax hot, and I will kill you with the sword; and your wives shall be widows, and your children fatherless (Ex. 22:22–24).[4]

> For the LORD your God is God of gods, and Lord of lords, a great God, a mighty, and a terrible, which regardeth not persons, nor taketh reward: He doth execute the judgment of the fatherless and widow, and loveth the stranger, in giving him food and raiment (Deut. 10:17–18).

This is a description of a blood avenger. God declares that He serves as the blood avenger of those who have no earthly next of kin to intervene on their behalf.

This was common knowledge in Israel. So, Solomon did not have to go into detail regarding the background of his command here. When a person secretly moves a landmark to gain a little extra property for his family, he takes a high-risk step that threatens to undo him. When God pleads a person's cause, the offender has nowhere to hide. The Psalmist described what such people can expect.

> They encourage themselves in an evil matter: they commune of laying snares privily; they say, Who shall see them? They search out iniquities; they accomplish a diligent search: both the inward thought of every one of them, and the heart, is deep. But God shall shoot at them with an arrow; suddenly shall they be wounded (Ps. 64:5–7).

The evil-doers do not experience immediate negative sanctions. This gives them confidence.

> LORD, how long shall the wicked, how long shall the wicked triumph? How long shall they utter and speak hard things? and all the workers of iniquity boast themselves? They break in pieces thy people, O LORD, and

---

4. Gary North, *Authority and Dominion: An Economic Commentary on Exodus* (Dallas, Georgia: Point Five Press, 2012), Part 3, *Tools of Dominion* (1990), ch. 48.

afflict thine heritage. They slay the widow and the stranger, and murder the fatherless. Yet they say, The Lord shall not see, neither shall the God of Jacob regard it (Ps. 94:3–7).

This proverb reminds such men that God does see what they do, and He will intervene in history to right such wrongs.

B. Beyond Cosmic Impersonalism

Thieves do cost-benefit analyses, just as other men do. They see how easy it is to move a landmark. They see how difficult this will be to detect, let alone prove in a court of law. They do not look beyond the social order to identify possible flaws in their plan. They do not believe that there is anything beyond the impersonal forces of history to bring them to judgment, should there be no human witnesses.

This is foolish, says this proverb. There is a God who intervenes in history. He judges in terms of a legal code. He does not withdraw indefinitely from the affairs of men.

It is not just modern man who views justice in history as a matter of power rather than ethics. In Solomon's day, there were men who took the same view of historical cause and effect as modern man does. While most people in Solomon's day may have believed in some sort of supernatural background for the universe, just as most moderns do, they did not regard this supernatural realm as sufficiently aware or sufficiently interested in men's affairs to intervene in order to bring justice to victims. Such intervention was too specific, too immediate, and too predictable to be taken seriously in a rational criminal's cost-benefit analysis.

Modern covenant-breaking men dismiss such a view of historical cause and effect as implausible. Modern covenant-keeping men accept this view as a statistical possibility, but they are not sufficiently persuaded of its validity to believe that God actually intervenes in specific cases when society refuses to enforce God's law. Most of them relegate God's Bible-revealed law to the Old Covenant. That is to say, they deny that the sanction described in this proverb is still a factor to be considered when thinking about the enforcement limits of written or customary law. Their view of God's intervention on behalf of the victim is not significantly different from covenant-breaking men's view. Both groups regard this proverb as expressing a view of God that is no longer relevant in modern times, because cause and effect no longer operate in this fashion.

This outlook makes law enforcement more expensive. It persuades criminals that their acts of theft will not expose them to negative supernatural sanctions in history. They fear only the civil government. Similarly, covenant-keepers are equally persuaded that criminals' acts of theft will not expose them to negative supernatural sanctions in history. So, covenant-keepers are tempted to increase the power of the civil government to extend its techniques of law enforcement. They trust an expanded state, just as criminals fear it. Neither side fears God as a blood avenger.

Conclusion

This proverb presents a covenantal view of cause and effect. It asserts that the God who revealed His law to Moses is also the enforcer of last resort in history. This means that civil government need not be trusted to provide anything like the degree of justice presented in this proverb. It must not be so trusted. God is omniscient; the state is not.

74

UNDISCIPLINED LIVING

Be not among winebibbers; among riotous eaters of flesh: For the drunkard and the glutton shall come to poverty: and drowsiness shall clothe a man with rags.

Wine-lovers and meat-lovers, drunkards and gluttons, and people who just cannot seem to keep their eyes open: they share a common destiny. They will eventually wind up in poverty. This proverb does not say why, but it takes little imagination to understand why. *They are undisciplined.*

It is not that they are all lazy. The sleepy fellow may be, but not the drunkard or the glutton. They share the same personality trait. *They do not say no*. The drunkard does not stop drinking. The party-goer does not stop attending parties. The glutton does not stop eating. They all waste time and money on excessive consumption. They are unwilling to make the adjustments necessary in their lives to bring their appetites under control. The self-discipline required to regain control over their lives is beyond their will.

It is not that they do not know what they are doing. They know, but they do not care enough to change their ways. This brief proverb identifies their character flaw. Solomon did not spend space by explaining why such behavior produces poverty. He merely reminded his readers of the existence of the cause-and-effect relationship between undisciplined living and poverty.

Thrift is based on deferred gratification. An individual sees something he would like to own or like to experience. It costs money. It costs time. The person then makes a judgment regarding time: now, later, or never. If he decides "now," then he must forfeit the money and time that he could have used to invest.

290

He can also use the money and time to enjoy something else. He can consume many things. These are singled out as producing poverty when consumed in large quantities: wine, meat, and food. They are irresistible to the people described in this proverb. Other things could be consumed in large quantities, but these are singled out. This one sounds odd to our ears: "riotous eaters of flesh." This is because meat in the modern world's industrial economies is so common that to eat it, even lots of it, is not considered deviant. Riotous parties where meat is consumed in large quantities are not common, not because riotous parties are uncommon, but because meat is so common. Until the mid-nineteenth century, meat was so expensive that a riotous party marked by high meat consumption would have been regarded as an expensive luxury available only to the rich. Anyone attending such parties on a regular basis would have had to be a party giver, not just a party attendee.

The person who is unable to say no to riotous, expensive parties, or to wine, or to food is a wastrel. He is wasting what could be exchanged for capital. He is consuming when he could be producing. More wealth is going out than is coming in. The end result is poverty.

A person who refuses to say no to his appetites is unable to budget. Yet budgeting is basic to success in a world under a cursed scarcity (Gen. 3:17–19). The curse was imposed in order to force men to choose among options. Left to themselves without the environmental restrictions imposed by scarcity, men would be murderous and destructive.[1] So, God has imposed limits on what men can accomplish with the resources they possess. This forces those who wish to maximize their accomplishments to allocate their wealth carefully. They must not surrender to their desire for present gratification. They must not allocate too much wealth to consumption.

Addiction to liquor, food, or partying is common in history. These seem to be irresistible for some people. This proverb warns readers that if they have difficulty resisting any of these, as well as sleep, then they should begin to exercise self-control now. The alternative is to risk becoming addicted. The reader is warned not to pursue a pattern of behavior based on self-indulgence. This is the warning: *to be addicted is to die in poverty*. The negative sanction of poverty is as universally feared as these behaviors are addicting. This proverb rests on a premise: poverty is to be avoided. If this were not the premise, then

---

1. Gary North, *Sovereignty and Dominion: An Economic Commentary on Genesis* (Dallas, Georgia: Point Five Press, [1982] 2012), ch. 12.

the threat of poverty in the long run could not overcome the lure of self-indulgence in the short run.

Conclusion

If you want to avoid poverty, avoid addictive behavior. Addictive behavior leads to the undisciplined consumption of wealth. It undermines thrift. It undermines capital formation.

Why do you and most other people want to avoid poverty? Because poverty is a negative sanction in history. As a general rule, he who owns very little can accomplish very little. He does not possess tools of production: capital.

Those who fear poverty because they fear restrictions on their consumption are warned that if they are not self-disciplined, they will find themselves in tighter straits than they prefer: fewer choices. Those who fear poverty because they fear restrictions on their ability to extend the kingdom of God in history are warned that if they are not self-disciplined, they will find themselves in tighter straits than they prefer: fewer choices. The negative sanction is the same in both cases.

75

THE PRICE OF PROSPERITY

I went by the field of the slothful, and by the vineyard of the man void of under-
standing; And, lo, it was all grown over with thorns, and nettles had covered
the face thereof, and the stone wall thereof was broken down. Then I saw, and
considered it well: I looked upon it, and received instruction. Yet a little sleep, a
little slumber, a little folding of the hands to sleep: So shall thy poverty come as
one that travelleth; and thy want as an armed man.

PROVERBS 24:30–34

This proverb has a structure different from all the others. It is not
in the form of detailed instruction, as with the first nine chapters
and chapters 30 and 31. It is also not in the form of pithy statements
that convey a single idea. Instead, it is in the form of an observation,
followed by an assessment of what Solomon had seen. The lesson
learned affirms what Solomon had already announced: "Yet a little
sleep, a little slumber, a little folding of the hands to sleep: So shall
thy poverty come as one that travelleth, and thy want as an armed
man" (Prov. 6:10–11).

Solomon says that he observed the condition of the capital assets
owned by a slothful person—perhaps two people—who had no understanding. The assets were a field, a vineyard, and a stone wall. All
showed signs of decay. The land was filled with thorns and nettles.
These were signs of God's curse of the ground in response to Adam's
rebellion. "Thorns also and thistles shall it bring forth to thee; and
thou shalt eat the herb of the field" (Gen. 3:18).[1] They had covered
over the ground. This was evidence of long-term neglect. The stone
wall was broken down. A stone wall does not fall apart overnight,

---

1. Gary North, *Sovereignty and Dominion: An Economic Commentary on Genesis* (Dallas,
Georgia: Point Five Press, 2012), ch. 12.

except in an earthquake. Whoever owned this property had allowed it to fall into autonomy.

A. Autonomous Nature

This proverb testifies to the existence of an environment that is hostile to mankind. Left to itself, it will cease to be productive in terms of the needs and desires of men. *Nature's autonomous productivity is a threat to mankind.* What nature produces on its own is contrary to the plans of productive men.

Solomon says that poverty is the outcome of men's acceptance of nature on nature's terms. Nature is uninterested in men. Men are interested in nature. They are supposed to bring nature under their dominion, which in turn brings nature under God's dominion. This is the requirement of the dominion covenant. "And God said, Let us make man in our image, after our likeness: and let them have dominion over the fish of the sea, and over the fowl of the air, and over the cattle, and over all the earth, and over every creeping thing that creepeth upon the earth" (Gen. 1:26).[2]

Solomon describes poverty as if it were active: like a person on a journey. He walks along and finds victims. The lazy person's lack of goods is also like the results of an attack by an armed thief. He who refuses to labor is like a person who disarms himself in a world of armed thieves. This indicates that *wealth is abnormal.* It is the product of labor. *Poverty is normal.* Do nothing, and it will arrive at your doorstep—your broken-down doorstep.

Things do not take care of themselves. Men must take care of them. *The environment resists alterations by man for man.* This is not passive resistance. It is active resistance. *That which is normal for nature brings poverty to man.* Men must therefore actively resist nature's normal operations in order to achieve their goals. "In the sweat of thy face shalt thou eat bread, till thou return unto the ground; for out of it wast thou taken: for dust thou art, and unto dust shalt thou return" (Gen. 3:19).[3]

It is clear throughout the Proverbs that *poverty is normal but not normative.* It is something to be avoided. Solomon pointed to sloth and slumber as two primary sources of poverty. He did not have to devote space to an explanation of why poverty is something to be avoided. *Poverty is a curse.* This fact is almost universally recognized.

---

2. *Ibid.*, ch. 3.
3. *Ibid.*, ch. 12.

B. Overcoming Poverty

The first step, Solomon teaches here, is to avoid the lifestyle of the slothful. *This takes a change of heart.* This is why Solomon keeps returning to this message. Reformed lazybones, through their capital accumulation and their increased productivity, raise the operational living standards of all men. Poverty is then redefined upward. The West has experienced this, beginning around 1780.

It takes work to clear away thorns and thistles, to replace the fallen stones in fences. Solomon calls his listeners and readers to a life of hard work. This is what it takes to roll back the kingdom of poverty. *Sloth is the default mode of mankind*, which is why God cursed the land. Men must be motivated to work. Overcoming scarcity is the primary motivation for most people to get out of bed.

There is a saying in the United States: "You can get rich if you work just half a day. It doesn't matter which half." This saying recognizes the centrality of labor in overcoming poverty.

Yet hard work alone is not sufficient to overcome poverty. Men must work in order to produce something valuable enough and scarce enough to get paid for. If no one is willing to pay, then the labor will not achieve the goal of overcoming poverty unless God intervenes because He honors the specific work being performed at no pay. *Poverty-overcoming work must be buyer-directed work.*

Conclusion

The environment was redesigned by God after Adam's Fall. It was re-designed to thwart man's plans. It now automatically imposes costs on him. He must give up the things he wants in order to gain things he wants even more. One of the things he must give up is leisure. He has no free time. All of his time must be paid for.

76

REWARDING OUR ENEMIES

If thine enemy be hungry, give him bread to eat; and if he be thirsty, give him water to drink: For thou shalt heap coals of fire upon his head, and the LORD *shall reward thee.*

PROVERBS 25:21–22

A. Treating Enemies Lawfully

Most of this passage was quoted by Paul:

> Dearly beloved, avenge not yourselves, but rather give place unto wrath: for it is written, Vengeance is mine; I will repay, saith the Lord. Therefore if thine enemy hunger, feed him; if he thirst, give him drink: for in so doing thou shalt heap coals of fire on his head. Be not overcome of evil, but overcome evil with good (Rom. 12:19–21).[1]

This passage establishes a principle of action: *we must treat our enemies according to God's law.* But we must then go the extra mile (Matt. 5:41).[2] We must show mercy to them. This has the effect of disarming them. It also disarms us. To do good to our enemies makes us less willing to inflict harm if we are ever in a position to do so. Vengeance is God's, not ours.

This command rests on a fundamental principle: *vengeance really is God's.* He brings negative sanctions. This passage indicates that he brings these sanctions in history. But the image of coals on a man's head points to the final residence of covenant-breakers.

---

1. Gary North, *Cooperation and Dominion: An Economic Commentary on Romans*, 2nd ed. (Dallas, Georgia: Point Five Press, [2000] 2012), ch. 10.

2. Gary North, *Priorities and Dominion: An Economic Commentary on Matthew*, 2nd ed. (Dallas, Georgia: Point Five Press, [2000] 2012), ch. 9:D.

It rests on a second principle: God brings positive sanctions in history. "The LORD shall reward thee." For showing mercy to an enemy, the covenant-keeper accomplishes two things: (1) he delivers his enemy into God's hands for judgment; (2) he gains positive rewards for himself. This is far better than sitting on the sidelines and seeing an enemy go hungry.

What is the cost? First, submission to a law of God. Second, some bread and water. The food is not the best. It sustains the beneficiary for a few hours. It gets him to the next step in his journey. Except in a famine or drought or a war, the cost is minimal.

The contrast between the low cost and the high return is striking. For the cost of bread and water, the covenant-keeper places his enemy under an extreme threat. He delivers him into God's court of justice. If the enemy is also God's enemy, this is a fearful place to be.

This proverb reminds men that their instinctive reaction is incorrect. They want to keep their enemies under a minimal restraint: either hunger or thirst. Their enemies' condition is little more than an annoyance to them, something that can be solved by bread and water. Instead of taking this approach, this proverb says, take an action that will bring the enemy under fearful sanctions.

B. Fearful Negative Sanctions

The passage rests on the assumption that God will impose fearful negative sanctions. This is an Old Testament passage, reaffirmed by Paul. The supposed contrast between the fearful God of the Old Testament and the loving Jesus of the New Testament is negated by this passage. The stated goal of this strategy is to place enemies under fearful negative sanctions. *The goal here is revenge, but revenge applied by a specialist in revenge.* Rather than revenge autonomously applied by withholding something of very little value, it is revenge of enormous proportions applied by God.

Negative sanctions are legitimate. They are necessary. They are part of the covenantal cause-and-effect system that governs human relationships. They are the foundation of positive sanctions shown to an enemy. But it goes beyond this. Negative sanctions are accompanied by positive sanctions shown to the person who shows low-cost mercy. Positive sanctions also are part of the created system of social causation in history.

This proverb calls covenant-keepers to show mercy in the name of God, who in turn will not show mercy when He gets the opportunity to deal with the recipients of His servant-mediated mercy. This promise points to hell (Luke 16:19–31) and the lake of fire (Rev. 20:14–15). Men receive God's common grace in history.[3] Those who remain covenant-breakers then must suffer eternally for their lack of gratefulness to God for His common grace. The more common grace they have received, the greater their torment in eternity.

> And that servant, which knew his lord's will, and prepared not himself,
> neither did according to his will, shall be beaten with many stripes. But he
> that knew not, and did commit things worthy of stripes, shall be beaten
> with few stripes. For unto whomsoever much is given, of him shall be
> much required: and to whom men have committed much, of him they will
> ask the more (Luke 12:47–48).[4]

The modern world hates Christianity, but people hate it more for its doctrine of hell than any other. Men in the West do not tolerate the thought that God does not tolerate them. This passage indicates just how complete God's hatred of them is. He calls His people to show mercy to them in order that He may punish them for more.

Negative sanctions are part of God's kingdom-building process. The extension of God's kingdom in history is accomplished by the rolling back of Satan's. By bringing the enemies of God under negative sanctions imposed by God, the covenant-keeper extends God's kingdom. The aid provided by bread and water is marginal. The negative sanctions invoked by this act of mercy are not marginal.

Conclusion

The covenant-keeper must show minimal mercy to his enemies. God will reward those who do. This reward includes the positive sanction of seeing one's enemies ruined. Covenant-keepers are encouraged to seek this end because God seeks it. He sets the pattern; His followers should imitate it. This is not the sort of God modern men want to believe in, but it is the only God there is.

This does not mean that covenant-keepers should not pray that their mercy will bring the recipients of mercy to repentance. *The goal is the expansion of God's kingdom in history*. This can be through either redemption or destruction. Both work well. God initiates both. But here, men are told that positive sanctions produce negative sanctions. The focus is on negative sanctions.

---

3. Gary North, *Dominion and Common Grace: The Biblical Basis of Progress* (Tyler, Texas: Institute for Christian Economics, 1987).

4. Gary North, *Treasure and Dominion: An Economic Commentary on Luke*, 2nd ed. (Dallas, Georgia: Point Five Press, [2000] 2012), ch. 28.

77

THE LABORER'S REWARD

Whoso keepeth the fig tree shall eat the fruit thereof: so he that waiteth on his master shall be honoured.

PROVERBS 27:18

The imagery of keeping the tree hearkens back to keeping the tree in Eden. "And the LORD God took the man, and put him into the garden of Eden to dress it and to keep it" (Gen. 2:15). Yet the Hebrew word for "keep" in Genesis 2:15 is the same as the word for "wait" in this proverb. The two tasks are similar.

The person who takes care of the fig tree establishes a moral claim to the fruit of the tree. Obviously, he is not a hired servant, whose pay is his reward for service. This case is different. The person invests time and effort in caring for the fig tree. He does not do this for the sake of the tree. He does it in expectation of a reward.

This is similar to a servant who serves a master, or should be, says Solomon. The Hebrew word for master here is used throughout the Old Testament for the person at the top of a hierarchy. So close was this master-servant relationship under the Mosaic law that it could be made permanent on request by the servant.

> If his master have given him a wife, and she have born him sons or daughters; the wife and her children shall be her master's, and he shall go out by himself. And if the servant shall plainly say, I love my master, my wife, and my children; I will not go out free: Then his master shall bring him unto the judges; he shall also bring him to the door, or unto the door post; and his master shall bore his ear through with an aul; and he shall serve him for ever (Ex. 21:4–6).[1]

---

1. Gary North, *Authority and Dominion: An Economic Commentary on Exodus* (Dallas, Georgia; Point Five Press, 2012), Part 3, *Tools of Dominion* (1990), ch. 32:D:3.

The servant is subordinate to his master. This proverb indicates that the servant is to exercise the same degree of concern for his master as a husbandman does for his fig tree, whose output he will own. The motivation of the tree-owner is eating or selling the figs. The motivation of the servant is to gain praise from the master. Praise is said to be the equivalent of eating the fruit of one's labor.

Praise here is seen as a major benefit. This should not be surprising. Entertainers who perform in front of a live audience respond favorably to applause, which is a form of praise. The American comedian Bob Hope was popular longer than any other American entertainer: seven decades. He set a world record with his 61-year contract with the same network (radio and television). *The Guinness Book of World Records* also lists him as the world's most honored entertainer. He was extremely wealthy, worth several hundred million dollars. Yet he refused to retire until he could no longer perform because of deafness. He died at age 100 in 2003. When asked at age 59 why he had cut short a fishing vacation, he replied, "Fish don't applaud."

Public honor for a servant is a special reward. The servant's task is to serve selflessly. He is not to call attention to himself. Things under his administration should run smoothly. His focus is directed upward, toward his master. The relationship is personal, yet it is also one of reward for services rendered. It is not a father-son hierarchy.

This proverb does not say how the servant will be honored. The Old Testament had no clear concept of final judgment, so the frame of reference was social. Within the context of his role as a servant, he would someday receive honor.

This honor is therefore owed to him, even as figs are owed to the person who cares for the fig tree. The master builds up a debit account over time, one which is not in a household ledger book, but which is a liability nonetheless. Faithful service is a rarity, so the servant is entitled to some form of public recognition. In corporations, a man with decades of service commonly has a party held in his honor at company expense upon his retirement. Superiors make speeches, and the man may be given a symbolic gift, which used to be a gold watch, which was a symbol of his years of predictable service. But this recognition is not the same as that owed to a servant. These men were very often middle-level employees. They were never bound by loyalty to their superiors, but only to the company.

The servant's loyalty is to his master's person. It is also to his master's household. The element of personal service marks the relationship. Honor received in recognition of such service in this context is personal. It is earned. To withhold it is regarded as worse than an oversight. Although it has no market value, because it cannot be sold, it is valuable. The master has an obligation to make public recognition of service rendered.

In Jesus' parable of the talents, this theme of public reward is basic. A ruler leaves his kingdom and places subordinates in charge.

> After a long time the lord of those servants cometh, and reckoneth with them. And so he that had received five talents came and brought other five talents, saying, Lord, thou deliveredst unto me five talents: behold, I have gained beside them five talents more. His lord said unto him, Well done, thou good and faithful servant: thou hast been faithful over a few things, I will make thee ruler over many things: enter thou into the joy of thy lord (Matt. 25:19–21).[2]

The grant of authority over many additional things was not part of the master's initial offer. He simply assigned each an area of responsibility: capital. They put this to productive use. They were doing this on his behalf. The parable appears in the section of the New Testament that deals with the final judgment.

So, the proverb regarding predictable praise has implications far beyond the master-servant relationship in a household. The relationship is central to the extension of God's kingdom in history. The servant's care for the master is a form of training. The goal is praise.

Conclusion

The laborer is worthy of his hire (Luke 10:7). In this case, because of the close personal relationship between master and servant, the final payment involves public honoring of the servant. This costs the master no money. It costs him only a public acknowledgment that the servant had made the master's own work more effective, that whatever the master had achieved rests heavily on the performance of his servant. This is too much for some masters to pay. But those who do will reap rewards: greater commitment from servants and hence greater output from them. Over time, those masters who understand and honor the motivation of their servants will replace those who do not. The free market is competitive. It rewards those who achieve greater output per unit of resource input. A servant is a resource input.

2. Gary North, *Priorities and Dominion: An Economic Commentary on Matthew*, 2nd ed. (Dallas, Georgia: Point Five Press, [2000] 2012), ch. 47.

78

REDEMPTION AND PRICES

Hell and destruction are never full; so the eyes of man are never satisfied.

PROVERBS 27:20

Hell in the Old Testament referred to the grave. As surely as graves will not fill up for as long as men are alive, so are the eyes of man not satisfied. The Hebrew word translated as "full" is the same word translated as "satisfied." To speak of the eyes of man as full does not convey the meaning. The word "satisfied" does.

From the economic point of view, this proverb rivals the importance of the verse describing curse of the ground (Gen. 3:18).[1] Free market economic theory teaches that demand is unlimited at zero price. It also teaches that supplies are always limited: the doctrine of scarcity. This was Adam Smith's starting point in *The Wealth of Nations* (1776). The world does not supply at zero cost all the things that men want to use or own. Out of men's study of the interplay of these two phenomena—demand and supply—has arisen the science of economics.

A. Mises on Discontentment

The economist who has made the most comprehensive use of the principle of permanent dissatisfaction is Ludwig von Mises. In his magnum opus, *Human Action* (1949), he included a section in Chapter 1 titled, "The Prerequisites of Human Action." The first prerequisite is discontentment.

---

1. Gary North, *Sovereignty and Dominion: An Economic Commentary on Genesis* (Dallas, Georgia: Point Five Press, [1982] 2012), ch. 12.

We call contentment or satisfaction that state of a human being which does not and cannot result in any action. Acting man is eager to substitute a more satisfactory state of affairs for a less satisfactory. His mind imagines conditions which suit him better, and his action aims at bringing about this desired state. The incentive that impels a man to act is always some sense of uneasiness. A man perfectly content with the state of his affairs would have no incentive to change things.[2]

Mises was open about the origin of this theory of human action. It rests on hedonism. "The idea that the incentive of human activity is always some uneasiness and its aim always to remove such uneasiness as far as possible, that is, to make the acting men feel happier, is the essence of the teachings of Eudaemonism and Hedonism."[3] This is Epicureanism, he says. It has never been refuted. "The theological, mystical, and other schools of a heteronomous ethic did not shake the core of Epicureanism because they could not raise any other objection than its neglect of 'higher' and 'nobler' pleasures."[4] Mises rejected all such criticisms. Why? Because the individual is autonomous. There is no higher court of appeal.

> The ultimate goal of human action is always the satisfaction of the acting man's desire. There is no standard of greater or lesser satisfaction other than individual judgments of value, different for various people and for the same people at various times. What makes a man feel uneasy and less uneasy is established by him from the standard of his own will and judgment, from his personal and subjective valuation. Nobody is in a position to decree what should make a fellow man happier.[5]

B. Destruction and Hedonism

Solomon compares death and destruction with human discontentment. Solomon had enormous wealth and power. In Ecclesiastes, he surveyed a representatively wide range of hedonism's options: the pursuit of pleasure and fame. It is all vanity, he concluded.

> I communed with mine own heart, saying, Lo, I am come to great estate, and have gotten more wisdom than all they that have been before me in Jerusalem: yea, my heart had great experience of wisdom and knowledge. And I gave my heart to know wisdom, and to know madness and folly: I perceived that this also is vexation of spirit. For in much wisdom is much

---

2. Ludwig von Mises, *Human Action: A Treatise on Economics* (New Haven, Connecticut: Yale University Press, 1949), p. 13.

3. *Ibid.*, p. 15.

4. *Idem.*

5. *Ibid.*, p. 14.

grief: and he that increaseth knowledge increaseth sorrow. I said in mine heart, Go to now, I will prove thee with mirth, therefore enjoy pleasure: and, behold, this also is vanity (Eccl. 1:16–2:1).

His conclusion was straightforward: "Let us hear the conclusion of the whole matter: Fear God, and keep his commandments: for this is the whole duty of man. For God shall bring every work into judgment, with every secret thing, whether it be good, or whether it be evil" (Eccl. 12:13–14).[6]

Mises and all those who claim ethical neutrality, methodological neutrality, and value-free analysis are wrong. Man is not autonomous. There are higher standards than those that men in their ethical rebellion adopt for themselves at any point in time. These standards apply in history and will govern the final judgment. God imputes—assigns and evaluates—value to all things, in terms of ethics and in terms of meaning. His imputation establishes the standard of value.

So, it matters what the source of dissatisfaction is. If it is the world's lack of conformity to God's standard of value, then dissatisfaction is legitimate. It reflects men's desire to make things better in history.

> Know ye not that they which run in a race run all, but one receiveth the prize? So run, that ye may obtain (I Cor. 9:24).[7]

> Wherefore seeing we also are compassed about with so great a cloud of witnesses, let us lay aside every weight, and the sin which doth so easily beset us, and let us run with patience the race that is set before us (Heb. 12:1).

In contrast, the quest for an unlimited and undefined "more" for oneself in history is illegitimate: the religion of mammon. This is an unbounded quest. That is why it is illegitimate: *man is finite and bounded.* Jesus warned: "No man can serve two masters: for either he will hate the one, and love the other; or else he will hold to the one, and despise the other. Ye cannot serve God and mammon" (Matt. 6:24).[8] Jesus spoke these words of warning to His disciples regarding the dead-end nature of this quest.

> And he said unto them, Take heed, and beware of covetousness: for a man's life consisteth not in the abundance of the things which he possess-

---

6. Gary North, *Autonomy and Stagnation: an Economic Commentary on Ecclesiastes* (Dallas, Georgia: Point Five Press, 2012), ch. 45.

7. Gary North, *Judgment and Dominion: An Economic Commentary on First Corinthians*, 2nd ed. (Dallas, Georgia: Point Five Press, [2001] 2012), ch. 12.

8. Gary North, *Priorities and Dominion: An Economic Commentary on Matthew*, 2nd ed. (Dallas, Georgia: Point Five Press, [2000] 2012), ch. 14.

eth. And he spake a parable unto them, saying, The ground of a certain rich man brought forth plentifully: And he thought within himself, saying, What shall I do, because I have no room where to bestow my fruits? And he said, This will I do: I will pull down my barns, and build greater; and there will I bestow all my fruits and my goods. And I will say to my soul, Soul, thou hast much goods laid up for many years; take thine ease, eat, drink, and be merry. But God said unto him, Thou fool, this night thy soul shall be required of thee: then whose shall those things be, which thou hast provided? So is he that layeth up treasure for himself, and is not rich toward God (Luke 12:16–21).[9]

And he said unto his disciples, Therefore I say unto you, Take no thought for your life, what ye shall eat; neither for the body, what ye shall put on. The life is more than meat, and the body is more than raiment. Consider the ravens: for they neither sow nor reap; which neither have storehouse nor barn; and God feedeth them: how much more are ye better than the fowls? And which of you with taking thought can add to his stature one cubit? If ye then be not able to do that thing which is least, why take ye thought for the rest? Consider the lilies how they grow: they toil not, they spin not; and yet I say unto you, that Solomon in all his glory was not arrayed like one of these. If then God so clothe the grass, which is to day in the field, and to morrow is cast into the oven; how much more will he clothe you, O ye of little faith? And seek not ye what ye shall eat, or what ye shall drink, neither be ye of doubtful mind. For all these things do the nations of the world seek after: and your Father knoweth that ye have need of these things. But rather seek ye the kingdom of God; and all these things shall be added unto you (Luke 12:22–31).[10]

C. Establishing Prices

In a free market, prices are established through competitive bidding. Individuals compete for scarce resources by offering something in exchange. The price system operates in terms of this general rule: "High bid wins."

The array of prices reflects the competing bids. Covenant-keepers and covenant-breakers compete for resources. They seek to achieve their ends through the means of private property. The New Testament speaks of redemption. Redemption means buying back something originally owned. Jesus bought back the fallen world from God's wrath (common grace). This included individual souls (special

---

9. Gary North, *Treasure and Dominion: An Economic Commentary on Luke*, 2nd ed. (Dallas, Georgia: Point Five Press, [2000] 2012), ch. 25.
    10. *Ibid.*, ch. 26.

grace).[11] "But when the fulness of the time was come, God sent forth his Son, made of a woman, made under the law, To redeem them that were under the law, that we might receive the adoption of sons" (Gal. 4:4–5). His work was definitive, meaning complete. His people's representative redemptive work on His behalf is progressive. "For we are his workmanship, created in Christ Jesus unto good works, which God hath before ordained that we should walk in them" (Eph. 2:10).

The price of everything reflects the efforts of all men to establish a kingdom in history: man's or God's. This is the war between mammon and God. It is a covenantal war that encompasses every area of life. The fact that evangelism is called redemption indicates the nature of the process. It involves purchasing the entire world, one item at a time, on behalf of Christ. This involves the whole world.

> For we know that the whole creation groaneth and travaileth in pain together until now. And not only they, but ourselves also, which have the firstfruits of the Spirit, even we ourselves groan within ourselves, waiting for the adoption, to wit, the redemption of our body (Rom. 8:22–23).[12]

> For he must reign, till he hath put all enemies under his feet. The last enemy that shall be destroyed is death. For he hath put all things under his feet. But when he saith, all things are put under him, it is manifest that he is excepted, which did put all things under him. And when all things shall be subdued unto him, then shall the Son also himself be subject unto him that put all things under him, that God may be all in all (I Cor. 15:25–28).[13]

Ownership is always stewardship. It is never autonomous. The distribution of property, like the array of prices, reflects men's stewardship on behalf of either mammon or God.

Conclusion

The eyes of men are never satisfied. There is always more to buy. The question is: By whom and for whom is it being purchased? Secular free market economics focuses on the consumer: the final owner. Socialist economics focuses on the state: the final owner. Biblical economics focuses on God: the original owner, present owner, and final owner.

Each approach has a doctrine of stewardship. The free market economist proclaims the individual as steward on his own behalf and

11. Gary North, *Dominion and Common Grace: The Biblical Basis of Progress* (Tyler, Texas: Institute for Christian Economics, 1987)

12. Gary North, *Cooperation and Dominion: An Economic Commentary on Romans*, 2nd ed. (Dallas, Georgia: Point Five Press, [2000] 2012), ch. 5.

13. North, *Judgment and Dominion*, ch. 16.

also on behalf of the highest-bidding consumer. The socialist proclaims the state bureaucrat as steward on behalf of the People, who are collectively sovereign. The Christian economist proclaims (or should proclaim) the individual and the association as stewards on behalf of the triune God.

The Christian should be dissatisfied with his previous performance, but not dissatisfied with its outcome.

> Not that I speak in respect of want: for I have learned, in whatsoever state I am, therewith to be content. I know both how to be abased, and I know how to abound: every where and in all things I am instructed both to be full and to be hungry, both to abound and to suffer need. I can do all things through Christ which strengtheneth me (Phil. 4:11–13).[14]

> And having food and raiment let us be therewith content (I Tim. 6:8).[15]

> Let your conversation be without covetousness; and be content with such things as ye have: for he hath said, I will never leave thee, nor forsake thee (Heb. 13:5).

---

14. Gary North, *Ethics and Dominion: An Economic Commentary on the Epistles* (Dallas, Georgia: Point Five Press, 2012), ch. 23.

15. Gary North, *Hierarchy and Dominion: An Economic Commentary on First Timothy*, 2nd ed. (Dallas, Georgia: Point Five Press, [2001] 2012), ch. 10:B:1.

79

ENTROPY AND CAPITAL

Be thou diligent to know the state of thy flocks, and look well to thy herds. For riches are not for ever: and doth the crown endure to every generation?

PROVERBS 27:23

This proverb is directed to those who have amassed capital. It focuses on what might be called the *entropy of capital*. Without an owner's attention to details, the entropy process takes control. Things grow more chaotic. Economic value declines. Solomon has already described this process. "I went by the field of the slothful, and by the vineyard of the man void of understanding; And, lo, it was all grown over with thorns, and nettles had covered the face thereof, and the stone wall thereof was broken down" (24:30).[1] Care of the flocks, like care of the fields, requires attention to details.

Riches are easily dissipated by heirs. "For riches are not for ever: and doth the crown endure to every generation?" Heirs can squander their inheritance. This reverses the expansion of family wealth over time. A family's dominion is thereby reduced. In the process of redemption—buying back the kingdom of Satan—the dissipation of family capital is a threat.

In good times, the owner is tempted to imagine that they are permanent. This proverb reminds owners that this is not the case. Circumstances change, and he who wants to maintain his capital must adjust accordingly. While successful men prefer to think that they deserve their wealth, this proverb points to the fact of capital dissipation. It takes active efforts to preserve capital.

There is a phrase in agricultural circles: "The best fertilizer is the

---

1. Chapter 75.

owner's shadow." Because he cannot oversee everything personally, the owner delegates authority to his employees. They are unlikely to take the same care with his resources as they do with their own. Furthermore, if they were as productive as the owner, they would not be employees. They would own their own businesses. Their skills at making a profit are limited. So, the owner has an economic incentive to monitor the management of his subordinates. This proverb encourages this kind of responsible oversight.

Solomon asks rhetorically: "Doth the crown endure to every generation?" It does not. What crown? Probably his own. Kingly crowns are passed from father to son. But sons who cannot defend their authority lose their crowns. This happened to Solomon's son, Rehoboam, with respect to the northern tribes: Israel. They revolted and separated from the nation. He retained authority only over Judah and the tribe of Benjamin (I Kings 12:21). God had revealed to Solomon that this would happen (I Kings 11:11–13).

Conclusion

This proverb is simple. It advises people with capital to "mind the store." Things do not autonomously take care of themselves. God requires owners and managers, as good stewards of His capital, to monitor it. Someone must monitor capital. This service is not done at zero cost. It must be paid for. This means that purely passive income is a form of capital consumption. This proverb warns against passive income. Passive income is an illusion.

80

THE MYTH OF VALUE-FREE ECONOMIC THEORY

Better is the poor that walketh in his uprightness, than he that is perverse in his ways, though he be rich.

PROVERBS 28:6

A. Righteousness Above Wealth

This proverb reminds men that righteousness is more important than wealth. It is an extension of Proverbs 1:1–4.[1] Few religions have ever taught anything else. Even murderous cults, such as thuggee, have a concept of ethics governing those inside the cult.

Throughout history, people have taught their children this principle. Also throughout history, men have pursued wealth at the expense of ethics. The lure of great wealth is so powerful that people with the ability to get rich through evil actions have done so. They have abandoned the ethical principles they learned in their youth and in school.

This proverb makes a value judgment. It does not pretend to be ethically neutral. It does not deal with means to the neglect of ends. It makes a judgment regarding ends and means. The end of great wealth, when attained through ethically perverse means, is not worth the cost. To make plain the extent of the high cost of perversity, Solomon compares the rich man with a poor man. The poor man is better off than the rich man. The deciding factor is ethics, not wealth.

Solomon does not hesitate to tell his listeners which condition is best. The suggestion of modern free market economists that such a judgment is not scientifically valid, because it makes interpersonal comparisons of subjective utility, would not have impressed Solo-

---

1. Chapter 1.

310

mon. This is because God does not begin with the hypothetically autonomous value scale of the acting individual. He begins instead with His covenant with mankind, which has established a system of moral cause and effect in society.

Christian economics makes no pretense of value neutrality. Value neutrality is a myth, and a highly unneutral one, given the fact of God's assertion of absolute sovereignty. *Value neutrality constitutes a rebellion against God and His covenant.* Its defenders assume that each individual is autonomous. But on such a basis, there can be no scientifically valid universal ethical system, including the ethics of neutrality.

Such an assertion of individual men's autonomy is inherently a form of *nominalism*: every man is a king, no man is a servant. Reality is whatever individual men think it is. Each person imputes meaning to the universe. But he does not impute corporate meaning. What he imputes has authority only for himself.

Under such a philosophy, the quest for wealth and power easily becomes an obsession. If the universe reflects what an individual thinks and does, then to gain immunity from other men's rival imputations and power, the self-proclaimed autonomous individual must seek to establish his own authority. This outlook leads to the error described in this proverb: seeking wealth perversely. Wealth is seen as a means of buying immunity and power.

Who imputes good or evil, success or failure, to anyone or any group? God does. Deny God this ability, and you must attribute it to something else. The state has been an obvious candidate through the ages. For a few theorists, the free market has replaced God as the agency of imputation. But the free market is merely the social arrangement that has developed as a result of the concept of private property. This concept rests on ethics: "Thou shalt not steal." "The Lord is not a respecter of persons." "Do not move thy neighbor's landmark." The free market has no external source of legitimacy in a world without God or permanent ethics. Everything is said to evolve. Power-seekers then seek to direct evolutionary forces to their benefit.[2]

B. Poverty

Poverty is best defined as a lack of affordable options. The individual poor man has fewer choices than a rich man does. It appears that a poor man operates at the mercy of the wealthy or else in the shadows,

2. Gary North, *Sovereignty and Dominion: An Economic Commentary on Genesis* (Dallas, Georgia: Point Five Press, [1982] 2012), Appendix A.

where the wealthy pay no attention. Poverty is the absence of immunity. Poverty is weakness.

Then why should Solomon insist that a poor man in his righteousness is better than a rich man in his perversity? What did he mean, *better*? The Hebrew word can be translated "good," in the sense of righteousness. As in English, it can also mean valuable, as in "good land." It can be translated as "prosperity." "Thou shalt not seek their peace nor their prosperity all thy days for ever" (Deut. 23:6). It can mean "better off." "And wherefore hath the LORD brought us unto this land, to fall by the sword, that our wives and our children should be a prey? were it not better for us to return into Egypt?" (Num. 14:3).

Then why is righteousness in poverty better than perversity in prosperity? This proverb does not say, but there is enough information in the Bible to answer the question. "Thou shalt be perfect with the LORD thy God" (Deut. 18:13). "Let your heart therefore be perfect with the LORD our God, to walk in his statutes, and to keep his commandments, as at this day" (I Kings 8:61). Jesus warned: "Be ye therefore perfect, even as your Father which is in heaven is perfect" (Matt. 5:48).

In contrast is the rich perverse man. His condition was summed up by Jesus. "For what is a man profited, if he shall gain the whole world, and lose his own soul? or what shall a man give in exchange for his soul?" (Matt. 16:26).[3]

Conclusion

There is no neutrality. There is also no neutral science. Neutrality is always a disguise for man's pretended autonomy. It begins with a presupposition: whatever is logical for all men is neutral. First, there is this problem: all men never agree on what is logical. There are many forms of logic, and lots of illogical men. Second, God establishes what is logical and true; men's individual minds do not.

There is ethical causation in history. The Bible teaches that societies that adopt laws that are more consistent with biblical laws get richer than societies whose laws are less consistent with biblical laws (Lev. 26; Deut. 28). In contrast, for individuals there can be anomalies (Ps. 73). So, this proverb brings us to the great religious rivals, God and mammon, by way of anomalies: righteous poverty and perverse wealth. Better the former than the latter, this proverb teaches.

---

3. Gary North, *Priorities and Dominion: An Economic Commentary on Matthew*, 2nd ed. (Dallas, Georgia: Point Five Press, [2000] 2012), ch. 35.

81

THE DISINHERITANCE OF COVENANT-BREAKERS

He that by usury and unjust gain increaseth his substance, he shall gather it for him that will pity the poor.

PROVERBS 28:8

This proverb is a variation of another: "A good man leaveth an inheritance to his children's children: and the wealth of the sinner is laid up for the just" (Prov. 13:22).[1] It presents a view of economic causation that is tied directly to ethics. Righteousness is a predictable source of wealth. The generous will inherit. This proverb is not saying that righteousness is its own reward. It is saying that righteousness brings positive economic sanctions in this life. It also announces that unrighteousness is a predictable source of impoverishment: gathering for others. Bad actions produce bad results. The world is not ethically random.

It takes things a step further. It says that he who devotes his efforts to unrighteousness ultimately is working on behalf of the person who deals righteously with people. Previously, Solomon announced that the wealth of the sinner is laid up for the just. Here, he repeats this assertion.

This system of covenantal economic causation does not announce that the good do well and the evil do poorly. It says that *the good do well at the expense of evildoers*. It is not that there are two fields of grain, with one field flourishing and the other field blighted. It goes far beyond this. It says that the output of one field will benefit the owner of the other field.

---

1. Chapter 41.

A. Dominion Through Inheritance

This proverb rests on a concept of inheritance that is unique to the Mosaic covenant. This concept of inheritance is symbolized by the conquest of Canaan. That was a conquest by force, a one-time event. But the nature of the transaction is clear from this proverb: *inheritance through disinheritance.*

> And it shall be, when the LORD thy God shall have brought thee into the land which he sware unto thy fathers, to Abraham, to Isaac, and to Jacob, to give thee great and goodly cities, which thou buildedst not, And houses full of all good things, which thou filledst not, and wells digged, which thou diggedst not, vineyards and olive trees, which thou plantedst not; when thou shalt have eaten and be full; Then beware lest thou forget the LORD, which brought thee forth out of the land of Egypt, from the house of bondage. Thou shalt fear the LORD thy God, and serve him, and shalt swear by his name (Deut. 6:10–13).

The covenant-breaker labors to build up an inheritance that he can pass on to his heirs. He makes himself a name. He leaves behind a legacy. The concept of intergenerational wealth transfer is inherent in humanity. This is an aspect of the dominion covenant. Adam was supposed to multiply and fill the earth. The concept of economic growth as stewardship on behalf of God is misapplied by covenant-breakers, who labor for themselves. The goal of dominion through expansion of wealth is legitimate (Deut. 28:1–14).[2] The question is: *Dominion on whose behalf?*

This proverb reinforces the earlier one, which clearly places wealth in the context of inheritance. The sense of long-term inheritance through the transfer of accumulated wealth is inescapable. This proverb is less forthright regarding the context of inheritance. The phrase, "he shall gather it for him that will pity the poor," does not specify a time frame. It does not indicate when the wealth transfer will take place: in the lifetime of the covenant-breaker or in his heirs' lifetimes. This proverb is silent on whether this transfer will be intergenerational or not. The man who uses unethical practices to accumulate wealth may not see his capital transferred to a righteous man of his own generation. But Solomon gives a warning to every such person: the end result of his efforts will be to enlarge the inheritance of his covenantal enemies.

---

2. Gary North, *Inheritance and Dominion: An Economic Commentary on Deuteronomy*, 2nd ed. (Dallas, Georgia: Point Five Press, [1999] 2012), ch. 69.

God's message to Satan throughout history.

B. Kingdoms in Conflict

The Kingdom of God will replace the Kingdom of satan in history.

This is God's message to Satan throughout history. The kingdom of God will replace the kingdom of Satan, not just in eternity, but also in time. "And the LORD God said unto the serpent, Because thou hast done this, thou art cursed above all cattle, and above every beast of the field; upon thy belly shalt thou go, and dust shalt thou eat all the days of thy life: And I will put enmity between thee and the woman, and between thy seed and her seed; it shall bruise thy head, and thou shalt bruise his heel" (Gen. 3:14–15). This will be manifested in civil rule.

> Why do the heathen rage, and the people imagine a vain thing? The kings of the earth set themselves, and the rulers take counsel together, against the LORD, and against his anointed, saying, Let us break their bands asunder, and cast away their cords from us. He that sitteth in the heavens shall laugh: the Lord shall have them in derision (Ps. 2:1–4).

> A Psalm of David. The LORD said unto my Lord, Sit thou at my right hand, until I make thine enemies thy footstool. The LORD shall send the rod of thy strength out of Zion: rule thou in the midst of thine enemies (Ps. 110:1–2).

This principle of dominion applies in economic affairs in the same way. The expansion of God's kingdom in history is not limited to one manifestation of His covenantal order, but extends to all. The conquest is comprehensive because redemption is comprehensive.[3]

This proverb teaches that the covenant-breaker may well be able to expand his control over wealth through usury. He can increase his wealth by lending at interest to covenant-keepers who are in poverty through no fault of their own. This proverb does not say that unrighteousness produces losses from beginning to end. On the contrary, it affirms that the covenant-breaker can build up wealth. It says only that this wealth will eventually wind up under the control of a covenant-keeper. This is the essence of the dominion covenant: *the steady replacement of covenant-breakers by covenant-keepers*. The social world operates in terms of a covenantal order that elevates ethics over all other sources of economic success.

Why is this historical process not obvious to covenant-breakers and covenant-keepers alike? Why are two proverbs necessary to remind economic actors of the nature of economic causation? One an-

---

3. Gary North, *Is the World Running Down? Crisis in the Christian Worldview* (Tyler, Texas: Institute for Christian Economics, 1988), Appendix C.

swer is that covenant-breakers suppress the truth (Rom. 1:18–22).[4] But this does not explain why covenant-keepers seem equally blind to economic causation. The most likely answer is the long-term nature of this process of wealth transfer. Asaph suffered from an inability to see that covenant-keepers' success would eventually lead to their destruction.

> For I was envious at the foolish, when I saw the prosperity of the wicked. For there are no bands in their death: but their strength is firm. They are not in trouble as other men; neither are they plagued like other men. Therefore pride compasseth them about as a chain; violence covereth them as a garment. Their eyes stand out with fatness: they have more than heart could wish. They are corrupt, and speak wickedly concerning oppression: they speak loftily (Ps. 73:3–8).

But Asaph eventually came to his senses. "Until I went into the sanctuary of God; then understood I their end. Surely thou didst set them in slippery places: thou castedst them down into destruction. How are they brought into desolation, as in a moment! they are utterly consumed with terrors" (Ps. 73:17–19).

Conclusion

Economic causation is covenantal. It is hierarchical, because God controls events. It is ethical, because God establishes rules of right and wrong. It is predictable, because God governs through a system of sanctions. Finally, it is eschatological, because of the structure of inheritance in history: inheritance through disinheritance.

This proverb reflects the covenantal structure of kingdom history. Satan is disinherited in history. This means that, for a time, he accumulates capital that is worth inheriting in history. He build up a kingdom. Then he loses it. Sometimes redemption is strictly by purchase. Covenant-keepers buy back the kingdoms of man. They offer for sale what covenant-breakers want. They exchange trinkets for ownership of long-term, culture-transforming capital. But they also inherit. The ideal way is through conversion. The heirs of rich sinners transfer allegiance to a new king and a new kingdom. In doing so, they disinherit their forefathers, who had other goals for their wealth.

---

4. Gary North, *Cooperation and Dominion: An Economic Commentary on Romans*, 2nd. (Dallas, Georgia: [2000] 2012), ch. 2.

82

PATHWAY TO SUCCESS

He that tilleth his land shall have plenty of bread: but he that followeth after vain persons shall have poverty enough.

PROVERBS 28:19

This is a variation of Proverbs 12:11: "He that tilleth his land shall be satisfied with bread; but he that followeth vain persons is void of understanding."[1] The contrast there is between steady though uninspiring physical labor vs. following the schemes and dreams of vain (empty) people. Here, the contrast is between plenty of bread and "poverty enough." This is a poetic phrase. Solomon could have said "poverty" and conveyed the idea. But "poverty enough" puts an edge to it, a kind of ridicule. It raises the question: Poverty enough to do what? The idea here is *sufficient poverty to make God's point.*

A. Unreliable Leaders

What is God's point? This: there are vain people in every society who lure unsuspecting and naive followers into making economically disastrous decisions. These people thrive on having followers. They get a sense of satisfaction out of the deference shown to them, even if this deference comes from people with minimal ethical awareness. Solomon reminds his readers of the danger associated with following such people. The end result is poverty.

But why would anyone follow vain leaders? The implication is that the followers are unwilling to submit to the requirements of conventional labor: tilling one's own land. Such labor is undistinguished in an agricultural society. The fact that a man owns land, tools, and seed

---

1. Chapter 36.

does not distinguish him from all the other farmers who also own land, tools, and seed. It distinguishes him from field hands who own no land, tools, or seed, but he does not have his eye on those whom he might employ. He has his eyes on his peers. He wishes to stand out from them in the way that he stands out from field hands: higher.

Most people dream of attaining personal distinction in life. They want to be remembered as people who stood out from the crowd in some way, even if this means joining another crowd. Becoming the follower of an unconventional person who has the gift of attracting followers seems to many people to be the pathway to distinction. Men seek distinction through being represented by significant people. The fact that these people are empty does not register in the thinking of their followers.

Solomon says that it is wise to stick with what is conventional and thereby put bread on the table rather than venturing into unknown realms as followers of vain people. Stick with the tried and true. If you fail to stand out from the crowd, but you have bread on your table, you are better off than dreaming of wealth untold in the entourage of vain people.

B. Conventional Roads to Success

This proverb affirms tilling as the road to success, with success defined as bread on the table. This is an affirmation of conventional labor, long and hard, in the mid-summer sun. It affirms a theory of conventional labor. He who wishes to escape from this conventional pathway to success is opening himself to poverty-inducing leadership by vain people.

Until the advent of mass agricultural production, which accelerated rapidly with mechanical harvesters in the 1840s, and also with the transportation revolution of the railroads, which began in the same decade, most people tilled the soil for a living. They did not produce enough food to support a predominately urban society. Most people lived on farms, whether they raised grains or edible-wearable animals. A farmer pursued a vocation that extended back into the mists of unrecorded history. This occupation has been the archetype of conventional production.

The Bible speaks of bread as the symbol of life: that which sustains life. It teaches that bread is necessary but insufficient for sustaining life. Moses spoke to the generation of the conquest, reminding them of God's four decades of miracles in the wilderness: "And he humbled thee, and suffered thee to hunger, and fed thee with manna, which thou knewest not, neither did thy fathers know; that he might make thee know that man doth not live by bread only, but by every word that proceedeth out of the mouth of the LORD doth man live" (Deut. 8:3). This was spoken about a generation that lived in the presence of constant daily miracles. These miracles occurred in order to confirm their faith in God. But the manna ceased after the nation crossed the Jordan River and entered the promised land (Josh. 5:12). Their faith in God was supposed to remain intact, despite the removal of daily miracles.[2] Jesus quoted Moses' words: "But he answered and said, It is written, Man shall not live by bread alone, but by every word that proceedeth out of the mouth of God" (Matt. 4:4). This was a warning against the quest for miracles—turning stones into bread—as a substitute for faith.[3]

In Canaan, farming replaced manna-gathering. The drudgery of daily labor in the fields became the basis of success from then on. But this was not the only basis of success. Adherence to God's covenantal legal order was also required (Deut. 28:1–14).[4] It was this combination of conventional labor and adherence to biblical law that repelled (and still repels) those who seek personal success by identifying with vain people, who offer other, less rigorous avenues to success.

Conclusion

The common visual representation of a traditional farmer tilling his fields is a picture of a man behind a plow. Pulling the plow is an ox or a mule or a water buffalo. The common visual representation of a traditional follower of vain persons is a picture of a huge political rally. At the center is a now-dead, notorious, and defeated politician raising his fist. His victorious enemies paint the pictures and publish the archived photos. These images are essentially correct.

There is a famous painting of an old man, head bowed, giving prayerful thanks for a loaf of bread. In front of him on the table is an old, fat book—probably a Bible—with his metal-rimmed glasses folded on top of it. This is the most accurate visual representation of all. He is no longer of working age, but he has a full loaf of bread in front of him. He did not follow vain men.

---

2. Gary North, *Inheritance and Dominion: An Economic Commentary on Deuteronomy*, 2nd ed. (Dallas, Georgia: Point Five Press, [1999] 2012), ch. 18.

3. Gary North, *Priorities and Dominion: An Economic Commentary on Matthew*, 2nd ed. (Dallas, Georgia: Point Five Press, [2000] 2012), ch. 1.

4. North, *Inheritance and Dominion*, ch. 69.

83

NO SHORTCUTS TO SUCCESS

A faithful man shall abound with blessings: but he that maketh haste to be rich shall not be innocent.

PROVERBS 28:20

He that hasteth to be rich hath an evil eye, and considereth not that poverty shall come upon him.

PROVERBS 28:22

These are reinforcing proverbs. A common warning is given to a person who is impatient in his goal to gain riches. Proverbs 28:20 indicates that riches are legitimate. What is not legitimate is riches as a goal. "Labour not to be rich: cease from thine own wisdom" (Prov. 23:4).[1] Even less legitimate is the desire to get rich quick.

A. Positive Sanctions in History

In verse 20, we are informed of the way to positive sanctions in life: faithfulness. Faithfulness is an attribute of God. "And the heavens shall praise thy wonders, O LORD: thy faithfulness also in the congregation of the saints" (Ps. 89:5). What this proverb says regarding an individual, Deuteronomy 28:1–14 says of Israel as a nation. "And all these blessings shall come on thee, and overtake thee, if thou shalt hearken unto the voice of the LORD thy God" (Deut. 28:2). "The LORD shall command the blessing upon thee in thy storehouses, and in all that thou settest thine hand unto; and he shall bless thee in the land which the LORD thy God giveth thee" (Deut. 28:8).[2]

---

1. Chapter 72.
2. Gary North, *Inheritance and Dominion: An Economic Commentary on Deuteronomy,*

320

This proverb says the blessings shall abound. This indicates considerable wealth. It is not speaking of a comfortable life. It is speaking of a life marked by exceptional blessings. This need not be limited to wealth. The passage in Deuteronomy 28 is comprehensive in its description of the variety of blessings. This proverb indicates something comparable for the individual.

Then why does Solomon warn against riches more than once? Why is something which is a legitimate outcome of faithfulness not legitimate as a personal goal? If there is a predictable covenantal relationship between ends and means, why are the means legitimate, the end legitimate, but not the goal of attaining the end? Why would Solomon encourage faithfulness by pointing to the positive sanctions that result from faithfulness, yet warn people not to pursue riches?

B. Success vs. Success Indicators

There are success indicators in life, yet they do not always indicate success. Here is a familiar example. A student is encouraged to learn. To aid him in his quest for knowledge, the teacher enforces a system of sanctions: grades. Poor grades indicate a lack of success in gaining knowledge. Good grades indicate success. The student is then motivated to achieve good grades. He learns the tricks of taking examinations. His grades rise. He learns how to take shortcuts on studying. His grades rise. He finds that he can cram for an exam the night before the exam and get better grades, although whenever he does this, he forgets most of what he has studied as soon as the exam is over. His grades rise. At some point, the pursuit of good grades undermines his quest for knowledge.

It may go beyond this. He may find ways to cheat on the exams. The quest for good grades then undermines his morality. The success indicators no longer measure his success. They measure his failure.

In every field of life, this dilemma appears. It is a universal problem. Success indicators do not automatically detect performances that are based on illegitimate means—means that are counter-productive to the end for which the indicators were designed. No matter what the objective indicators of success are, they can be misused by performers when adopted as ends in themselves.

Money is a universal success indicator. There are few others that are valued more highly. Of those indicators that are readily measured, only life extension is higher on most men's scales of value, at least when death is imminent. Yet even here, mere temporal extension of life can become a false standard. A man may be granted a longer life for betraying something or someone. Every society has standards that are said to be superior to life extension. But these are not equally measurable: honor, integrity, and reliability. Money and time are supremely objective and universally honored. This is why they are morally dangerous. But money is more dangerous than time, for it is exchangeable at all times. There may not be a buyer for whatever one is willing to give up in order to gain extra time. There is always a ready market for money.

The Bible is clear on this point: *riches alone are illegitimate as a success indicator*. Blessings are more comprehensive than riches. To the extent that someone defines success exclusively as riches, he has misunderstood life's proper goal. Such a person is easily tempted to adopt means to riches that are inconsistent with covenantally defined blessings. If a person's sole end is money, the means selected are likely to be illegitimate. If the means are illegitimate, the end will be the opposite of the goal sought. "He that hasteth to be rich hath an evil eye, and considereth not that poverty shall come upon him" (v. 22).

Conclusion

God's blessings are a legitimate goal in life. They are basic to covenantal cause and effect. *But the moral cause is more precious than the measurable effect*. Men should remain faithful to God even in cases where the immediate effect is negative. The positive blessings are God's means to confirm the legitimacy of the moral means. Moral cause and positive effect together confirm God's covenant. "But thou shalt remember the LORD thy God: for it is he that giveth thee power to get wealth, that he may establish his covenant which he sware unto thy fathers, as it is this day" (Deut. 8:18).[3]

Riches are the outcome of a life of covenantal faithfulness. He who seeks shortcuts to wealth is like the student who seeks shortcuts to wisdom. He will not only not achieve his goal, he will achieve its opposite: poverty.

---

3. Gary North, *Inheritance and Dominion: An Economic Commentary on Deuteronomy*, 2nd ed. (Dallas, Georgia: Point Five Press, [1999] 2012), ch. 22.

84

THE POOR MAN'S JUDICIAL CAUSE

The righteous considereth the cause of the poor: but the wicked regardeth not to know it.

PROVERBS 29:7

The issue here is the system of justice. A poor person comes into a court of law, and the righteous person considers his case. The wicked pay no attention. This is what Jeremiah later identified as the ethical condition of Israel.

> Your iniquities have turned away these things, and your sins have with-holden good things from you. For among my people are found wicked men: they lay wait, as he that setteth snares; they set a trap, they catch men. As a cage is full of birds, so are their houses full of deceit: therefore they are become great, and waxen rich. They are waxen fat, they shine: yea, they overpass the deeds of the wicked: they judge not the cause, the cause of the fatherless, yet they prosper; and the right of the needy do they not judge. Shall I not visit for these things? saith the LORD: shall not my soul be avenged on such a nation as this? (Jer. 5:25–29)

The context is civil judgment. God warned the Israelites that they had to obey His law. "Ye shall do my judgments, and keep mine ordinances, to walk therein: I am the LORD your God" (Lev. 18:4). This is repeated over and over in the Mosaic law. The rule of law was to govern Israel. "Ye shall have one manner of law, as well for the stranger, as for one of your own country: for I am the LORD your God" (Lev. 24:22).[1] Everyone inside the boundaries of Israel came under biblical

---

1. For the exegesis of this principle, see my comments on Exodus 12:49. Gary North, *Authority and Dominion: An Economic Commentary on Exodus* (Dallas, Georgia: Point Five Press, 2012), Part 1, *Representation and Dominion* (1985), ch. 14.

law. "Ye shall not respect persons in judgment; but ye shall hear the small as well as the great; ye shall not be afraid of the face of man; for the judgment is God's: and the cause that is too hard for you, bring it unto me, and I will hear it" (Deut. 1:17).[2]

This proverb, like the Mosaic law as a whole, in no way authorizes the perversion of justice on behalf of the poor. It does not teach, nor did the Mosaic law teach, that the poor man is entitled to anything except an impartial application of the Mosaic law to his case. "Ye shall do no unrighteousness in judgment: thou shalt not respect the person of the poor, nor honour the person of the mighty: but in righteousness shalt thou judge thy neighbour" (Lev. 19:15). This law is opposed to the welfare state's programs of coercive wealth-redistribution.[3]

The wicked person ignores the cause of the poor man. Note: this does not say that he ignores the cause of the poor man's poverty. He ignores his cause, meaning his judicial case against an opponent. This is a strictly judicial matter, not an economic matter. The Mosaic law was clear: the judge must not respect persons, meaning favor one person or the other in a lawsuit based on the person's national origin or economic condition. The New Testament is equally clear. "For there is no respect of persons with God" (Rom. 2:11). God's court is the model. "But he that doeth wrong shall receive for the wrong which he hath done: and there is no respect of persons" (Col. 3:25). A court must not care what a person owns, only what he has done. It must seek to reflect God's judgment.

The wicked man in this proverb pays no attention to the poor man's cause or case. He is unconcerned with the outcome of the court. He has no concern with justice. He is ignorant of the principle of the rule of law. He is unaware of such matters. This proverb does not say that he is a self-conscious oppressor. He is barely conscious at all, judicially speaking.

This is a wicked person, this proverb says. Such a lack of concern with the law of God is the mark of a wicked person. To turn a blind eye to the judicial cause of the poor is to imagine that God is equally blind and also does not care. The Bible insists that God does care. "Shall I not visit for these things? saith the LORD: shall not my soul be avenged on such a nation as this?" (Jer. 5:29).

---

2. Gary North, *Inheritance and Dominion: An Economic Commentary on Deuteronomy*, 2nd ed. (Dallas, Georgia: Point Five Press, [1999] 2012), ch. 4.

3. Gary North, *Boundaries and Dominion: An Economic Commentary on Leviticus*, 2nd ed.(Dallas, Georgia: Point Five Press, [1994] 2012), ch. 14.

Conclusion

He who turns a blind eye to the poor's judicial cause is a wicked person. Why? Because he disregards the rule of law. But if this is the reason, then he who turns a blind eye to the rich man's judicial cause is also a wicked person. "Ye shall do no unrighteousness in judgment: thou shalt not respect the person of the poor, nor honour the person of the mighty: but in righteousness shalt thou judge thy neighbour" (Lev. 19:15).

The modern-day defender of the welfare state turns a blind eye to the judicial cause of the rich man. The law punishes the rich man, not for breaking a statute, but for achieving success.

Both the rich man and the poor man should be protected by the terms of biblical law. They should both be secure in their property, their marriages, and their liberties. Both should seek to extend God's kingdom in history. Neither should therefore infringe on the other's God-assigned stewardship responsibilities.

85

A MIDDLE-CLASS LIFESTYLE

Two things have I required of thee; deny me them not before I die: Remove far from me vanity and lies: give me neither poverty nor riches; feed me with food convenient for me: Lest I be full, and deny thee, and say, Who is the LORD? or lest I be poor, and steal, and take the name of my God in vain.

PROVERBS 30:7–9

Here, Solomon equates vanity and lies with both poverty and riches. Yet he was very rich. He was rich enough to support 700 wives and 300 concubines (I Kings 11:3). Why would he warn men against riches? Possibly because of what he had learned from having 700 wives and 300 concubines.

A. A Warning Against Riches

Are the two requests related? Yes. A person with great wealth is under constant pressure to spend his money in ways that benefit suppliers of motivation. These motivation-suppliers are called salesmen. They sell vanity. They also sell lies. Of course, vanity and lies are not sold as vanity and lies. They are disguised. They are packaged as must-have and must-do items. They are sold by means of deception, so their essence is lies. Inside the packaging is vanity: emptiness.

Solomon uses food as the representative symbol of what he seeks. He asks for neither too much nor too little food. If he has too much food, he will become full. When he is full, he will deny God. He will say, "Who is the Lord?" This response is what Moses had warned against. God had fed them in the wilderness with manna, Moses reminded the generation of the conquest. Here was the great temptation: "And thou say in thine heart, My power and the might of mine hand hath gotten me this wealth. But thou shalt remember the LORD thy God: for it is he that giveth thee power to get wealth, that he may establish his covenant which he sware unto thy fathers, as it is this day" (Deut. 8:17–18).[1]

On the other hand, a person with too little food is hungry. He may capitulate to his hunger by stealing food. The heart of this sin is to bring God's name into disrepute, to "take the name of my God in vain." Why is this the case? Because of the five-point covenantal structure of the Ten Commandments: a parallel pair of five commandments, the first priestly and the second kingly.[2]

The third commandment places a legal boundary around God's name. "Thou shalt not take the name of the LORD thy God in vain; for the LORD will not hold him guiltless that taketh his name in vain" (Ex. 20:7).[3] Boundaries are an aspect of part three of the five-point biblical covenant.[4] Commandment three is in the first group of five commandments, dealing with priestly matters. The eighth commandment is the prohibition against theft. "Thou shalt not steal" (Ex. 20:15). This commandment is the third in the second series of five, dealing with kingly matters. It places a legal boundary around property.[5] By stealing, which is a boundary violation of property, a covenant-keeper necessarily also takes God's name in vain. As a covenantal representative of God, he brings God into disrepute.

B. Middle-Class Income

The proper goal is middle-class income. Whatever the distribution of wealth is at any point in time, the covenant-keeper should seek middle-class income. He should not seek poverty, which is generally a curse. He should not seek riches, which is generally a curse. The cursed aspect of the first condition is more readily apparent than the second condition, but this proverb indicates that both are more likely to be curses than blessings. Poverty is a curse because it reflects the curse of the ground (Gen. 3:17–19): more weeds than fruit. Riches

---

1. Gary North, *Inheritance and Dominion: An Economic Commentary on Deuteronomy*, 2nd ed. (Dallas, Georgia: Point Five Press, [1999] 2012), ch. 22.

2. Gary North, *Authority and Dominion: An Economic Commentary on Exodus* (Dallas, Georgia: Point Five Press, 2012), Part 2, *Decalogue and Dominion* (1986), Preface.

3. *Ibid.*, ch. 23.

4. Ray R. Sutton, *That You May Prosper: Dominion By Covenant*, 2nd ed. (Tyler, Texas: Institute for Christian Economics, [1987] 1992), ch. 3. Gary North, *Unconditional Surrender: God's Program for Victory*, 5th ed. (Powder Springs, Georgia: American Vision, [1980] 2010), ch. 3.

5. North, *Authority and Dominion*, ch. 28.

are a curse because they bring great temptation. Jesus affirmed this cursed status of riches when He said, "Verily I say unto you, That a rich man shall hardly enter into the kingdom of heaven. And again I say unto you, It is easier for a camel to go through the eye of a needle, than for a rich man to enter into the kingdom of God" (Matt. 19:23b–24).[6]

When men seek riches, they do not compare riches in history with poverty in eternity. "For what is a man profited, if he shall gain the whole world, and lose his own soul? or what shall a man give in exchange for his soul?" (Matt. 16:26).[7] Instead, they compare riches in history with poverty in history. They then choose riches over poverty.

So, the question of wealth arises: "Compared to what?" Most Americans, Canadians, Western Europeans, Australians, New Zealanders, and Japanese are middle class. They think of themselves as middle class. Yet in terms of the distribution wealth worldwide, they are upper class. They are the dominant groups in the top 20% of the world's population, who own 80% of the capital. To be in the middle class in the United States in the early years of the twenty-first century is to be wealthy by the world's standards.

So, when people think of themselves as middle class, they think of their neighbors. In the United States, we have a phrase: "Keeping up with the Joneses." The Jones family lives next door, or else lives in the circle of acquaintances in which we travel. We judge our economic success in terms of what we can see of theirs. Presumably, they do the same with us.

This is a serious error. First, we do not know about their level of consumer debt. They may be at the ragged edge of bankruptcy. Second, they are not representative of the masses of the world's population. There are billions of people who live in such poverty that middle-class Westerners cannot empathize with them. We have no criteria for comparison. Even the poor people we may see on the streets are wealthy by comparison. We see a mentally disturbed person walking up and down a downtown sidewalk, pushing a shopping cart full of junk. That shopping cart represents a capital base not shared by a billion poor people in the unpaved streets of Asia.

---

6. Gary North, *Priorities and Dominion: An Economic Commentary on Matthew*, 2nd ed. (Dallas, Georgia: Point Five Press, [2000] 2012), ch. 38.

7. *Ibid.*, ch. 35.

C. Class Morality

It has long been common among the heirs of upper-class fortunes to dismiss middle-class morality. From Great Britain's Puritan era in the late sixteenth century to the Victorian era in the late nineteenth century to the jet set today, middle-class people have been likely to be tradesmen, entrepreneurs, and skilled professionals. For centuries, they were dismissed by the landed ruling classes as either middle class or on their way to becoming newly rich. Money-grubbing was not for the rich. The Puritans and their social successors, the Protestant dissenters, favored hard work, thrift, attention to business details, and customer service. This was correctly viewed as middle-class morality by the ruling classes, whose wealth was protected by primogeniture laws (oldest son inherits all) and entail laws (forbidding the sale of an oldest son's land). Members of the ruling landed class could gamble their land away, but their gambling peers were of the same class.

The working classes had a similar contempt for middle-class morality, much preferring the lifestyle of the rich and famous, which was their lifestyle, but without the money to fund it. The features of these lifestyles were the same, but the poor could afford them only part-time: leisure (unemployment), gambling, partying (gin mills), and mistresses (prostitutes).

Middle-class living has a tendency over time to produce economic growth. It produces steadily rising income. From monks who took vows of poverty in the medieval era, and whose orders grew rich over centuries as a result of hard work and reinvested capital, to immigrant Jews whose sons became lawyers and accountants, and whose grandsons became media moguls and real estate tycoons, the story has been the same: middle-class morality produces society-wide economic growth and occasional individual wealth. Two percent growth per annum, compounded over two and a half centuries, has produced the modern world. In contrast, the lifestyle of the rich and famous rests on capital consumption. Eventually the heirs run out of money.

Middle-class morality is biblical morality. It is the bedrock foundation of wealth accumulation. When men pray for middle-class income and then work for it, their heirs become incomparably rich by the criteria of their grandparents. My grandparents were born in a world without automobiles, airplanes, commercial electricity, radio, and most of the other common features of middle-class life in the West. Their grandparents were born in a world without railroads, steamships, anesthetics, or even something as common as toilet paper. Their grandparents'

grandparents were born in a world that would have been recognizable by Moses. This transformation of the world did not take very long.[8]

Two percent per annum, either up or down, is barely observable in any area of life. Yet over decades, such slow, directional change will transform the social landscape. Middle-class morality can be maintained in the conditions of compound economic growth, just as it was in North America from 1750 to 1960. But if it declines at a steady rate—the divorce rate or the illegitimacy rate—over time, it erodes the foundations of positive growth (Deut. 28:15–68). Such social orders are eventually replaced (Deut. 8:19–20).[9]

D. Compounding Responsibility

As wealth grows, responsibility grows. Ownership is inescapably a social function.[10] The owner of every asset is a steward acting on behalf of God the Creator, but this stewardship must be manifested in history. Other men, made in God's image and also acting as His stewards, bid for ownership or control over every scarce resource, which is what defines a scarce resource. The owner must decide what to do with his property. Whose bid will he accept, including his own? He can consume it, invest it, let it waste away on its own, or give it away. He must make a choice. There are no choices without personal responsibility. The more we own, the more choices we have, and therefore the more responsibility we have. Jesus warned:

> And that servant, which knew his lord's will, and prepared not himself, neither did according to his will, shall be beaten with many stripes. But he that knew not, and did commit things worthy of stripes, shall be beaten with few stripes. For unto whomsoever much is given, of him shall be much required: and to whom men have committed much, of him they will ask the more (Luke 12:47–48).[11]

This being the case, there had better be a parallel development: moral decision-making and economic decision-making. A person

---

8. John Tyler, President of the United States in 1841–45, was born in the first term of George Washington's presidency (1790), less than a year after the French Revolution began. His grandson, Harrison Ruffin Tyler, is still alive (2021) and lives on his grandfather's land. His brother Lyon died in 2020. I interviewed Lyon in December 2010.

9. Gary North, *Inheritance and Dominion: An Economic Commentary on Deuteronomy*, 2nd ed. (Dallas, Georgia: Point Five Press, [1999] 2012), ch. 23.

10. Gary North, *An Introduction to Christian Economics* (Nutley, New Jersey: Craig Press, 1973), ch. 28.

11. Gary North, *Treasure and Dominion: An Economic Commentary on Luke*, 2nd ed. (Dallas, Georgia: Point Five Press, [2000] 2012), ch. 28.

had better get rich slowly, because he improves his understanding of moral causation slowly. He develops his moral skills slowly. Theologians call this process *progressive sanctification*. Wealth accumulated over decades is not the threat to a person that overnight wealth is. Overnight wealth is far easier to achieve than overnight moral maturity. The only widely sought-after goal more dangerous than "get rich quick" is "get power quick."

A man should learn how to handle his wealth through experience—experience evaluated in terms of God's Bible-revealed law. He should learn from others' experience, too. These others are likely to be people in his own social circle and economic class. The upper classes' contempt of newly rich people has rested on an accurate insight. The newly rich do not "mind their manners," i.e., are unfamiliar with the rules of polite society, which is confident about its future because it has long held the reins of both wealth and power. The newly rich are still intent on "making it," when their concern should be focused on "conserving it." Yet the rich and powerful are rarely reliable judges of what is required to conserve social order. They have abandoned middle-class morality.

Conclusion

This proverb warns against both riches and poverty. We readily understand the warning against poverty. But few people pray, or have ever prayed, against riches. Solomon did not pray soon enough. He prayed for wisdom (II Chron. 2:10), received wisdom (I Kings 4:29–30) and riches (I Chron. 29:4), and then lost wisdom (I Kings 11:4). His son lost most of his kingdom. Solomon would have been better off with wisdom in a cave than wisdom and riches in a palace. He would have been a far better prophet than a king. We would still read two of his books, which are more prophetic than kingly. As for his Song, one wife would have been sufficient. Better one wife like her than 699 like the other ones he married, let alone the 300 concubines without dowries.

86

. VIRTUE AND PRODUCTIVITY

Who can find a virtuous woman? for her price is far above rubies.

PROVERBS 31:10

A. A Virtuous Woman

This introduces the longest section in the Bible describing the charac-
teristics of a virtuous woman. The advice comes from a woman. "The
words of king Lemuel, the prophecy that his mother taught him"
(Prov. 31:1). The passage leads to a conclusion. "Favour is deceitful,
and beauty is vain: but a woman that feareth the LORD, she shall be
praised" (31:30). This is surely good advice to every son. Solomon
ignored it on a scale unmatched in recorded history. But his end confirmed it.

> And he had seven hundred wives, princesses, and three hundred concu-
> bines: and his wives turned away his heart. For it came to pass, when Sol-
> omon was old, that his wives turned away his heart after other gods: and
> his heart was not perfect with the LORD his God, as was the heart of David
> his father. For Solomon went after Ashtoreth the goddess of the Zidonians,
> and after Milcom the abomination of the Ammonites. And Solomon did
> evil in the sight of the LORD, and went not fully after the LORD, as did
> David his father (I Kings 11:3–6)

> Wherefore the LORD said unto Solomon, Forasmuch as this is done of
> thee, and thou hast not kept my covenant and my statutes, which I have
> commanded thee, I will surely rend the kingdom from thee, and will give
> it to thy servant. Notwithstanding in thy days I will not do it for David
> thy father's sake: but I will rend it out of the hand of thy son (I Kings
> 11:11–12).

332

B. Value Measured in Rubies

There is a familiar phrase, "as good as gold." The phrase here presents an even more favorable comparison: "Her price is far above rubies." It indicates that a man with a virtuous wife would be foolish to sell her for rubies if such a market existed. This is poetic, not literal. It does not mean that there was an active market for wives in Solomon's day, in which men bid for other men's wives. (Such a practice did exist—illegally but traditionally—in Great Britain for several centuries, ending only in the late nineteenth century. A man who was tired of his wife would bring her into the town square, where men bid for her. The highest bidder got her.)[1]

The comparison is economic: the price of a wife in terms of the price of multiple rubies. Yet the passage deals with a virtuous woman. The connection between her virtue and her family's increased wealth is inescapable. There is no passage in the Bible that is more detailed in this regard. Proverbs presents a series of pithy snippets on the ways to wealth. It then culminates with this, the key passage in the Bible on the ways to wealth.

C. Trustworthy

"The heart of her husband doth safely trust in her, so that he shall have no need of spoil" (v. 11). What has spoil—confiscated military booty—have to do with a wife? Nothing. The translators did a poor job here. The New American Standard Bible is on target: "He will have no lack of gain." The rest of the chapter describes why he will have no lack of gain.

This raises a question: What has his trust in her got to do with his prosperity? There are two answers: income and outgo. She makes money as an entrepreneur, and she also buys carefully. She watches the ledger.

The woman is reliable: trustworthy. "She will do him good and not evil all the days of her life" (v. 12). What is the nature of this good? "She seeketh wool, and flax, and worketh willingly with her hands" (v. 13). The Hebrew word translated as "willingly" is elsewhere translated as "pleasure" or "desire." It indicates an active, enthusiastic performance of duties. "She is like the merchants' ships; she bringeth her food from afar" (v. 14). A merchant journeys to distant places in search of underpriced, undiscovered bargains to bring back home in

---

1. Samuel Menefee, *Wives for Sale: An Ethnographic Study of British Popular Divorce* (New York: St. Martin's, 1981).

order to sell at a high mark-up. So does the virtuous wife. She goes looking for bargains in out-of-the-way markets, where there are fewer buyers making competitive bids and therefore lower prices.

This woman has a servant's heart. "She riseth also while it is yet night, and giveth meat to her household, and a portion to her maidens" (v. 15). She serves her maidens, whose job is to serve her. This shows kindness, but this fact appears in the midst of a passage describing economic productivity. Why should the person in charge of the household sacrifice time and effort for her servants? Because of the response. The maidens will see that they are not slaves, but are members of a working household. The evidence of this is the service rendered downward from the wife to the maidens. The wife works extra hard for everyone in the household. The maidens perceive themselves as parts of this household. What is the morally correct response? To work at least equally hard. The entire household then benefits. The division of labor increases everyone's output. A maiden, left on her own while the wife looks for bargains in distant markets, will be less likely to reduce her efforts. It would look bad to the other maidens. She would appear to be a slacker, not a model to be imitated. The model to be imitated is the wife. This model was adopted by Christ as the model for leadership in the church.

> But Jesus called them unto him, and said, Ye know that the princes of the Gentiles exercise dominion over them, and they that are great exercise authority upon them. But it shall not be so among you: but whosoever will be great among you, let him be your minister; And whosoever will be chief among you, let him be your servant: Even as the Son of man came not to be ministered unto, but to minister, and to give his life a ransom for many (Matt. 20:25–28).[2]

It is not just that the virtuous wife is thrifty and hard working. She also is an investor. "She considereth a field, and buyeth it: with the fruit of her hands she planteth a vineyard" (v. 16).

"She girdeth her loins with strength, and strengtheneth her arms" (v. 17). She works hard physically. Her body reflects this commitment to hard work. She has strong arms. She does some heavy lifting. She is not spending time at the local gymnasium, a Greek invention and a place for men. She does not need an exercise program.

"She perceiveth that her merchandise is good: her candle goeth not out by night" (v. 18). She understands that she has a competitive

---

2. Gary North, *Priorities and Dominion: An Economic Commentary on Matthew*, 2nd ed. (Dallas, Georgia: Point Five Press, [2000] 2012), ch. 41.

edge in what she produces. She keeps at it late into the evening. Yet she also rises early. "She riseth also while it is yet night." Late to bed and early to rise.

She sews. "She layeth her hands to the spindle, and her hands hold the distaff" (v. 19). She gives. "She stretcheth out her hand to the poor; yea, she reacheth forth her hands to the needy" (v. 20). "She is not afraid of the snow for her household: for all her household are clothed with scarlet" (v. 21). As the colloquial phrase puts it, she has everything covered. Come what may, her family is prepared.

She dresses well. "She maketh herself coverings of tapestry; her clothing is silk and purple" (v. 22). Purple clothing was for rich people in the ancient world. Purple dye was expensive. She recognizes that her success is reflected in how she dresses. She dresses well. Her attire reflects the level of her performance. She has given to the poor. So, she thinks nothing of spending a lot of money on clothing. She is not guilt-ridden about this. Queens dress well, Queen Elizabeth II's hats to the contrary. She is not putting on airs. Her clothing reflects her status as biblically virtuous.

"Her husband is known in the gates, when he sitteth among the elders of the land" (v. 23). Her husband has leisure to serve as an advisor. He has leisure because she generates income for his household. She has social status in the community because he has social status. He has status because she knows how to make money and run an orderly household. He is not tied down at home, making decisions and settling disputes.

She is running a small business. "She maketh fine linen, and selleth it; and delivereth girdles unto the merchant" (v. 24). The merchants rely on her as a source for products to sell. This means that her product line has a good reputation. It is in constant demand. More than one merchant understands this. She makes them look good to their customers. This guarantees repeat business and higher prices: more bidders for her products.

She is already well known. "Strength and honour are her clothing" (v. 25a). She will become even better known: "and she shall rejoice in time to come" (v. 25).

She has good judgment. "She openeth her mouth with wisdom; and in her tongue is the law of kindness" (v. 26).

"She looketh well to the ways of her household, and eateth not the bread of idleness" (v. 27). We are back to the earlier description: care about others as head of the household, and not one to waste time.

D. Her Great Reward

She has a good reputation. She has a vineyard. She has a successful business. Her family's income serves as protection in cold times: scarlet clothing. Yet the culmination of her life of successful production is the praise her family will give her. "Her children arise up, and call her blessed; her husband also, and he praiseth her" (v. 28). Her husband tells her, "Many daughters have done virtuously, but thou excellest them all" (v. 29). He pronounces judgment. His judgment matters to her. This is a powerful positive sanction.

She labored within her household. She ran businesses. She was a real estate developer. She slept little. But she never forgets her assignment: to serve her children, her maidens, and above all, her husband. She was not in this for the money. The money was a tool of dominion. Her household's dominion expanded: in business, in real estate, in charity, and in her husband's influence in the gates, i.e., civil authority and judgment.

Then comes the warning of the king's mother: "Favour is deceitful, and beauty is vain: but a woman that feareth the LORD, she shall be praised" (v. 30).

The book concludes with this: "Give her of the fruit of her hands; and let her own works praise her in the gates" (v. 31). This is of course poetry. Her works do not literally praise her. It means that those who see her works praise her. They are objectively superior, a fact perceived subjectively by those who are aware of what she has accomplished.

Conclusion

A good-looking good woman is hard to find and harder to marry. But a virtuous woman is much harder to find. If a woman is one in a hundred in looks, one in a hundred in wisdom, and one in a hundred in business savvy, then she is one in a hundred times a hundred times a hundred, i.e., one in a million. These odds are against even kings, let alone the average guy. Reduce these odds, the king's mother advised. If the prospect is one in a hundred in wisdom and one in a hundred in business savvy, she is one in ten thousand. One in ten thousand is as much as any husband can legitimately expect. So, sacrifice good looks for wisdom and business savvy.

Solomon understood this from experience. "As a jewel of gold in a swine's snout, so is a fair woman which is without discretion" (Prov. 11:22). He married more than his share of women without discretion.

CONCLUSION

The overall theme of the Book of Proverbs is the contrast between the wise man and the fool.

The supreme economic theme in the Book of Proverbs is this: *biblical ethics is the basis of personal success*.[1] Proverbs deals with success. It identifies what success is: diligent living in conformity to God's Bible-revealed laws.[2] Diligence is required.[3] Solomon contrasts success with success indicators. Success indicators can sometimes be the product of diligent living in defiance of God's Bible-revealed laws.[4] Personal success generally includes visible riches.[5] Success is not limited to riches. Biblical wisdom counts for more than riches.[6] Nevertheless, biblical wisdom generally brings riches.[7] The goal of riches is to serve as a means of exercising dominion.[8] This requires stewardship, which in turn requires private ownership.[9] It also requires the accumulation of assets for the purpose of inheritance.[10]

The Book of Proverbs' distinguishing feature, compared to other rule books for personal success, is its assertion of *God's providential system of cause and effect*. Biblical causation is based on the concept of cosmic personalism. The universe is under God's sovereignty because it was created out of nothing by God's verbal command. So, economic causation operates in terms of God's Bible-revealed laws.[11]

---

1. Chapters 1, 3, 4, 5, 19, 20, 21, 25, 30, 41, 64, 78, 80, 81, 85.
2. Chapters 14, 16, 62, 79.
3. Chapters 61, 71, 77.
4. Chapters 33, 48, 49, 53, 73, 83, 85.
5. Chapters 6, 17, 18, 23, 24, 25, 26, 35, 38, 82, 83.
6. Chapters 1, 4, 5, 9, 17, 18, 53.
7. Chapters 9, 18, 20, 63, 80.
8. Chapters 4, 8, 21, 25, 26, 34, 81.
9. Chapters 67, 70, 75, 85.
10. Chapters 3, 9, 18, 27, 33, 34, 40, 41, 55, 56, 61, 79, 81.
11. Chapters 2, 3, 5, 7, 8, 9, 20, 21, 27, 30, 32, 61, 64, 73, 81.

If there is success, then there is also failure. What produces poverty, which is a universally recognized mark of personal failure? Two things are identified: laziness[12] and debt.[13]

What are the supreme marks of biblical ethics in an economy? Honest weights and measures.[14]

Solomon compiled these proverbs at the height of Israel's power and wealth. After Solomon, things went downhill rapidly and never recovered. There is no better evidence in history of the causal relationship between visible success and temptation unto destruction, which was the theme of Deuteronomy 8. No sooner had Solomon attained visible success than he began violating the terms of kingship set forth in Deuteronomy 17. He began accumulating gold and horses (I Kings 10:26–28). He also accumulated foreign wives. The wives tempted him to worship their gods (I Kings 11). No sooner had Solomon died than his son and his counselors hiked taxes (I Kings 12). The result was Jeroboam's successful revolt and the separation of Israel into two rival kingdoms, northern (Israel) and southern (Judah).

This reminds us of a painful principle: "Nothing fails like success." Biblically speaking, this statement is incorrect. It should read: "Nothing fails like positive success indicators in a covenant-breaking society." Moses said it best:

> And thou say in thine heart, My power and the might of mine hand hath gotten me this wealth. But thou shalt remember the LORD thy God: for it is he that giveth thee power to get wealth, that he may establish his covenant which he sware unto thy fathers, as it is this day. And it shall be, if thou do at all forget the LORD thy God, and walk after other gods, and serve them, and worship them, I testify against you this day that ye shall surely perish. As the nations which the LORD destroyeth before your face, so shall ye perish; because ye would not be obedient unto the voice of the LORD your God (Deut. 8:17–20).

Solomon was wise enough to compile the Book of Proverbs. He was not wise enough to implement them in his own life or in the life of the civil government that he commanded. His failure, as well as the failure of his son, testifies to the fundamental message of the Bible, from Genesis to Revelation: *knowledge does not save. Grace saves.*

He knew this. He then forgot. He was God's servant. Servants have a common characteristic: "A servant will not be corrected by

---

12. Chapters 21, 22, 37, 38, 50, 58, 68, 69, 74, 75.
13. Chapters 9, 10, 11, 60, 67, 69.
14. Chapters 29, 52, 56.

words: for though he understand he will not answer" (Prov. 29:19). God spoke to him, but he did not listen (I Kings 11:10). So, God corrected him by telling him that his son would lose the kingdom which he would inherit from his father (I Kings 11:11–12).

The truth of the Book of Proverbs is found in its opening words.

> A wise man will hear, and will increase learning; and a man of understanding shall attain unto wise counsels: To understand a proverb, and the interpretation; the words of the wise, and their dark sayings. The fear of the LORD is the beginning of knowledge: but fools despise wisdom and instruction. My son, hear the instruction of thy father, and forsake not the law of thy mother: For they shall be an ornament of grace unto thy head, and chains about thy neck. My son, if sinners entice thee, consent thou not (Prov. 1:5–10).[15]

This truth is consistent with the closing words of Ecclesiastes.

> And further, by these, my son, be admonished: of making many books there is no end; and much study is a weariness of the flesh. Let us hear the conclusion of the whole matter: Fear God, and keep his commandments: for this is the whole duty of man. For God shall bring every work into judgment, with every secret thing, whether it be good, or whether it be evil (Eccl. 12:12–14).[16]

Solomon's example down through the ages testifies against the fundamental error of Greek philosophy, which proclaimed that to know what is good is to do what is good. Greek philosophy proclaimed a *two-step religion*: salvation by knowledge leading to salvation by works. The history of Western civilization has been marked by a struggle between Greek philosophy and biblical wisdom. Biblical wisdom points to the need for God's grace. If Solomon became the wisest fool in history, then the precepts of wisdom are not sufficient to save. This was the message of the prophet Habakkuk: "Behold, his soul which is lifted up is not upright in him: but the just shall live by his faith" (Hab. 2:4). This is why the proverbs, for all their specific wisdom, point to the New Covenant.

> For by grace are ye saved through faith; and that not of yourselves: it is the gift of God: Not of works, lest any man should boast. For we are his workmanship, created in Christ Jesus unto good works, which God hath before ordained that we should walk in them (Eph. 2:8–10).

---

15. Chapter 3.
16. Gary North, *Autonomy and Stagnation: An Economic Commentary on Ecclesiastes* (Dallas, Georgia: Point Five Press, 2012), ch. 45.

Made in the USA
Middletown, DE
22 July 2023

35570471R00195